T0326517

Oil Producing Countries and Oil Companies

From the Nineteenth Century to the Twenty-First Century

P.I.E. Peter Lang

Bruxelles · Bern · Berlin · Frankfurt am Main · New York · Oxford · Wien

Alain BELTRAN (ed.)

Oil Producing Countries and Oil Companies

From the Nineteenth Century to the Twenty-First Century

International Issues
No.14

Conference organised by CNRS and Total Cy
on September 18th and 19th, 2006, in Paris (France).

© P.I.E. PETER LANG S.A.,
Éditions scientifiques internationales
Brussels, 2011
1 avenue Maurice, B-1050 Brussels, Belgium
info@peterlang.com; www.peterlang.com

Printed in Germany

ISSN 2030-3688
ISBN 978-90-5201-711-2
D/2011/5678/69

Library of Congress Cataloging-in-Publication Data
Oil producing countries and oil companies : from the nineteenth century
to the twenty-first century / Alain Beltran (ed.).
p. cm. -- (Enjeux internationaux, 2030-3688 ; 14)
Includes index. ISBN 978-90-5201-711-2
1. Petroleum industry and trade--History. I. Beltran, Alain.
HD9560.5.O3685 2011   338.2'728209--dc22   2011006112

CIP also available from the British Library, GB.

Bibliographic information published by "Die Deutsche Nationalbibliothek"
"Die Deutsche Nationalbibliothek" lists this publication in the "Deutsche National-bibliografie"; detailed bibliographic data is available on Internet at <http://dnb.d-nb.de>.

Table of Contents

Introduction

Alain BELTRAN

Research Director, National Center for Scientific Research, France

Following the 2003 colloquium on the subject of national oil companies, this second international conference, organized with the cooperation of Total and of the CNRS (the French National Center for Scientific
Research), attempts to describe the diversity of the relationships between producing countries and oil companies, in time and in space, so as
to develop a still-summary typology thereof, pending the future work.
The following presentations are often highly original and point to a
certain number of research leads. The 2006 colloquium made it possible
to take account of the regions that had not been dealt with previously,
such as Romania, Latin America, and Near and Middle East. But in spite
of everything, there are still a few geographical areas that have not been
mentioned, Germany, for instance, as a major consumer country, or else
the USSR-Russia, which has been hypersensitive since the 1980s to
fluctuations of the oil manna.

The experts expressing themselves here give us, first of all, a certain
number of long-term petroleum statistics making it possible to isolate
long-term policies, as well as interruptions or course changes. Then too,
looking beyond the price criterion alone, we note that the relationships
between economic partners are also sensitive to economic conditions, to
the appraisal of geopolitical risks, to the force relationships between
States, and in a nutshell to geo-strategic thinking, of which oil is one of
the most reliable indicators. Alliances may dissolve, the companies may
go it alone, and the "raison d'État" may prevail over strictly economic
considerations. Similarly, it is established that companies belonging to
one and the same country may react differently and develop original
strategies in the face of nationalizations, embargoes, etc. However, oil
has long been a strategic commodity, and that fact presupposes a certain
continuity in supplies, whether in physical or in price terms. Whence the
apparent need for States as well as for the companies to develop special
relationships with certain suppliers. Such a trusting relationship is

developed over time and does not necessarily involve oil. In the long run, arms sales, technological cooperation and cultural relationships create a framework for winning supplier loyalty, and several such cases are mentioned in these pages. This desire for stability is echoed by many factors making for change, if not a whole new ball game. First of all, there was the arrival of new players ready to change the rules of the game so as to get installed in the oil landscape, as Enrico Matei or certain American independents did. Without destabilizing the system, they changed the previous relationship between companies and producers. Then the 1970s enabled the producers, in a way, to take power. Actually, the game became more complex, more subtle, less regulated and sometimes difficult to follow (whence numerous fantasies): the majors, which provided price stability at the expense of the producers, lost their touch to a great extent – but that does not mean that the major powers, beginning with the United States, were henceforth offside.

The most recent period added some factors making for change, if not destabilization. On one hand, the emerging countries request, or even demand, their share of oil (and of natural gas) to power their economic takeoff or strong growth. But at the same time, the sensitivity to the environment and the awareness that fossil energies are a finite resource have added some new factors, making the oil landscape more complex. The oil companies are thinking about diversifying, but they are also going to look for non-conventional types of petroleum. The producing countries with the smallest reserves already have to think about the long term and the post-oil era. All of those factors should have the result of exacerbating tensions. Actually, looking beyond the conflicts, pragmatism often carries the day over resentment, since oil remains the world's most marketed – and most marketable – product. The notions of independence or of acquisition of independence remain a relative matter in the oil world: the sellers have to sell all the same.

So we are witnessing the emergence of a new kind of relationship between producing countries and companies. Certain emerging countries have decided to adopt an offensive policy with respect both to exploration and to technology. They are constructing a real oil policy for the long term. For others, the hydrocarbon resources remain an essential source of foreign currency and are vital, but, more rapidly than they expected, they are being forced to factor in the need for profiting from this advantage so as to transform it into sustainable development infrastructures. The conversion to free-market economics, which has affected the world since the decade of the 1980s, has not managed to transform oil into a market exactly like the others. Fantasies are still there making oil the ultimate explanation of the world's transformations. Reminding people that there is also a market – characterized by often obscure rules

– is not among the least of the benefits from the work of the experts grouped here. The oldest businesses are concentrating their efforts to cope with ever-larger investments, while their Brazilian, Mexican and Chinese counterparts are pushing for their own places in the world rankings. In such a fast-changing world, it is even more necessary than before to find reference points, whence a necessary and even helpful review of history.

PART I

OIL SUPPLY IN FRANCE
(NINETEENTH-TWENTIETH CENTURIES)

France's Oil Sources and Supply Networks (1861-1950)

Morgan LE DEZ

Le Havre University, France

The purpose of this communication is to offer a brief panorama of France's oil supplies between 1861 and 1950. The sources used are the statistical data of the French Customs Agency mentioning imports of crude and refined oil by country, this since 1863. The period under study ends in 1950, a year marked by the return to the same level of imports as in 1939 and by the end of the exceptional supply system instituted at the beginning of the Second World War.

The image of oil changed during that period. It was a negotiable good at the outset, in the same way as cotton or coffee, but oil became a raw material, a mainly utilitarian source of energy as lighting, becoming indispensable or even strategic due to its new applications and uses, mainly in the transport sector. Hence that period is the one marking the birth and development of a new industry. The very existence of oil had been known for centuries, but it was in the middle of the nineteenth century that this energy source started to be used on a large scale for lighting. That success in a fast-growing field, due to its quality, its abundance and its low cost, resulted in exploration for it all over the planet.

In the interest of a better understanding of the historical stages involved in French oil supplies, we will take an interest first of all in the producing and exporting countries, and then in France, a mainly importing and consumption country, by studying the volumes, the structure and the origin of its supplies. Finally, we will mention the development of the French oil industry by way of its supply and transport networks.

I. Panorama of World Oil Exploitation

We will see, in this initial part, the producing countries from which France could obtain supplies and the French position in their exports.

A. The Extension of Oil Exploitation

Fig. 1 groups, in a table, all the producing countries from which France obtained crude oil until 1950. That table shows the first year of significant production of those countries, that is, the beginning of lasting and organised production that could generate profits. The table also mentions the year of their first exports of crude to France appearing in the statistics of the French General Customs Department (Direction des Douanes, *Tableau général du commerce et de la navigation*, Paris):

Fig. 1 Main producing countries exporting to France 1857-1950

AREAS	COUNTRIES	YEAR OF FIRST SIGNIFICANT PRODUCTION	YEAR OF FIRST FRENCH IMPORT
NORTH AMERICA	USA	1859	1861
LATIN AMERICA	Colombia	1919	1928
	Ecuador	1917	1931
	Mexico	1901	1931
	Peru	1884	1932
	Venezuela	1910	1930
EUROPE	Galicia	1861	1908
	Rumania	1857	1903
RUSSIA	Russia	1863	1866
MIDDLE EAST	Arabia	1936	1945
	Iraq	1927	1934
	Kuwait	1938	1949
	Persia	1908	1929
SOUTH-EAST ASIA	British East Indies	1889	1933
	Dutch East Indies	1885	1932
	Before 1900 AD		Since 1900 AD

Sources: d'après CPDP (Éléments statistiques) & Statistiques des Douanes françaises
© M. LE DEZ – Université du Havre-UMR IDEES/CIRTAI Sept. 2006

According to that document, France obtained crude supplies until 1903 mainly from the United States of America, but also from Russia starting in 1866. On the French market[1], one must await the year 1893, all the same, for Russian oil to really compete with the United States by means of regular and comparable imports.

The table brings out the fact that the number of producing countries increases above all after 1900, in other words, that France seemed to diversify its supply sources: from other European States, such as Rumania, and then from the producer countries of Latin America and Southeast Asia, and finally from the Middle East. But it mentions only the years of the initial French imports, without offering any perspective on the regularity or changes in the national origin of the imported crudes. Between 1861 and 1950, there are a total of fifteen producer countries that, in succession or simultaneously, meet French needs for crude. Do those changes in the supply sources correspond to geographical changes in oil world production?

Fig. 2 illustrates those transformations, which may partly explain the changes in French "purchasing strategies" for crude oil. The crude geography of hydrocarbon production fluctuates over the long term. The fact is that at every moment, it reflects the status of geological prospecting and the oil companies' investment opportunities.

Fig. 2 World oil production areas 1860-1950

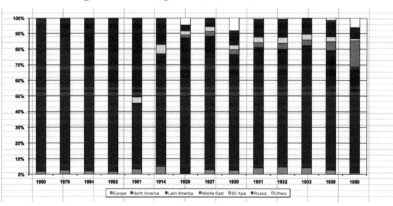

Sources: Redwood (Sir Boverton), *A treatise on petroleum*, London, 1910; Raymond Foss Bacon, *The American Petroleum Industry*, New York, 1916; CPDP, Éléments statistiques, 1955

© M. LE DEZ – Université du Havre-UMR IDEES/CIRTAI Sept. 2006

---

[1] Special agreements between Russia and France signed in 1892 encouraged imports of russian oil.

This chart only indicates general tendencies, since the data concerning world oil output remain imprecise and very partial. For the period of interest to us, the national production of each country may be evaluated in terms of mass or of volume, depending on the case, in "quintaux" or in barrels, the content thereof sometimes being mentioned (in principle, 42 US gallons). These remarks also apply to the customs statistics of the importing countries, such as France. That document, associated with a few data concerning the production volumes, enables us all the same to emerge with a few major findings.

The production increase is multiplied by 10 every decade on average until the 1880s, then the growth rate declines and becomes ever more regular, with a doubling on average every decade until the first oil shock: 66,693 tons in 1860, 700,818 tons in 1870, a million tons being exceeded in 1873, two million five years later, and four million tons in 1881. But the growth displayed by the first few decades is already attenuated: 9 million tons are exceeded in 1890, and 19 million in 1900. During the first half of the twentieth century, world output exceeded 54 million tons in 1913, and 203 million in 1933, but a slowdown is noted during the decade of economic recession prior to the Second World War: 293 million tons being produced in 1940, and some 524 million in 1950. Production does not get back to a regular and increasing growth rate until after the war, this applying until the oil shocks. A billion tons of oil was produced toward 1960, the amount doubling before the end of the decade. Three billion tons of crude produced is reached as of 1978. This sharp slowdown in production growth is confirmed by the 2003 figures: 3.6 billion tons of crude oil in the world.[2]

Between 1860 and 1950, there is a change in the growth rate of world oil production characterised by a rate slowdown toward by the 1880s. Referring to Fig. 2, we note that the said decade corresponds to a period of initial diversification on the part of the producing countries. Russia was the first to attack the North American monopoly toward 1876, going so far as to grab half of the world output in 1901. The First World War isolated Russia from its customers, the effect being a search for new petroleum deposits in order to meet constantly increasing demand. Some new producer countries emerged, mainly in Latin America, Southeast Asia and the Middle East, but also in Europe. In spite of everything, the United States and Canada together produced 60% of the world's crude until the Second World War. Oil was then a new world product, dominated more particularly by the United States and Venezuela. Those two countries were still the leading oil producers in 1950

---

[2] Source: CPDP, *Pétrole 2003: Éléments statistiques*, p. E15. Cf. aussi www.cpdp.org.

(67.8% of world output), in spite of the emergence of the Middle East. This diversification of producer countries is paired with diversification of consumer countries. The development of refining as well as of consumption in the industrialised countries, particularly in Europe, contributed to this "globalisation" of production.

It remains true all the same that, quantitatively and historically, the leading producer during that period was the United States. What countries received that nation's production in the first few years?

B. The Destinations of the First American Exports

We have just seen that the United States accounted for the entire world output of oil, and hence trade therein, until the takeoff of Russian production in 1865. The initial American petroleum deposits, located in the Great Lakes region, and to be more precise in the state of Pennsylvania, were so productive that the initial exports of oil to the Old World took place as of 1861, only two years after the beginning of exploitation.

Fig. 3 groups the destinations and the respective quantities and number of barrels for the first three years of American exports. The gross data are taken from one of the oldest monographs in French concerning oil, published in Geneva in 1865,[4] but the author does not mention his sources. As he indicates, that table is incomplete, since it does not contain a large number of other ports receiving American oil. Furthermore the importing ports that are mentioned or are absent from the table received some quantities of oil from other producing countries. Hence that table's data give indications of magnitude with respect to the destination of the oil exported by the world's leading producer, as well as concerning the position of the main French import ports by comparison with their European counterparts.

Fig. 3 Destination of US crude oil exports (1861-63)

From United States to:	1861		1862		1863		Progression rate 1862-63
	Barrels	%	Barrels	%	Barrels	%	
Liverpool	1,872	17.29%	17,845	26.53%	59,128	20.29%	231.34%
London	1,156	10.68%	11,349	16.87%	51,297	17.60%	352.00%
Total U.K.	3,028	27.97%	29,194	43.41%	110,425	37.89%	278.25%
Le Havre	737	6.81%	7,955	11.83%	54,562	18.72%	585.88%
Marseille	160	1.48%	1,357	2.02%	26,725	9.17%	1869.42%
Bordeaux	-	0.00%	20	0.03%	258	0.09%	1190.00%
Cette	-	0.00%	43	0.06%	111	0.04%	158.14%
Dieppe	-	0.00%	617	0.92%	5,600	1.92%	807.62%
Total France	897	8.29%	9,992	14.86%	87,256	29.94%	773.26%

Anvers	91	0.84%	8,231	12.24%	24,826	8.52%	201.62%
Brême	321	2.97%	4,525	6.73%	8,996	3.09%	98.81%
Hambourg	423	3.91%	2,294	3.41%	9,631	3.30%	319.83%
Gibraltar	18	0.17%	49	0.07%	2,783	0.95%	5579.59%
Gênes	7	0.06%	210	0.31%	2,407	0.83%	1046.19%
Lisbonne	47	0.43%	541	0.80%	1,860	0.64%	243.81%
Total Europe	4,832	44.64%	55,036	81.83%	248,184	85.15%	350.95%
China	28	0.26%	397	0.59%	2,531	0.87%	537.53%
Africa	44	0.41%	608	0.90%	987	0.34%	62.34%
Australia	1,683	15.55%	2,337	3.47%	6,169	2.12%	163.97%
Brazil	588	5.43%	2,427	3.61%	5,191	1.78%	113.89%
Others ports	3,650	33.72%	6,454	9.60%	28,401	9.74%	340.05%
TOTAL	10,825	100.00%	67,259	100.00%	291,463	100.00%	333.34%

Source: REY (A.), *L'Huile de pétrole*, 1865, p. 26
© M. LE DEZ – Université du Havre-UMR IDEES/CIRTAI Sept. 2006

With respect to France, the customs statistics for the first time mention imports "of oil of crude or refined oil", to use the expression contained in their registers, starting in 1863. But other statistics, concerning ports or secondary, like that table, show us that France had been importing crude or refined oil since 1861. Those initial arrivals are generally occasional, not consistent, containing small quantities in a way typical of sales of a new product. It is established that oil was imported into France for the first time via Le Havre in 1861. It was the British schooner "Theresa" coming from Liverpool, that brought in the first three barrels of American oil on 31 May 1861. Those barrels had transited via Great Britain because, in fact, it was starting at the end of 1860 that US oil, actual exploitation of which had gotten underway in August 1859, began to be exported in very small amounts to Europe. The first barrels coming directly from New York arrived in Le Havre on 8 October 1861 on board the French brig "Tour Malakoff" (60 barrels), according to the *Le Journal du Havre* at the time.[3]

Moreover in the years 1861 to 1863, the US exports of crude oil went mainly to the European countries, to an extent of about 85% (Great Britain, France, Belgium, German states, Italian states, Portugal), the rest being shared among Brazil, Australia, China and Africa.

In terms of traffic, the leading European country receiving such cargos was Great Britain, followed by France. Located on the trans-Atlantic commercial lines, the ports of Northern Europe along the

---

[3] Marseilles and Bordeaux followed the Havre example according French Commerce Ministry archives.

English Channel, of the North Sea and of the Baltic were also the largest beneficiaries of such exports.

In France, Le Havre and Marseille were the first ports to receive US oil, but in much smaller quantities than Liverpool and London. The flows became concentrated with the years in Europe, mainly in the British and French ports. But the table brings out tendency reversals for only these three years of exports: Antwerp accounted for 0.84% of American exports in 1861, and then 12.24% in 1862, but finally falling to 8.52% in 1863, whereas its traffic rose by 201.62% between the latter two years. In terms of absolute values, the exports of crude oil increased by 333.31% between 1862 and 1863, years in which all of the European ports mentioned in the table are affected.

This traffic increase rate between 1862 and 1863 is highly variable between one port and another or one country or another. Gibraltar, Marseille and then Bordeaux are among the ones displaying the highest rates, but represent, respectively, only 0.95%, 9.7% and 0.9% of the exports of American crude.

Finally, as we noted in the case of Antwerp, the oil traffic fluctuates sharply if the study is widened to include the first decade. This somewhat puts the data and tendencies shown in this table, created in 1865, into perspective.

However, before studying the traffic for France, this document has the merit of providing a few indications concerning the position of French ports in the American crude oil trade at its beginning, and of specifying the pioneering nature of a large number of European ports.

II. General Characteristics of the French Oil Traffic

In the first part we established the fact, mainly on the basis of statistical sources, that France was a pioneering country in the oil trade, the same applying to numerous other European countries. We must now determine the nature and structure thereof and quantify that traffic, so as to explain transformations noted in it.

In this second part, we will study, in succession, the changes in quantities of crude oil and of imported products, their breakdown, and the reasons for that breakdown.

A. An Importing-consuming Country, but also an Exporter

Fig. 4 puts changes in the volumes and composition of French oil imports into perspective. That chart represents the total oil imports as well as the components thereof, those of crude and those of products already refined between 1861 and 1950.

Fig. 4. French oil imports structure 1861-1950

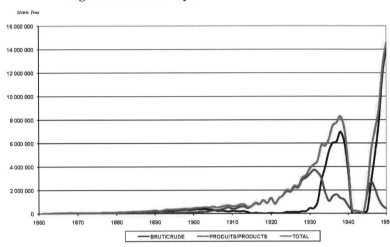

Sources: Statistiques générales des Douanes françaises

As one can see in the "Total" curve, the increase of imports of hydrocarbons generally was gradual, and then speeded up as of the start of the twentieth century, taking off in the 1930s, as well as after the Second World War.

One could simply explain that this surge in imports was the result of the development of all techniques using products coming from the refining process: automobiles, heating, ship propulsion, locomotives, aviation, etc. in addition to lighting. But that is not the only reason. It was also the fruit of an economic and political choice.

If one considers the curve of crude imports, 100,000 tons is exceeded in 1884, 400,000 tons in 1903, and 1 million tons in 1932, to reach a maximum of about 7 million in 1938 (a level again found in 1948). To supplement this chart, we must mention the fact that the customs statistics indicate that during the entire period under study, except during the Second World War, France exported crude oil and products to the other European countries, but also to Mediterranean and South American States, as well as to its overseas possessions (without its being possible to determine whether part of the oil produced[4] in France was exported itself). These "reexports" at certain times represent only a very small share of imports, except during the first decade of our period.[5] However,

---

[4]   Maximum production: 72,000 tons (1938).

[5]   In 1863, France imported 9,475 tons of crude oil and exported 4,260 tons. In 1900, 349,974 tons and 50 tons; in 1950, 14,135,488 tons and 8,759 tons.

the values of French crude imports represent only a tiny part of world output: approximately 3% toward 1870, 1% in 1890, and even a mere 0.06% in 1925. But the revival of crude imports at the start of the 1930s increased this rate to 1.5% toward 1933. In 1950, French imports of crude accounted for 2.69% of world production at that time.

On the other hand, the curve for the "Products" variable displays a trend opposite to crude. Hence we can see, in the chart, inversions of tendencies between the curves for crude imports and for refined products: first of all toward 1905, but also at the beginning of the 1930s. But until the dawn of the twentieth century, it does not enable us to see the details concerning such imports or to distinguish possible inversions of the crude and refined curves. Another graphic representation is needed to tackle and make detailed comparisons between those two statistical series, so as to explain their variations.

B. Importing Crude or Products? The "Oil Question" between Taxation and Strategic Reasons

The study of the volumes of crude and of refined oil indicated tendency inversions to us in the choice of the kind of hydrocarbons to be imported to meet national demand. This question of choosing between importing crude or already refined oil implies the question as to whether or not the country should have a refining industry. This "oil question", mentioned by a certain number of French authors[6], is debated depending on the times and the players on the basis of taxation or strategic grounds. A study of the crude/refine breakdown of oil imports will point to a very useful period segmentation in order to characterise these choices of a taxation or strategic type.

Fig. 5 represents the breakdown between crude and imported products in France between 1861 and 1950. These two curves confirm the inversions, already mentioned in Fig. 4, found in 1933 and 1947, but they also bring out some new ones. What is the explanation of this?

---

[6]   For instance: GASCHEAU (Maurice), *La question des pétroles en France*, 1903.

Fig. 5 Crude & oil products imports (1861-1950)

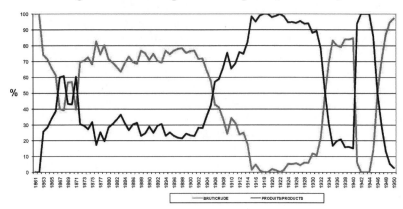

Sources: Statistiques générales des Douanes françaises
© M. LE DEZ – Université du Havre-UMR IDEES/CIRTAI Sept. 2006

The fact is that one sees that they coincide perfectly with changes in customs legislation. In that connection, let's consider the stages of each trend inversion in the curves:

– The years from 1861 to 1870 constitute a period of uncertainty for manufacturers, since following the law of 4 June 1864, the difference of customs duties between crude and refined is insufficient and they hesitate in making their choice, whence a balance between the percentages. That was also the time of the beginnings of an industry, or rather one can say of "refining" or "purification" craftsmanship by traders in or manufacturers of plant oils, which viewed oil as a source of extra profits.

– The laws from 1871 to 1873, which surtaxed refined oil, promoted crude imports, the government having desired the emergence of a national refining industry.

But in 1903 a new customs law, establishing what was known as a "manufacturing" tax on refining, reduced the differential rate on crude (the crude-refined taxation difference increased), a fact that encouraged refiners to import products, rather than crude. The effects of that law were felt immediately, and the trend reversal occurred in 1905.

While being accentuated during the First World War, that effect lasted until the 1928 laws, which reformed the customs treatment of products and defined a new oil importing approach. Their main consequence was the institution of a veritable refining industry in France, with an increase in crude imports.

However, the application of the customs legislation of 1928 was suspended in September 1939, and the State then managed the national supply. That exceptional situation lasted until 29 June 1950, the date on which the 1928 legislation was put back into effect: the rationing period ended.

In the meantime, the Second World War cut France off from its imports of crude oil, but not from imports of products arriving either from Germany, from Rumania, or from the United States (until 1941).

At the end of hostilities, imports of refined oil needed for restarting the national economy were reduced as of the time of recommissioning of the refining tool.

In the foregoing two charts (see Figs 4 and 5), we showed the changes, the continuities and the breaks in supplies of France in the light of availability of the raw material, of the needs, but also of the political events and of customs legislation. We also brought out the increasing interest of French political and economic leaders in everything related to oil. That raw material became ever more necessary to operation of the national economy. Hence the questions relating to its supply, shipment and distribution were of ever greater interest to French economic players.

III. Transport Issues at the Heart of the Supply Networks

Let us now think about the origins of the crude oil and also about the companies importing that oil and which formed the refining industry in France.

A. The Origins of Crude Oil

Fig. 6 brings out the origins of the crude oil imported by France between 1861 and 1950. In that connection, we have collected the supplier countries grouped in six geographical spaces, so as to facilitate the reading of the chart.

Fig. 6 French crude oil imports by origin (1861-1950)

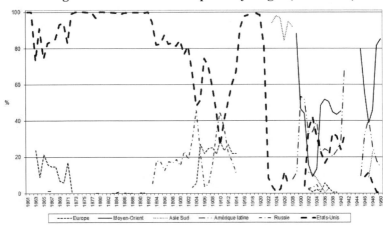

© M. LE DEZ – Université du Havre-UMR IDEES/CIRTAI Sept. 2006
Sources: Statistiques générales des Douanes françaises

Africa is absent, since no real production had yet emerged on that continent outside Egypt, which we have included in the Middle East zone.

Until 1892 the geographical distribution of imports was marked by the virtual US monopoly, for the simple reason that it was the largest producer and that the quality of the crude was such as to make it possible to obtain excellent lamp oil. The presence of imports coming from other European states from 1863 to 1872 is explained by the fact that the American crude transited, in particular, via Great Britain and Belgium. The fact is that special commercial and customs agreements linked those countries with France, making the purchase of oil in them attractive. You will also note a few imports coming from Russia, but they did not become significant until 1893.

Who are the importers during this period? In the first few years, the imports were the doing of Paris traders or traders established in the large French maritime ports. They bought the oil on the futures market of the importing port to resell it. But there were others than traders. There were also manufacturers that, already involved in the production of plant oil, launched out into "oil refining". For instance, as of 1861 the firm of Fenaille et Châtillon, specialising in production of greases and oils, bought a few barrels of oil in Le Havre to study all of the possibilities for using that product. Others followed (such as Desmarais Frères, which gave rise to Total group), and in 1863 France had 17 refineries. They were often small workshops that multiplied during that first decade. But of the 26 industrial establishments existing in 1882, only 20 remained in 1891. Those refiners got supplies almost solely from Standard Oil.

Between 1892 and 1918, there was an initial diversification of supplies. In 1892, the majority of French refiners were grouped in a "Chambre syndicale" (trade association), whereas already the three firms in Paris (Fenaille and Despeaux, Deutsch and Desmarais) had already established a special group that had powerful contacts with the foreign producers. That "Chambre syndicale" was established in order to more effectively meet the demands of the producing companies with respect to prices, and in that year of 1892 it had 14 members when a new supply agreement was concluded with Standard Oil.

During that period, there was a lasting and growing reappearance of imports of Russian oil, which was beginning to compete with US production. That resulted from Franco-Russian agreements and from the appearance of a tariff distinction made depending on the origin of the oil. Europe (outside Russia) was also present, but at this time it was Rumania that exported to France starting in 1903. Another reason for importing oil from various countries was the difference in crude grades. The oil imports from the United States were richer in lamp oil quality than the ones coming from Russia, which contained more lubrication oils and residues. Thus the product range was widening.

In 1902, there were 15 refiners in France, but the 1903 laws forced them to reduce their refining activities and to become, rather, importers of finished products. It was at that time that the foreign companies set up shop in France, including, for instance, Vacuum Oil Company in 1893 and Standard Oil of New Jersey in 1902.

When the First World War broke out, France was cut off from its supplies of Russian oil from the Black Sea and from the Caucasus, as well as from the other European producers, such as Austria-Hungary and Rumania. As a result, crude supplies were provided by the United States, but as we have seen earlier, this chart is deceptive, since actually France imported almost exclusively products.

With respect to the companies that were above all importers of products, in 1914 the French oil market was in the hands of ten "maisons" known as the "Cartel of ten", which held a de facto monopoly on the market, favoured by the State until the end of hostilities.

Between 1918 and 1928, following the First World War, the US share dropped to the benefit of the Southeast Asian countries between 1924 and 1928, France importing refined oil from them. But during that period, the imports of crude remained low, below the level of the products.

On a world scale, following the armistice, Standard Oil requested suppression of the interallied oil conference, which organised supplies during the war. In December 1918, the trusts, that is, Standard Oil Company (New Jersey), Royal Dutch Shell and the Anglo-Persian Company, were free and dominated world output. In France, that new situation brought a complete reorganisation of the old companies to the benefit of new ones, formed under the impetus of those three major producers. Those Majors tried to find outlets for their oil and to create distribution and sales networks. To do so, they created or developed their subsidiaries, absorbing or merging with the existing French companies. In France, to partly counter such trusts, a mixed company was established in 1924 independent of the big oil groups, Compagnie Française des Pétroles (CFP). That company was established following the award to France of 25% of the shares of Turkish Petroleum Company, a concession holder of oil fields in the Middle East. Thus France had supply sources that it controlled and a national company, not only for distribution, but also for production, and soon for refining.

The period from 1929 to 1940 was marked by the diversification of supplies. The fact that the law favouring refining went into effect brought a diversification of sources of crude. This law resulted from the discovery of oil deposits in Mesopotamia in 1927, but that crude was not imported by France until 1934. In the meantime, French imports came mainly from Persia as of 1929 (80% of imports of crude in 1929) and from others states in the Middle East. But that share gradually declined as imports of crude from Latin America increased. The new refining companies that were established following the law of 1928 (subsidiaries of majors already established in France, but also a subsidiary of the CFP, Compagnie Française de Raffinage) obtained supplies from the production sites of their own parent companies. For instance, Royal Dutch Shell took an interest at that time in the crude coming from Venezuela. Its French subsidiary, Société des Pétroles Jupiter, equipped its refinery at Petit-Couronne near Rouen to mainly handle the crude coming from that country as soon as it went into operation in 1929.

The share of North American crude still amounted to 40% in 1933, but then declined, particularly to the benefit of imports from Iraq, but also from Latin America and even from Rumania, which again became a French supplier in 1931.

On the eve of the Second World War, the refining companies established in France processed crude in the following proportions: 45% from the Middle East, 35% from the United States, and 20% from Latin America. Crude oil then accounted for more than 80% of French imports of hydrocarbons.

The war and the Occupation isolated France from its crude oil supplies until 1945. It was necessary to wait until 1946 and the first re-commissionings of refineries to find significant imports of crude.

Two producing regions then emerged in the post-war period: the Middle East and Latin America. In 1950, France supplied itself from producing states in those two regions of the world to an extent of over 90%!

This chart shows that since 1861 France has been obtaining supplies from distant states on all continents, except Africa. Hence the issues of maritime transport and of the weight of a few ports concentrating that traffic will be vital in order to understand the organisation of oil activities in France.

B. The Weight of the Maritime Ports in the Choice of Industrial Developments

There is one aspect of the oil supply of a European consuming country like France that has taken on primordial importance: the aspect relating to transport, particularly maritime transport.

We have seen by way of the various documents studied that a great part of the world production of crude oil was the object of international trade over maritime routes, this since the beginning of its history. The lasting nature of the commercial links between France and a small number of producing countries (15 between 1861 and 1950 according to Fig. 1 and the customs statistics) was to contribute to the appearance of a few major maritime routes.

Needless to say, those routes follow changes in the geographical breakdown of supply of and demand for crude oil. The trans-Atlantic lines with North America and Latin America were joined, as of 1929, by the ones linking the French ports with the ports in the Eastern Mediterranean, such as Tripoli or Haifa in the 1930s. This marked the beginning of Iraqi production. Just after the Second World War, a new maritime route developed, the one linking the oil fields in the Persian Gulf with the Western ports via the Suez Canal.

With respect to France, those maritime lines all ended at a small number of ports, almost all located in the mouth or at the end of estuaries of the major rivers. Fig. 7 informs us about this. One is dealing here with some very old major commercial ports for which, at the beginning, oil constituted a traffic among others, but which came to specialise in that so special merchandise with the development of the industrial activities connected with it: refining, and then, much later, petrochemistry.

Fig. 7 Oil import & refining in France (1861-1950)

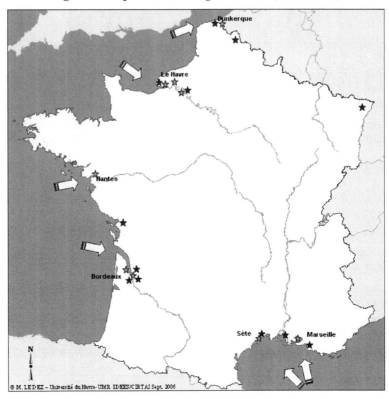

<u>Key</u> :

Le Havre : Main import place
★ : 1st generation refineries (ab.1863-ab.1923)
☆ : 2nd generation refineries (from 1929)

© M. LE DEZ – Université du Havre-UMR IDEES/CIRTAI Sept. 2006

Thus those major maritime ports captured the oil traffic of a certain number of neighbouring secondary ports. For instance, that was the case with Sète (formerly written Cette), a pioneer port[7] that came under the influence of Marseille in spite of the nearby establishment of refineries in Frontignan.

---

[7] See Figs 3 and 7.

Thus the period between the two world wars witnessed the concentration of oil imports around the ports of Marseille, Bordeaux, Nantes, Le Havre, Dunkirk and their hinterlands. That is where the "second generation" refineries, resulting from the customs laws of 1928, established themselves in the 1930s.

The French manufacturers, importers and refiners, set up shop near the import ports enjoying easy access to the interior part of the country, since shipment of the raw material is less expensive then moving numerous and varied oil products characterised by higher value added. But it is true that this depends on the level of consumption and on the location of the population centres.

The location of the refining tool is an indicator of the supply model selected. In the case of a former producing country, the refineries are close to the production area. Thus in France there was a refinery in Merkwiller, near the Pechelbronn oil field in Alsace, close to the German border[1], a fact that explains its remoteness from the import ports. The great majority of French refineries were built near a consumption centre or along a communication artery, such as a river, in order to facilitate shipment of the imported crude and of the oil products toward the interior part of the country.

This distribution of oil activities in France, established as of the end of the nineteenth century, lasted until the 1950s. Subsequently, with the increased consumption of oil products, oil pipeline networks were constructed, and two main axes were selected:

– the Seine axis, linking the port of Le Havre with the Paris region;
– the one in the valley of the Rhône, linking Marseille with Germany.

In both cases, the pipeline networks connected the import port with depots, with new refineries known as "inland", and with industrial or urban consumption centres marked by increasing needs.

Hence those ports, interfaces between the places of production and places of consumption, remained the basic link in France's oil supply.

In Conclusion

Between 1861 and 1950, oil remained a "New World" product, in spite of the discovery of new deposits on almost all continents. The French customs statistics bring out the existence of oil exchanges with other European consumer states as of 1863. In France, as in other countries that only consumed, the hydrocarbon supply followed the development both of that resource and of its applications, but also political events. Following the First World War, there was an increasing awareness of the role played by oil in the national economy, with consequences:

– for the structure of imports: crude/refined

– for industrial policy: the choice of a refining industry on the national territory

– concerning the choice of supplies of crude oil: diversification with control of new deposits, transport means and distribution.

The ports receiving oil in France in the nineteenth century were, to a great extent, the same ones as now. The fact is that the map of France's oil facilities was established on the eve of the Second World War. That was followed by some adaptations to increase traffic and demand. However, the supply issues were more than ever at the centre of political concerns in the second half of the twentieth century.

Bibliography

BACON (Raymond Foss) & HAMOR (William Allen), *The American Petroleum Industry*, 2 Vols., McGraw-Hill Book Company Inc., New York, 1916.

COMITE PROFESSIONNEL DU PETROLE, *Éléments statistiques*, Rueil Malmaison, C.P.D.P. éd., Publication annuelle depuis 1955.

DIRECTION DES DOUANES, *Tableau général du commerce et de la navigation*, Paris, Publication annuelle depuis 1832.

REDWOOD (Sir Boverton), *A Treatise on petroleum*, 3 Vols, Charles Griffin & C° Ltd, London, 1913.

REY (Alphonse), L'Huile de pétrole: connaissance de l'huile de pétrole dans les temps anciens, importance de son exploitation, procédés employés pour l'extraire et la raffiner, applications diverses de ses dérivés, Genève, Impr. Pfeffer & Puky, 1865.

SCHUHMANN (Jacques), *Le Transport maritime des pétroles*, Paris, éd. A. Pedone, 1937.

A Few Strategic Considerations Concerning French Imports of Oil Products between 1946 and 2005

Roberto NAYBERG

Panthéon-Sorbonne University, France

This communication considers oil imports as a whole (both crude oil and finished products), to the exclusion of condensates of natural gas, natural gas and other gaseous hydrocarbons, trade in which is specific to them (imports from a small number of countries, distinct operators and distribution networks), and of vaselines, paraffins and waxes, which are of diverse mineral origins.

Its only ambition is to bring out, by examining five charts showing the development of imports over the 60 years in question, a few significant tendencies and their implication from a geo-strategic viewpoint.

I. The Quantities Imported

A. Changes in Amounts Imported

Fig. 1 Oil imports total in France

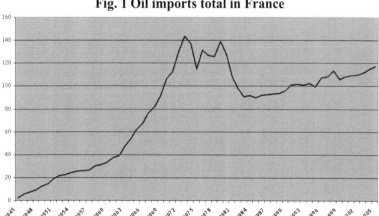

In spite of the discoveries and of the exploitation of a few deposits in mainland France (in Alsace, the Landes, in Lacq and in the Paris Basin), the constant feature of that period, as was also true of the previous one, is still the disproportion between the needs and indigenous output. The coverage rate never exceeded 5%.

The most striking fact is that, until 1973 inclusive, there was a very strong increase in imports. As of 1948, they exceeded their 1938 level (namely a little more than 8 million metric tons), to reach the record level of more than 143 million tons in 1973, which represents a multiplication of tonnage by a factor of 16 in 25 years. The increase was particularly spectacular in the 1964-73 period, with annual increases often exceeding 10% (16% in 1970, 15% in 1972). That 10-year period witnessed a near tripling of imports, from less than 54 million tons in 1964 to more than 143 million in 1973.

After the first oil shock, imports fell suddenly, reaching an initial low in 1975 (-20% by comparison with the 1973 peak), and then recovered markedly. In 1979, they almost got back to their 1973 level at almost 139 million tons.

But the second oil shock dealt imports a fatal blow. They suddenly collapsed (almost 35% less in four years). In 1983, they represented less than two-thirds of the levels reached in 1973 and 1979. For several years they stagnated at a level of around 90 million tons a year, that is, at the level reached in 1969, some 15 years earlier.

Since 1986, there has been a slow uptrend, utterly out of line with the triumphant upswing noted in the period 1948-73, which all the same brought imports in 1991 to over a hundred million tons, a level they had not reached since 1981, the figure of 117 million tons being reached in 2005, meaning – by comparison with the relative low reached in 1985 –, a 30% rise in twenty years.

In 2005, imports as a whole got back to their level of 1971 or 1975.

B. The Structure of Imports

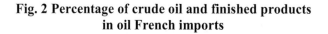

**Fig. 2 Percentage of crude oil and finished products
in oil French imports**

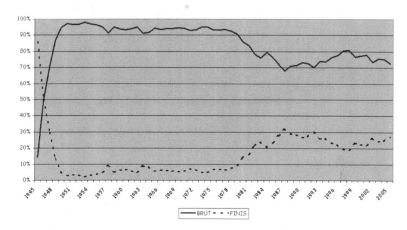

Fig. 2 describes the trend of imports expressed in percent, representing crude oil and finished products. This development can be broken down into three stages or main moments:

– While in 1938, crude imports accounted for almost 85% of the total, in 1945 the situation was almost reversed, imports of crude constituting less than 15% of the total. This sudden and spectacular reversal was due to the dependence on American supplies, consisting essentially of finished products, and to the destruction suffered by industrial facilities during the war.

– As of 1946, imports of crude and of finished products were in balance, and as of 1948, the share of crude oil in total imports slightly exceeded the percentage reached in 1938, while in 1949, it went over the 90% mark.

This astonishing rise in the proportion of crude (from 14% to 95% in five years) bears witness both to the tenacity of the French political and administrative figures in their desire to make re-creation of a national oil refining industry possible, and to the strength of the effort to reconstruct an adequate industrial tool.

The 1949-79 period found the share of crude constantly maintaining itself above 90%, with peaks of 97 or 98% between 1950 and 1954. That period really experienced the most complete realization of the political will that had conceived the laws of 1928 and had them voted by Parliament.

It coincides very exactly with the very strong growth rates of imported tonnages.

We remind you that the decision to create, in France, an industry refining crude oil and to bring about the conditions required for this had been made by the Higher Council of National Defence at its plenary session held on 10 November 1923 and had been based on strictly strategic considerations (wider choice of the origins of imports, the development of industrial stocks added to the buffer reserves).

As happened with the imported quantities, the second oil shock proved to be decisive. As of 1980, and for the first time since 1948, imports of finished products exceeded one-tenth of total imports. In less than ten years, from 1979 to 1987, their share increased from 9 to 32%. Since then, the amount has maintained itself within a range of 20 to 30%, with a slight drop until 2000 (23%), and then an advance in the last few years (27% en 2005).

This communication does not concern itself with detailing the reasons explaining this history, but one may put forth the hypothesis that it results from the conjunction of a modification of the economic conditions of operation of oil refining (decline of the profit margin, competition offered by foreign refineries, particularly those in Europe, benefiting from more advantageous operating conditions) and from a change in the structure of consumption of finished products (development of the use of gas-oil) and in the distribution procedures for fuels (sale at hypermarkets).

II. Origin of the Imports

A. The Main Moments

Fig. 3 Origins of oil imports in France

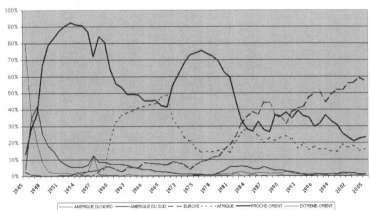

The countries that supplied France with oil products have been grouped within six geographical areas:

- North America (excluding Mexico);
- Central and South America (including Mexico and the insular states in the Caribbean);
- Europe (including Russia and the European states of the former USSR);
- Africa (including Egypt);
- The Near and Middle East (including Turkey);
- Eastern and insular Asia (including the states of former Soviet Central Asia).

This convention, which is questionable as such, made it possible to simplify the details of the national flows, which were too fragmentary.

Thus one can distinguish five main moments in the period of interest to us.

1945: While the Americas in 1938 represented 55% of all imports (including 34% for North America) and the Near East 39%, in 1945 the war circumstances and the conditions surrounding the liberation of Western Europe gave the United States, very temporarily, a share of the French market (80%) that it had not held since 1923. That restoration came at the expense of the Near East and of South America, whose market shares fell to 13 and 4%, respectively.

1946-59: As of 1946, the share held by North America returned to its 1938 level, with 36% of total imports. But that return to the pre-war situation was only a fleeting moment in an irreversible process of decline. The North American share fell to less than 5% as of 1949, and thenceforth did not exceed 3%, with the notable exception of the year 1957. That relative sidelining of a major French supplier since the nineteenth century constituted the originality of the period following the Second World War by comparison with the previous period.

In an initial phase, the North American decline boosted South America, which supplied France with up to 42% of its imports in 1947. But here again, this market share dropped suddenly, going below the 10% level as of 1951. It did not get back above that level, also with the exception of the year 1957.

The big winners of this commercial battle, needless to say, were the Near and Middle East, which combined the double advantage of being relatively close to France geographically speaking and of having an abundant offering of oil products. As of 1947, that region almost recovered the market share it held in 1938 (38% of total imports). It got over the 80% mark in 1950 and over 90% in 1952. The consequences of the

Suez affair in 1956 reduced its share somewhat, as it fell back to 72% in 1957. But it recovered the next year, to 84%, and still stood at 81% in 1959.

The predominance of the Near East, not previously noted in French supplies, reached its relative peak in the 1950s. The only possible comparison is with the years 1915 to 1920 for American oil, but that was a wartime and immediately post-war period. It was unprecedented since the beginning of the twentieth century for France, in peacetime, to have depended so strongly for its oil imports on one geo-political zone – moreover one that was not among the most stable. In addition, it is odd to note that it was at a time when France was suffering the political consequences of Arab nationalisms in the Near East and in North Africa, and when its Near Eastern policy had never been so favourable to the young state of Israel that it accepted such dependence. That situation, which is explained by economic and historical considerations (Near Eastern interests held, sometimes for a long time, by oil companies operating in France, the front rank of which naturally included Compagnie française des pétroles), found its sanction in the supply difficulties resulting from the Suez crisis.

1960-70: These 11 years witnessed the continuation of tendencies that had emerged in the previous period. South America's share continued to decline (7% in 1960, 2% in 1970) while Europe's rose (5% in 1960, 7% in 1970), while remaining marginal.

The really novel feature lays in the reduction of the Near East's share: 81% in 1959, 65% as of 1960, 42% in 1970. But in tonnage terms, that decline is found only between 1958 (more than 25 million tons) and 1961 (less than 21 million tons). As of 1962, the uptrend returned, the figure exceeding 44 million tons in 1970.

This relative decline was to the benefit of the African continent, where substantial deposits were discovered and went into production at the end of the 1950s (Algeria, Libya, Nigeria, Gabon). Representing 1% at most of the French imports until 1957, it began to progress in 1958 (3%), and in 1970 reached the level of almost half (49%) of the French supply. The surge was no less spectacular in tonnage terms: less than a million tons in 1958, and more than 52 million in 1970, a level never again reached subsequently – far from it.

In 1970, for the first time since the initial shipments of Iranian oil were received in 1915, Africa's share exceeded that of the Near East.

How can one explain this African success?

First of all, to be sure, by the same economic reasons that accounted for the Near Eastern success: the relative geographical proximity and the abundant supply. But also by political considerations: certain such oil territories (Algeria, Gabon, Congo) were part of the French Union until 1962. That was the time at which certain writers, impressed by this African mirage, talked about "French oil". Even after independence, the economic links were not broken. In certain countries, particularly in West Africa, French political influence lived on. And there was also the fact that the French companies, in particular the ones grouped within ELF-Aquitaine, played a non-negligible role in exploration of those countries and quite naturally shipped to mainland France the oil produced in the areas for which they held concessions.

To sum up, in the 1960s, the French supply of oil products got back to a balance between several geo-political zones with respect to imports, a balance it had experienced at the end of the 1930s and, fleetingly, in 1946-47. To be sure, that balance was more fragile than the one obtained 20 or 30 years previously, since it was based on only two zones instead of three. But it looked equally satisfactory to the people handling that matter.

1971-76: During these six years, the Americas no longer accounted for any more than 2% at most of imports, and Europe remained below 10%.

The most striking phenomenon was the collapse of African oil: 49% of French imports in 1970, and 14% in 1976. This trend is equally remarkable when expressed in percentage terms: more than 52 million tons in 1970, less than 34 million in 1973 (at the peak of French imports), and less than 19 million in 1976. That makes a fall of 64% in seven years, whereas the total decline of imports resulting from the first oil shock was only 20%.

This dizzying plunge, which thus began before the first oil shock, is attributable first of all to the nationalization without indemnity or compensation of Algerian oil, which occurred in 1971 and hit the French companies hard, as well as to the Libyan political convulsions.

It shows once again, in the history of oil, that outside possession of oil deposits in the national subsoil, there is no guaranteed salvation and that situations that seem as safe as houses are always at the mercy of the decisions made by the indigenous political authorities.

This relative and absolute decline of Africa was to the benefit of the Near East, which halted the decline of its market share that had been almost uninterrupted since 1958: 84% of total French imports in 1958, 42% in 1970, but 55% as of 1971 and 76% in 1976. While getting back to an extremely strong dominant position, since it provided three-fourths of French imports in the mid-1970s, it did not reach the heights of the 1950s all the same.

When expressed on terms of tonnage, the imports from the Near East increase continuously from 1962 until 1974. They rise from a little less than 21 million tons to almost 100 million, a virtual quintupling in 13 years. The increase was particularly marked in the years 1970-74, since it exceeded 125% in five years.

1977-2005: This period experienced a new and spectacular reversal of the situation.

The Near East's share began to decline as of 1977, initially slowly (74% in 1977, 69% in 1979), and then very rapidly following the second oil shock (63% in 1980, 28% in 1987). After having represented three-fourths of imports in 1976, that region supplied only a bit more than a fourth 11 years later. From more than 99 million tons in 1976, imports plunged to less than 26 million tons in 1987, a 74% drop.

The share recovered slightly starting in 1989 (37%), remained at a relatively high level of 30 to 40% until 2000 (31%), and then declined again to the lower level (23% in 2002, 24% in 2005). In tonnage terms, by comparison with the bottom reached in 1988 (a bit less than 25 million tons), the 1990s also witnessed an increase (a bit more than 41 million tons in 1998), followed beginning in 2001 by a marked decline (about 26 million and a half tons in 2005), marking a return to the levels of the 1980s.

The beneficiaries of this decline were, to a small extent and in an initial phase, the Americas and Africa. North America gained one to two points in market share, South America four to five, and African a dozen. But those areas again declined as of 1989, falling back to their prior level: in 2005, the Americas accounted for 2% of the French supply; and Africa for 16%. One even notes a downtrend for Africa, weakly marked, since 1984, which also appears in tonnage changes: 26.5 million in 1984 and barely 18 million in 2005, making a drop of 31% in 22 years.

But this was mainly to the benefit of Europe, which reached the level of 10% in 1977, crossed it as of 1978, and in 1987 – for the first time since 1913 – hit 44% of total imports. The tonnage, less than 12 million tons in 1976, exceeded 41 million in 1987.

After a very slight decline in 1989-92, which found Europe going below the 40% level (32% in 1991), the advance continued to go over 50% in 1996, getting close to 60% in 2004-05. The tonnage reached almost 54 million in 1996 and 67 million in 2004. In 30 years (1976-2005), imports from Europe rose by almost million tons, more than quintupling.

Those imports from Europe had a triple origin:

– North Sea (United Kingdom, Norway);

– Eastern Europe (ex-Soviet Union);

– Various other countries, mainly members of the European Union.

Even if the first two consist of indigenous oils, the third has an indefinite origin, sometimes non-European. It consists of finished products and replaces imports of crude oil that were previously refined in France. Hence this increase for Europe was partly a consequence of the crisis, and then of the economic repositioning of the French refining sector.

In addition, the weight of the Near Eastern countries within the Organization of Petroleum Exporting Countries and the political instability characterizing that region (let us mention for the record, and only as examples, during that short period, the Lebanese civil war, the Islamic revolution in Iran, the war between Iran and Iraq, and the two wars against Iraq) encouraged the French importers to emphasize supply sources that, if not more reliable, were at least more stable.

Due to that fact, starting in 1983 French supplies were relatively balanced between three major source zones: Europe, which in 1984 became the main supplier for France (with reservations that we expressed above as concerns the indigenous origin of certain European imports), the Near East and Africa. At the end of the period, the respective weights of those three zones stood at 57, 24 and 16% (64, 26 and 18 million tons), hence accounting for almost 97% of the French supply for around 109 million tons.

B. The French Dependence

To simplify the analysis, we have taken only three types of products: crude oils, naphtha, and aviation fuel, which represent both a major fraction of imports of mineral oils and products of an obviously strategic nature.

Fig. 4 Dependence intensity

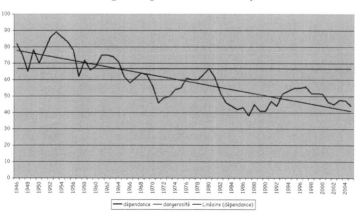

Fig. 4 brings out what we will call the intensity of the dependence. Expressed in percentage terms, it represents the proportion of the three leading countries supplying the products indicated above in total imports of such products.

The higher that proportion, that is, the more intense the dependence, the greater the fragility of the position of the importing country. The fact is that the latter is proportional to the concentration of the number of suppliers, and any importing country should follow the rule of minimizing the risk inherent to its situation of dependence by spreading the risk out over the largest possible number of import sources.

The paradox lies in the fact that the multiplicity of links attenuates the danger. We have considered here that the intensity of the dependence reached a critical threshold, designated in the chart as the "seuil de dangerosité" (danger threshold), when it exceeded two-thirds of the Y-axis.

An examination of this chart shows, looking beyond the ups and downs of the business cycle, a very marked long-term trend toward a decrease of the intensity of the dependence. With three exceptions, the index remains equal to or greater than the "danger threshold" from the year of the beginning of our study until 1964 inclusive, namely for 20 years all the same (and one could maintain this assertion going back to 1913). Starting in 1965, it goes back below the two-thirds level, no longer exceeding it except for one year, 1980, and even at that by just a single point. For more than a quarter of a century, it has oscillated within a range of 40 to 55%, making that the most favourable situation since the beginning of the twentieth century.

Roughly speaking, one can distinguish three stages in this development:

– After having reached peaks during the Second World War, under conditions of a collapse of quantities imported and of the number of supplier countries, the index falls back to 82 as of 1946. This downtrend was extended during the following years and there is a decline to as low as 70 in 1950.

– Starting in 1951, the index goes back up, as of 1952 crosses the level of 80 (with 89 in 1953), and still posts 78 in 1956, the year of the Suez crisis.

– Starting in 1957, the index fell suddenly. While it was still often over 70 until 1964, it hovered around the 50-60 level in the years 1965-79, experienced a sudden thrust in 1980 (67) following the second oil shock, but then oscillated between 40 and 45 in the 1980s, with a record of 38 coming in 1987. In spite of a slight deterioration of the index in the 1990s (with a high of 56 in 1997), the situation again improved at the beginning of the twenty-first century (44 in 2005).

Fig. 5 portrays the trend of primary dependence over the same period and for the same products. Expressed in percentage terms, this indicator represents the share of the leading supplier country in total imports of those products. Hence it makes it possible to measure the highest degree of dependence reached by France in its relationships with a supplier country. It supplements and specifies the previous indicator, which pointed more generally to the general and structural fragility of the oil supply.

Fig. 5 Primary Dependence

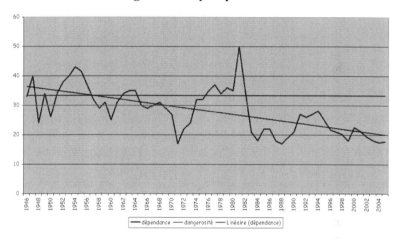

We put the danger threshold at one-third along the Y-axis, feeling that this is the limit of the risk acceptable to a country importing a strategic product, and that beyond that point, in case of a sudden break in supplies coming from the main supplier, it may become very difficult to find, overnight, one or several suppliers to provide the required amounts.

An examination of the chart shows a choppy curve, which demonstrates a tendency toward improvement over the period. One can distinguish five segments in it:

– In the immediate post-war period, the American continent recovers, temporarily, the predominance it exercised between 1913 and 1934: the United States of America in 1945 (index 69), and Venezuela between 1946 and 1948 (indices of 33, 40 and 24).

– Between 1949 and 1960, the Near East returns to the position held in the pre-war period (between 1935 and 1940) with indices between 25

43

and 43, but in addition to Iraq, which remained one of France's main suppliers throughout that period and held first place between 1953 and 1956, and also again in 1959 and 1960, two newcomers appeared: Saudi Arabia (index 34 in 1949) and above all Kuwait between 1950 and 1952, and again in 1957-58.

– The 1960s were characterized by the Algerian interlude, with a very rapidly rising level (index 1 in 1958, 2 in 1959, 20 as of 1960, and 31 in 1961), culminating at 35 in 1963 and 1964, then stagnating at a slightly lower level at the danger threshold.

– The nationalization of Algerian oil put a sudden end to the "African" decade of oil supply (the Algerian index falling from 27 in 1970 to 9 en 1971), and Saudi Arabia wrested first place away from it from 1971 to 1998, with the exception of the years 1984, 1985 and 1987, for which the United Kingdom was ahead of it. The Saudi Arabian index oscillated around the critical threshold in the 1970s, with a sudden push to 50 in 1981, but it then fell back to a range of 17 to 29, a very low level.

– Since 1999, Norway has held first place in the French supply (an index of 18 in 2005), followed by Russia (15) and Saudi Arabia (12). This is the lowest primary dependence since 1913.

III. Five Crises

Without going into a detailed examination of the consequences for oil imports of the five crises of 1956 (Suez), 1973 (first oil shock), 1979 (second oil shock), 1990-91 (first Gulf War) and 2003 (second Gulf War), which would go beyond the framework of this communication, it seemed interesting to us to provide a bit of information and commentary.

A. Suez

France contributed to the triggering of the Suez crisis in a situation in which its dependence on imports from the Near East had never been so high. That crisis forced it to call, temporarily, on some suppliers that had been somewhat neglected for a dozen years.

The Near East's share suddenly dropped from more than 90% to 72% in 1957, to the benefit of North America (which gained 12 index points) and of South America (up 7 points). At that time, as had been the case before the Second World War, the Americas could still cope with urgent additional demand, for relatively limited amounts (on the order of 3,350,000 tons). Hence they were still, but for the last time, the backup in a crisis situation.

That obligation, a humiliating one in the context of the situation, entailing recourse to the Americas, and particularly to the United States, was one element among others constituting a good illustration of the weakness of the French position at that time, since France had to call precisely on the country that had made the biggest contribution to its political failure. So, taking only its oil interests into account, France could not afford to give rise to hostility among the Arab countries in the Near East and to irritation of its American ally.

Nevertheless, as we have seen, the immediate consequences of the crisis did not last for more than a few months, and as of 1958, the Near East's share recovered.

B. The First Oil Shock

The 1973 shock hit France at a time when it was moving away from Africa to once again make the Near East its main supplier.

Hence the war in October 1973 wrong-footed France. However, since France at that time was obtaining supplies mainly from the members of the Organization of the Petroleum Exporting Countries, one can maintain that there was no really good solution for it. Maintaining the previous situation (African predominance) would not have spared it from the economic shock resulting from the higher prices of imported oil.

The best proof of this is that, unlike what happened in 1956, 1973 did not bring a break, even a brief one, as had occurred at the time of the Suez crisis, in the continuity of the movements characterizing that period: the share of the Near East continued to increase until 1976, and Africa's share to decline, while the shares of the Americas and of the Far East did not change, maintaining themselves at a very low level; Europe's share stagnated at 7 to 9% until 1976.

Hence the oil shock, manifesting itself in changes in imported quantities, did not result in even a temporary reshuffle of import sources.

C. The Second Oil Shock

On the other hand, the 1979 oil shock accelerated and precipitated changes that had set in two or three years previously, in addition to leading to a very sharp reduction of imported quantities and to an increase in the share of finished products, which we have already mentioned.

The share of the Near East, which had already dipped from 76% in 1976 to 69% in 1979, plunged suddenly to 27% in 1985. That decline was a bit to the benefit of Africa, which rose from 15% in 1979 to 29% in 1984, but above all of Europe, whose market share jumped from 12% in 1979 to 35% as of 1984, reaching 44% in 1987.

To be sure, that European success was due to various and "technical" factors, such as the discovery of off-shore deposits, geographical proximity, and competition offered by foreign refining, but it was also based on "political" reasons, such as the desire to call on non-OPEC producers located outside the continuous field of instability represented by the Near and the Middle East.

Hence the second oil shock, to a much greater extent than the first one, precipitated changes than had begun to emerge as of 1977 and cast doubt on the foundations of oil imports.

D. The First Gulf War

Twelve years later, the situation was so changed that the crisis resulting from Iraq's invasion of Kuwait in the summer of 1990 did not affect France as it would have done in 1976.

To be sure, in 1990 the Near East still accounted for more than a third of French imports (36%), after having declined to 27% in 1988, but that was equalled by Europe (35%), followed by Africa (accounting for 23%).

Thus the halt to imports from Iraq and Kuwait did not create any immediate major problem, and did not endanger the security of French oil supplies – at least in the short run.

E. The Second Gulf War

In 2003, even more than 13 years previously, the bulk of the French supply was European (56% of imports, against 35% in 1990 and 32% in 1991); the Near East's share had fallen from 36% to 21%, while Africa's share had contracted from 23 to 18%.

Hence from the viewpoint of the security of the oil supply, the situation during a period of serious international crisis had never been so assured, and moreover no supply shortages were noted.

One simply notes – within the category of the European share – a significant shift from British origin to Russian, a trend dating back to 2000, the United Kingdom's share slipping from an average of 15 to 16% in the second half of the 1990s to 12%, and then to 9% in 2003 and 6% in 2005, while the Russian share suddenly rose from 6% in 2000 to 17% in 2003 and 15% in 2005, Russia thus trailing only Norway as France's leading supplier.

Thus the 60 years covered by this communication can be broken down into five periods, although the last one lasted for almost 30 years. During those six decades, the French oil supply was subject to numerous vicissitudes.

During the first 30 years covered, the Near East succeeded the Americas as the major source of imports of oil products. That role was very conspicuous at certain times, but was disputed by Africa at other times. During the following 30 years, Europe played the lead role. In this perpetually changing game, in which the market shares held by one or another geographical area experience sudden and rapid changes, the supply balance is necessarily a fleeting one. This balance, the expression of a relative and rough equality between two or three major import zones, is the best guarantor (except for energy saving or substitution) of the continuity of the oil supply, beyond the many political uncertainties characterizing today's world.

In case of inability to minimize the risks inherent to a given zone, they should be spread out over the greatest possible number of areas. Moreover such diversification of import origins has been constantly sought since the beginning of the twentieth century by the French persons handling this issue.

PART II

CRISIS AND SECURITY OF SUPPLIES

The French Presidency, the National Companies and the First Oil Shock

Armelle DEMAGNY-VAN EYSEREN

Paris-Sorbonne University, France

When it comes, in discussions of the oil issue, to the question of relationships between the national companies and the producing countries, the end of Georges Pompidou's presidency, the period from October 1973 to March 1974, constitutes a highlight in terms of a redefinition of French oil strategy. The fact is that the French president's death in March 1974 coincided with the installation of a new energy policy, the main lines of which were actually sketched out beginning in 1971, at a time at which the first signs of a turnaround on the oil market were becoming perceptible. The immediate analyses and the first measures adopted to deal with the upheavals on the oil market in 1973-74 express the reactivity of the institutional players – first of all of governmental authorities, and then in a second phase those of the national oil companies, which acted as vital relays expressing the French state's will in a French context of strong state intervention in oil matters since 1928.

The first upheavals on the oil market became perceptible as of the start of the 1970s and resulted more specifically for the French companies in the loss of Algerian oil. An analysis of that swing period will then make it possible to go more deeply into the presidency's reactions in the face of the changes on the oil market, as well as into the new strategies assigned to the national oil companies by the government following the oil shock.

I. The French Oil Situation on the Eve of the Oil Shock: Dependence on Resources

A. Increasing and Conscious Dependence on Oil ...

The substitution of oil for coal that occurred during the 1960s had the very concrete result for France of raising the energy dependence rate from 35% in 1960 to 77% in 1973, although the averages in the European Economic Community were, respectively, 30% and 60%. Thus France was more dependent than the Federal Republic of Germany, but less so than Italy. That dependence was mainly due to the consumption of oil products, which accounted for 70% of energy consumption in 1973 (13% for solid fuels, 9% for primary electricity and 8% for gas).[1] At that time, three-fourths of the imports of crude oil came from the Middle East.

But until the end of the 1960s, relative cohesion among the oil companies and dissension among the producing countries, due to each producer's desire to see its output increase faster than its neighbors' production, had kept oil prices at a relatively low level. Thus the tax per barrel of the producing countries had gradually risen, in terms of current dollars, from 80 to 90 cents/barrel (+15% in 10 years), but actually it declined by around 15% in terms of constant dollars because of world inflation fueled by the abundancy of the American currency.

That finding led the producing countries to strengthen their cohesion within OPEC. That strengthened concertation wound up in a series of agreements negotiated between the oil companies and the producing countries between the first half of 1971 (the agreements of Teheran, Tripoli and Baghdad) and January 1972 (the Geneva agreements following the devaluation of the dollar in December 1971), which contributed to an initial substantial increase of the price per barrel.[2]

At the same time, a pause in new petroleum discoveries in the world reduced the relative amplitude of reserves, so that a period of temporary under-investment in exploration caused bottlenecks in terms of availability, all the more so in that certain producer countries, such as Libya and Kuwait, in the light of persistent worldwide inflation, considered that their interest no longer called for boosting production rates, but rather for preserving their wealth in the form of "black gold" rather than in dollars. In the light of highly expansionary economic conditions and of, on one hand, oil's position in the economies of the industrialized countries and on the other hand of the absence of substitute energy, that situation resulted at the start of the 1970s in tension on the international oil market – tension fed by the disappearance, announced by the United States at the end of 1969, of the production capacities of the American

---

[1] See the diagrams concerning energy dependence rates and consumption for each source of energy in A. Beltran, "The energy question in France from 1960 to 1974: dependence, crisis and role of the State", in *Georges Pompidou in the face of economic changes in the West, 1969-74*, Paris, PUF, 2003, pp. 389 and 390.

[2] OPEC successively obtained inclusion of the oil fee in operating charges, an increase of the tax rate applied to the companies, and elimination of the rebates due to competition.

reserves and of that country's massive intervention as buyer on the oil market starting in 1972.

The trend of French consumption toward a situation of dependence on oil and the gradual movement toward more expensive oil (even if it was not really expensive) were well known to analysts and politicians, as is shown by this note from Bernard Esambert, technical advisor to President Pompidou for industrial questions:

> In 1970, the needs for primary energy amounted to 220 million tons of coal equivalent (Mtec), and the breakdown by energy forms was as follows: solid fuels 26%, oil products 59%, gas 6%, primary electricity (hydraulic and nuclear) 9%.
>
> This shows the very marked predominance of oil products in the French supply. The reversal noted in the price trend of oil products since the end of 1969, following a certain number of economic and political events, clearly brought out the uncertainties weighing on the cost of our supply; the other European countries and Japan, poorly endowed with energy resources, are generally in a position analogous to ours.
>
> Thus when one wonders about the future trend of energy prices, it does indeed seem that the price downtrend in terms of constant francs noted during the last decade reached its end at the end of 1969 and that one must expect, following the substantial readjustments in 1970 and 1971, and particularly in view of the tax increase provisions included in the recent agreements with the producing countries, a period during which energy prices expressed in current currency will rise as a whole at a rate that could be close to that of GDP prices. Moreover a more unfavourable trend is possible, particularly if economic conditions lend themselves to new demands by producing countries. In spite of this less favorable price trend, it is wise to anticipate, for the near future, that the expansion of needs for primary energy will be maintained, at least if economic growth continues at the rates provided for in the Plan. Those needs will continue to increase at a rate of about 5%, so that they might reach about 280 Mtec in 1975. For the longer term, however, one may expect lower growth connected with the lagged effect of the trend of energy prices, less favorable than in the past, and with certain phenomena of relative saturation of needs.[3]

B. ... *Aggravated by the Algerian Nationalizations*

Starting in 1945, French oil policy had emphasized the acquisition of national resources, and that priority wound up with the Saharan discoveries of oil and gas beginning in 1956. But in 1971, France lost control

---

[3] Note by B. Esambert intended for the French President with a view to the restricted cabinet meeting held on 29 July 1971, devoted to energy policy, 28 July 1971, AN, 5AG2/1046.

of that Algerian oil, and the imperatives of French oil policy, as resulting from the oil law of 1928 and reaffirmed in July 1971, created a twin challenge to the authorities: guarantee reliable supplies while maintaining competitive energy.

As of the end of spring 1968, Algeria had already nationalized the assets of the foreign oil companies and of the French engineering businesses. That was little doubt that in the long run, President Boumediene would tackle the assets of the French oil companies, but the French government nevertheless wanted to settle the taxation dispute that had been pending since the suspension in June 1970 of the negotiations with the Algerian government. The fact is that by virtue of article 27 of the 1965 agreements, the tax base of the French oil companies doing business in Algeria had to be revised. In January 1971, following the call made by the Algerian foreign minister, Abdelaziz Bouteflika, on the French minister for industrial and scientific development, François-Xavier Ortoli, the latter decided on payment, by the French companies, of a substantial down-payment on tax arrears, by virtue of the 1965 agreement. It seems that the minister acted at his own initiative, since in this respect, the Department of Fuels (DICA) of the Ministry of Industrial and Scientific Development was formally opposed to that move, and Georges Dominjon, who was the minister's chief of staff at the time but above all had been assistant director for fuels from 1962 to 1969, had urged the minister not to deprive the French oil companies of bargaining chips in case of nationalization, which seemed ever more likely[4] and which in fact occurred in February 1971. The remark made by Georges Pompidou to Chancellor Brandt during a tête-à-tête in January 1971 shows, unsurprisingly, that it was no surprise at all, and above all puts the Algerian nationalization back in the center of the President's energy and geo-strategic concerns:

> We are in discussions with the Algerians and it's very tough. Those people want to nationalize oil eventually, that's for sure. The problem for us is that in the long run, we will be unable to oppose this. But we have to seek some supply guarantees and participation in production for a certain time. Still, sooner or later Algeria will nationalize oil, on its own initiative or by negotiation. Thus Algeria will eliminate the foreign companies' role. If it were only the Algerians, I would tell them to do it right away and pay. But I don't want to damage the Teheran conference and set an example for others. The solidarity of the consumers, and particularly of the Europeans, must be affirmed. America will be tempted to obtain supplies at home, in Canada, in Venezuela, even in the Persian Gulf, and to console itself in the final analysis with the idea that Europe will wind up paying more for its energy. There

---

[4]   Talk of Georges Dominjon with Armelle Demagny, 10 September 2001, Archives nationales (AN), Association Georges Pompidou (AGP), 1AV 817.

is a serious problem that will lead us to promote the production of atomic energy. The latter is far from making up for oil, but it will be necessary all the same to try to avoid complete dependence on oil. That will be a long and expensive process.[5]

On the strength of that analysis, the French government left it up to the French oil companies to negotiate with the Algerian companies. Compagnie française des Pétroles (CFP, the future TOTAL Group) quickly agreed to renegotiate its Algerian partnership, and it signed an agreement as of July 1971, incorporating the approach in effect in the other OPEC countries. Algerian crude, which represented a little less than one-fourth of the group's resources in 1970, was to be gradually reduced to 10%. On the other hand, the transition was more painful for ELF-Erap. Not only did Algeria symbolize, for France's second-biggest oil group, the "roots of their development"[6] but above all the young company still had many assets to be amortized in that country. With the end of Saharan oil, it was 80% of its crude resources that it had to reconstitute. Hence signature by ELF-Erap of an agreement in December 1971 with the Algerian government inaugurated a difficult period during which its needs for crude oil always exceeded the resources.

C. ... but Taken into Account as of 1971

As of 1971, a restricted cabinet meeting on energy laid down a certain number of objectives for the national oil companies on behalf of reducing dependence on the Arab oil producing countries.

The point was to continue to seek a balance on the French market between the foreign companies and the French companies (ERAP-CFP) while at the same time developing and consolidating the situation of the French companies internationally. In the light of the upheavals experienced by the two firms in terms of access to crude oil, the emphasis was on diversification of resources and on the concern for profitability. The national companies were "invited" to boost their exploration efforts in the "safe areas", meaning on the European continental shelf and in non-OPEC countries, as well as with respect to the new sources, oil shale and bituminous sandstone[7], and the very deep seas. Diversification within the Persian Gulf countries was also desired by the Fuels Depart-

---

[5] Second tête-à-tête between President Georges Pompidou and Chancellor Willy Brandt, at the Élysée Palace, on Monday, 25 January 1971, from 4:30 to 6:10 pm, AN, 5AG2/105.

[6] Letter from Pierre Guillaumat to François-Xavier Ortoli, 5 February 1971, mentioned in A. Beltran, S. Chauveau, *Elf Aquitaine. Des origines à 1989*, Paris, Fayard, 1998, p. 159.

[7] Which became profitable as of the time of doubling of the crude oil price.

ment. The financial effort devoted to prospecting, set at a minimum level of 1.2 billion francs per year, mainly concerned CFP and the Société Nationale des Pétroles d'Aquitaine (SNPA) because of the ERAP constraints in the face of reconstitution of its supply sources. However, the trend of the breakdown of effort among the three exploration teams (ERAP, SNPA and CFP) led the government to hope, by 1975, to reach an objective of "three equal thirds".[8]

The results of this diversification policy in the exploration field show that between 1965 and 1973, the French companies discovered more than a hundred oil deposits. Those reserves were found to an extent of 51% in the Middle East[9], 28% in Africa[10], 14% in Europe[11], 5% in America[12] and 2% in the Far East[13]. Some 55% of those reserves were discovered by CFP and 43% by ERAP[14]. However, CFP did not manage to diversify its resources, since 87% of its new reserves were in the Middle East[15]. Moreover in Iraq, the nationalization of the Irak Petroleum Company in June 1972, forced CFP in February 1973 to sign a contract for purchasing Kirkuk oil for 10 years, following a Franco-Iraqi governmental agreement.

Thus when the oil shock hit, resulting between November 1973 and January 1974 in a quintupling of the oil price (the price per barrel zooming from 2.89 dollars at the end of October 1973 to 11.65 dollars at the end of January 1974), France had already initiated a policy aimed at diversification of supplies in order to increase the security of its economy. Its crude oil supplies came from three main sources[16]:

– 70% of supplies came from oil supplied by the international oil companies to their French subsidiaries at the price called "tax paid cost" increased by the company margin, namely about 0.70% of the posted

---

[8] Note by Bernard Ésambert to the President with a view to the restricted cabinet meeting on 29 July 1971, undated, AN, 5AG2/62.

[9] Mainly the Emirates, Iraq and Iran.

[10] Particularly Émeraude and Loanga in the Congo, Grondin and Barbier in Gabon, Ashtart in Tunisia, and Stah in Algeria.

[11] Including the satellites of Ekofisk in Norway, Alwyn in Great Britain, and Amposta in Spain. The North Sea, pursuant to the authorities' wishes, attracted the bulk of the investments.

[12] Particularly Rainbow in Canada.

[13] Particularly Bekapaï in Indonesia.

[14] Good results were recorded starting in 1971. Its roduction increased by 23% between 1972 and 1973 against 12% for CFP.

[15] Confidential note from the Fuels Department, Comments on oil exploration, 3 January 1974, Ministry of Foreign Affairs (MAE), series Direction des Affaires Économiques et Financières (DAEF), sub-series Affaires Générales (AG), 389.

[16] Note from the general delegate for energy, 26 December 1973, AN, 5AG2/174.

price (used as the calculation basis for taxes due to the producing countries).

– 20% consisted of oil bought by the companies from the shareholder governments of the concessionaire companies.

– The remainder, namely 10%, came from the free market, mainly from the resources of the producing governments.

II. The New Challenges Stemming from the Oil Shock

A. The Presidency's Analyses

In a speech in January 1974, Georges Pompidou, reacting to recent events in the oil world, analyzed the logic and, in a certain way, the need for the action of the producing countries, while criticizing the method.

Hence the industrialized world and Europe, the European countries, were pulled, to varying degrees, into an ever more rapid movement, and one had to expect that at a given time, there would be a time for a halt and, if not a crisis, at the very least a slowdown. That is where the situation talked about above all today was grafted onto the situation: the oil crisis. An oil crisis of which I would like everybody to understand all of the aspects. First of all, there is a political aspect, the Arab oil producers wanting to use that "weapon" to wind up with the solution they desired to the Middle Eastern conflict, or in any case to help in that.

But behind that political aspect, one can see and one had to see deeper and longer-term ulterior motives, and first of all the idea that that the resources of the subsoil, whether they be oil or be raw materials, belong first of all to the countries on whose territory they are located, and that it may be in the interest of those producers not only to control their wealth, but also to slow production thereof so as to spread out over time the profits and the benefits that they draw from them in the interest of their own development, as well as on behalf of their own financial power, if any …

It is certain […] that since the era of colonization is behind us, all countries, small and large, aspire to independence. It is normal for the producing countries to consider themselves as masters of their production. Hence the policy that must be followed by the consumer countries is a policy of understanding with a view to the common interest shared with the producers, without any of the various parties attempting to impose its will. Here again we can say that our position was an easy one and that we did not have to change our attitude. But one must say that economic activity, which was intense the last few years, and the temptation, while producing less, to earn more have led the producing countries to indulge in the following reasoning: "We will produce less, but charge more for it." I don't question the justification for certain reactions. For half a century and more, those producer countries have seen the consumer countries and the big oil companies set the prices, which were certainly low and which were to the particular benefit of the European countries. But it seems to me that the goal has been overrun and that prices have become excessive, both in terms of absolute value and with respect to the speed of their increase. In any case, this considerable increase of the price of energy is having important consequences for us.[17]

Those excessive prices denounced by the French president very seriously upset the French economy, as well as all other European economies: higher inflation (see the table), trade imbalances due to the share of energy products in imports, which increased from 12.2% in 1973 to 22.6% in the next year[18], reduction of national income estimated at 2.5% of GNP[19], a rise of industrial cost prices, and finally a slowdown of the economic growth rate.

1. Increase in Prices of Oil Products in January 1974[20]

I. Prices ex-refinery (in francs per tonne)

	Former prices	New prices
Petrol	363	770
Super	396	830
Domestic fuel oil	266	435
Heavy gas-oil	128	253.5

II. Consumer prices in Paris (incl. tax and in francs/hectoliter)

	Former prices	New prices
Petrol	125	161
Super	135	175
Gas-oil	86.5	104
Domestic fuel oil	36.4	53
Heavy gas-oil	137.5	263

Even if the President's remarks bore witness to a certain anticipation and understanding of events, the article in February 1974 by René Granier de Lilliac, the brand-new boss of CFP-Total, on the other hand offered very violent criticism of the unpreparedness of the authorities and of the political class generally:

---

[17] Speech given at the City Hall of Poitiers on 24 January 1974, in Georges Pompidou, *Entretiens et discours 1968-1974*, Tome II, Paris, Flammarion, pp. 297-298.

[18] The trade surplus of 6.7 billion francs recorded in 1973 gave way to a deficit of 16.9 billion in 1974, the value of crude purchases in the meantime having increased from 15 to 48 billion francs. Cf. "The French oil problem", in Note et Études documentaires, No. 4279, 1976.

[19] According to an estimate by the Ministry of Industry, cf. *Ibid.*

[20] AN, 5AG2/174.

The reactivation of the Israeli-Arab conflict only precipitated measures that were predictable [...]. That was not due to a lack of warnings [...]. One must note that such warnings were most often disregarded by administrations eager to avoid annoying their citizens accustomed to abundance or by public opinion leaders for whom there must be no obstacles to economic growth, whether technical or political. The lack of foresight of some and the lack of realism of others ran up against the facts.[21]

B. The New Priorities of French Energy Policy: Energy Savings, Diversification of Supply Sources and the Launch of Civilian Nuclear Energy

Even if the CFP president considered the anticipatory measures ahead of changes on the oil market as markedly insufficient, they were real all the same, as we have seen, with the installation by the oil companies, and hence by CFP itself, of a diversification of supplies. However, those measures appeared insufficient in 1973-74 to counter the amplitude of the price increase, and new alternatives were sought.

The French government's new energy guidelines were announced at the time of the restricted cabinet meeting held on 5 March 1974. The most decisive aspects of the new energy policy were, on one hand, the launch of the civilian nuclear electricity plan, called the Messmer plan, and on the other hand a call for controlling energy consumption and its rationalization by improving the energy efficiency of technology. The energy saving measures developed by the new general delegate for energy, Jean Blancard, aimed, for 1974-75, at stabilizing energy consumption at the level reached in 1973, and at subsequent growth of such annual consumption at a rate close to 3% as against the previous 5%. Let us remind you of a few of the main measures: speed limited to 90 km/hr on the roads (decree of 3 December 1973); no lighting of empty offices; luminous advertising and decorations prohibited from 10 p.m. to 7 a.m., and abbreviated evening TV newscasts ...

As to the oil sector in the proper sense, the Fuels Department wanted participation by the French oil groups in the world exploration and production effort to increase by more than 40% by comparison with 1973. The North Sea was to attract the bulk of the French investments in exploration with a little more than 20% of the total. Then came North Africa and North America.[22] To that end, mastery of the techniques needed for exploration and development of the "great sea depths" was

---

[21] R. Granier de Lilliac, "The lesson of a crisis", in *La Revue des Deux Mondes*, February 1974.

[22] Comments on oil exploration, DICA, 31/01/1974, MAE, DAEF, AG, 389.

sought, thanks to a special program bearing that name, for which an EEC financial contribution was requested.

The minutes concerning the CFP general meeting held on 27 June 1974 for financial year 1974 makes it possible to judge the reactivity of the oil companies in the face of the new challenges resulting from the oil shock. In his introductory speech, René Granier de Lilliac first of all indicates a softening of the producing countries' attitude in view of the difficulties of getting rid of their production and of the negotiations aimed at stabilizing crude oil prices as a function of their grades. He continues by insisting on the emphasis placed on exploration in the North Sea (Ekofisk deposit and continuation of reconnaissance of the Alwyn deposit), the start of production from deposits in Indonesia (to the east of Kalimantan, ex-Borneo, the Bekapaï deposit) as well as a contract signed with Burma's state-owned company (Myanma Oil Corporation – MOC) for an exploration and operating permit. Finally, the policy of diversification of CFP supplies in countries considered "safe" also resulted in an accentuation of exploration and the acquisition of interests by Total Petroleum North America in Labrador, in Florida, Utah and Montana, as well as in the Gulf of Mexico.[23]

C. A more Disputed Decision: the State-to-state Agreement with Saudi Arabia

Among the urgent governmental measures in the 1973-74 period, another major new feature was the priority attached to signature of a supply contract between states.

Thus in November 1973, France signed a contract with Saudi Arabia bearing on 27 million tons of crude, to be delivered from 1974 to 1976. Similarly, in January 1974, following a visit by Foreign Minister Michel Jobert, a "major contract" was planned with that state, including delivery of crude to France in exchange for construction of a refinery and of a refinery and of petrochemical and mining installations in Saudi Arabia.

Why Saudi Arabia? The choice of the kingdom of King Faisal was made following a series of analyses, of which we will recall the main stages here. In an initial phase, the government reviewed the possible candidates, as is attested by a letter from Prime Minister Pierre Messmer to Foreign Minister Michel Jobert in 1973:

> I want to have […] your opinion […] concerning the choice of the State or States with which an agreement could be sought and about the way in which the negotiations should be carried out. I am particularly concerned about the choice to be made among Saudi Arabia, whose resources are the largest,

---

[23] General meeting on 27 June, 1975, financial year 1974, archives TOTAL.

Iraq, with which the Compagnie française de Raffinage is already linked, and Iran. There seem to be chances for a rapid conclusion with the latter State, but there is perhaps also the risk that an agreement would compromise the subsequent development of our oil relationships with certain Arab States. Hence your opinion is particularly needed on these difficult points in order to clarify the choices that the government will have to make.[24]

It was also necessary to choose a producing State that had not yet committed itself to too great an extent with a consuming country in exchange for an industrial participation. Thus Bernard Esambert, in a note in the autumn of 1973, reviewing the "free" countries, notes that West Germany, Great Britain, Belgium but also the United States contemplate conclusion of a contract with the NIOC, the Iranian national oil company, and he concludes: "The absence of a Saudi and Iraqi project is explained by the fact that those two countries do not have a national oil company. Moreover we could perhaps help them develop that tool, which is vital to conclusion of industrial agreements with our groups."[25]

The French finally chose Saudi Arabia, perhaps because of the particularly cordial relationship between Georges Pompidou and King Faisal. Let us remind you that the contemplated contract personally bound the two men, the main consequence of that fact being that it lapsed when Georges Pompidou died in March 1974. The question of determining the price of the Saudi oil remained on the agenda. As is recalled by the general delegate for energy in a note dated February 1974: "The stakes are considerable in view of the volume of crude oil involved: 35 million tons in 1977, increasing to 50 million tons in 1980 and reaching a ceiling of 60 million tons starting in 1984 [...], making an amount of 3,300 million francs in 1977 and 4,750 million francs in 1980."[26] Concluding that kind of contract amidst a situation of high prices could constitute a precious trump card in case the amounts of crude deriving from the concessions dried up, but also a real burden in case of stabilization and then a price decline. Unfortunately the bet did not pay off – quite the contrary.

Thus an article of February 1974 stigmatized the price to be paid by the consumer for supply security, who – once the embargo and the production restrictions vanished – would not feel so threatened:

---

[24] Letter from the Prime Minister to the Foreign Minister, 26 September 1973, AN, 5AG2/1037.

[25] Note from B. Esambert to the President, dated 16/09/1973, AN, 5AG2/1065.

[26] "Price of the crude oil bought by France under the long-term contract to be concluded with Saudi Arabia", note from the General Delegate for Energy, dated 5 February 1974, for the prime minister, AN, 5AG2/1037.

Two months ago, through Mr Pierre Messmer, France chose, as its oil poli-cy, obtaining a supply by long-term contract between States. The era of the great international companies is ending, he added. A policy is judged by its fruits. This one has so far only produced an agreement with Saudi Arabia. That country has undertaken to deliver 30 million tons to us over a period of three years, in exchange for equipment for the oil and petrochemical indus-try. That crude will be divided between the two French groups, Compagnie Française des pétroles and ELF-Erap-Antar.

For four weeks now, we have been witnessing a curious ballet between the two companies, each having the major purpose of "unloading the baby" on the other. As of now, the division of the 10 million tons per year has not been determined.

Even if that agreement was the subject of great publicity and was portrayed as a success, one capital issue was left obscure: the price that France has to pay for that crude. But there's the rub for the French companies. We think we can say that the contract was concluded on the basis of 10.80$ per barrel. At the same time, one of the two French companies is discussing a long-term contract with an American company taking part in ARAMCO (the sole operating company for Saudi Arabian oil) in which the seller is demanding 8.50$ and the purchaser is offering 8.30$. The deal will no doubt be struck at 8.40$, namely 2.4$ less than the state-to-state contract. Hence the differ-ence will be 70 francs per tonne! If France were supplied only under nation-al agreements, it would be necessary again to increase oil products by 15% ... One can see why the agreement on 800 million tons is pending. [...] Mr Messmer has set a price scale that does a disservice precisely to ELF-Erap-Antar and even to CFP.[27]

The change in the presidency was, precisely in the case of the supply contract with Saudi Arabia, a real relief. The fact is that it made suspen-sion of the long-term contract possible, the contract having been con-cluded *ad nominem*. Thus France's energy salvation lay in its civilian nuclear program, in its energy-saving program, and in its policy aimed at diversification of its oil supplies.

But there was still the issue of managing the monetary impact of that crisis, as analyzed in a note sent to the French president's office in January 1974:

Oil prices have reached such a level that the producing countries in the Middle East and Libya will hardly be able to spend, on work performed in their countries, more than a third of the foreign currencies received. The floating money that will be available to them may enable them to quickly control the price and the level of production of the majority of the commodi-ties imported by Europe and Japan (constitution by the Arabs of a stockpile

---

[27]   Roger Priouret, "Oil: two dollars more", in *L'Express*, 11 February 1974.

to artificially reduce the available quantities). If there is no reaction by the West and Japan *vis-à-vis* the cartel of oil-producing countries, Europe and Japan will be at great risk of quickly sliding into economic chaos. The more the industrialized countries hasten, as they are now doing, to promise the earth to the Arab leaders in exchange for poorly defined supply contracts, the more arrogant the latter will become, and they will consider themselves entitled to receive wealth and power in exchange for what Allah has put in their subsoil. However, if one wishes to be determinedly optimistic, one may say that the industrialized countries are actually only giving paper in exchange for the OPEC oil, and that, in some way or other, they will be clever enough to get their paper back.[28]

At the end of this study, which has intentionally emphasized the archives, we should emphasize the extent to which the options chosen from 1971 to 1974 by the French presidency and relayed by the national companies made it possible not only to cushion the economic and strategic impact of the oil shock, with a few exceptions due to the unpredictability of the Israelo-Arab conflict, but also and above all to stimulate the main turning points in connection with energy (energy saving, civilian nuclear, North Sea deposits, exploration of the great depths), which were to be confirmed at the time of the second oil shock.

---

[28] "Oil crisis of 1974, note dated 30 January 1974", Note sent to B. Esambert, no doubt emanating from the Ministry of Industrial and Scientific Development, AN, 5AG2/174.

The Risks, Costs and Benefits of Importing Oil

Fuel Import Policy in Britain, France and the United States since 1945

Martin CHICK

University of Edinburgh, United Kingdom

For the twenty-five years after the Second World War, the international fuel economy was dominated by the increasing exploitation of Middle East oil reserves. The enthusiasm for extracting Middle Eastern oil was due to its exceptionally low costs. By the mid-1960s, the *maximum economic finding cost* of Middle East oil lay between ten to twenty cents per barrel, which was about 5-10% of the realised free on board price that had been set on world markets by the oil companies in the 1950s.[1] Offering such substantial economic rents, oil production boomed in the Middle East after the Second World War. As such, Middle East oil presented a challenge both to the domestic oil-producing industry of economies like that of the United States as well as to coal-producing economies like that of Britain. The price threat to US oil producers was stark. By the late 1940s, with oil selling for around 2.50 dollars a barrel, such that stripper-well operators in Texas could earn a 10% profit, Middle East oil with a total cost of around 85 cents a barrel, was already highly price competitive.[2] By the start of 1949, oil imports into the United States were increasing at a rate of 25% a year, contributing to a daily excess supply of 300,000 barrels and making it likely that domestic oil prices would fall from over 3.00 dollars per barrel to 2.00 dollars per barrel within a few years. There was a danger that the major US

---

[1]   D. Yergin, *The Prize: The Epic Quest for Oil, Money and Power*, New York, Simon & Schuster, 1991, p. 432.

T. Weyman-Jones, *Energy in Europe*, London and New York, Methuen, 1986, p. 55.

M. Adelman, *The World Petroleum Market*, Baltimore and London, Resources for the Future, John Hopkins University Press, 1972, p. 77.

[2]   F. Parra, *Oil Politics: A Modern History of Petroleum*, London and New York, I.B.Tauris, 2004, p. 40.

companies who not only produced oil in the Middle East but also bought from the small independents in the United States might switch over to a greater reliance on imports.[3]

Cheaper oil imports also threatened the domestic coal-mining industry in the United States and Britain. This became particularly pertinent in Britain from 1958 as surplus coal began to pile up at pitheads across western Europe. In the case of coal, the industry's calls for protection brought the issue of the cost-benefits of importing oil to the fore, but it was an economic issue which permeated national energy policy beyond the specific interests of the coal-mining industry. In urging the case for the protection of oil imports, the detrimental effects of oil imports on existing employment in domestic fuel industries was a given that could not be urged too insistently without appearing to be other than what it was; special pleading by vested interests. More devious and much less vulnerable to accusations of special interest-group pleading, was to make the case against fuel imports on grounds of national security. Such national security arguments rested on two assumptions. Firstly, that fuel imports were fundamentally insecure, this insecurity being heightened by the reliance of the armed forces and vital industries on oil.[4] The second assumption was the corollary of the first: that if fuel imports were insecure, then domestic fuel production was inherently secure. As we will see, both of these assumptions were questionable. But they held a distinctive appeal, embracing the collective concern with national security while also providing a rationale for the protection of domestic fuel industries. Against the interests of national security, what did it matter that the economy and its citizens were paying more for fuel than they needed to?

---

[3] R. Vietor, *Energy Policy in America since 1945*, Cambridge, Cambridge University Press, 1984, p. 95.

Parra, *Oil Politics*, p. 44.

[4] M. Chick, "Sécurité nationale, conflit et ravitaillement en carburant et en énergie électrique dans la Grande-Bretagne en guerre", in D. Varaschin (ed.), *Les entreprises du secteur de l'énergie sous l'Occupation*, Arras, Artois Presses Université, 2006, pp. 235-247.

**Imports, exports and bunkering as a percentage
of total primary energy production (%)**

	IMPORTS	EXPORTS	BUNKERS
USA			
1950	5.6	3.8	1.2
1955	7.2	5.3	1.5
1960	9.4	3.2	1.4
1965	11.7	3.2	1.1
1970	13.2	3.6	1.0
1974	23.1	3.0	1.2
FRANCE			
1950	64.0	12.7	3.2
1955	87.9	23.5	4.7
1960	93.6	16.4	4.2
1965	152.6	21.3	5.2
1970	295.7	24.9	11.4
1974	499.5	37.8	18.6
UK			
1950	13.0	8.1	4.0
1955	29.0	10.0	4.7
1960	43.6	9.7	4.6
1965	64.8	10.5	4.3
1970	107.4	18.1	5.5
1974	117.7	13.5	5.2

Source: United Nations, World Energy Supplies, 1950-1974: Statistical Papers, Series J,
No. 19, United Nations, New York, 1976, Table 2

The above table presents a broad indication of what might be termed
the "energy dependence" of the UK, French and US economies between
1950 and 1974. The data confirms the common impression of the fuel
endowments of each country. While the United States has, in general,
balanced and significant endowments of coal, oil and natural gas, this
was clearly not the case in France. In fuel-poor France, from the Jeanneney Plan for the contraction of the French coal-mining industry from
1960s onwards, governments explicitly pursued a policy favouring oil
imports, albeit from what were deemed to be "French" sources. In
between France and the United States, was the United Kingdom which
had large coal reserves as well as considerable interests through British
Petroleum and Shell in oil development and trading. While protection
was offered to the British coal-mining industry, so too did the economy
steadily, if arguably too slowly, shift to a more oil-based primary fuel
policy.[5]

---

[5] M. Chick, "The marginalist approach and the making of fuel policy in France and
Britain, 1945-72", *Economic History Review*, 2006, LIX (1), pp. 143-167.

In examining the relationship between each economy's fuel endowment and its subsequent policy towards fuel imports, a fundamental paradox of political-economy needs unpicking. A fuel-rich economy such as the United States had the greatest ability to accommodate fuel imports and yet, because of the strength of domestic fuel-producing interests, it was also an economy in which strong fuel protectionists interests existed. Conversely, in fuel-poor France, there was both a greater need to import fuel, and as such a greater potential vulnerability to any cessation or interruption of fuel imports. Thus, the economy in which the risks of importing fuel were greatest was also the economy which pursued a fuel policy placing the greatest reliance on fuel imports.

What then explains this correlation between the security risk of importing fuel and the extent of the reliance on fuel imports? Part of the explanation is provided by the differing national views, born of their differing national histories, of the security of domestic fuel resources. While it appeared to be an unchallenged assumption of US and UK fuel policy that domestic fuel reserves were inherently secure, this was not the case in France. When French energy policy was being subject to a fundamental reappraisal by the Minister of Industry, Jean-Marcel Jeanneney, the Commissariat Général du Plan, and the government-advising Economic and Social Council from the end of the 1950s, there was no predilection to accept the security of domestic fuel resources as a given. In a France which had hosted invading armies during the Franco-Prussian war 1870-71, the First World War and the Second World War, France and its coal mines had a worrying tendency to be occupied in time of war, while her overseas sources of supply remained comparatively secure.[6] Had overseas oil reserves existed during the Second World War, they might well have assisted the efforts of the Free French.[7] In this context, it was possible to argue that in the interests of future French national security, it was vital that French economic performance be improved.[8] To this end, securing fuels on the most efficient and competitive basis was an issue of national security which overrode the particularist claims of French coalminers. As part of the review of French energy policy which was initiated by Jeanneney in 1959, the issue of the value of the "security" benefits of domestic fuel production was addressed by the advisory Economic and Social Council (ESC). Its

---

[6]   FONT 920430/42, (Ministry of Industry archives, Fontainebleau) oral evidence of Jeanneney, Conseil Économique et Social, 24 September 1959.

[7]   FONT 80AJ205/930275, "Note préliminaire sur une politique de l'énergie", 29 July 1959, p. 11.

[8]   F. Lynch, "Resolving the paradox of the Monnet Plan: national and international planning in French reconstruction", *Economic History Review*, 1984, 2nd ser., 37, (2), pp. 229-243.

report on French energy policy was of the view that "security of energy supplies ought not to lead to insecurity for the whole of our economy in international competition" and that the "fear of certain undefined risks ought not to cause malthusian reflexes".[9] Or as the dominant economist on the ESC, Maurice Allais argued: "All history shows that the inconveniences of a certain insecurity are relatively temporary, while a protectionist policy carries a permanent cost." While regarding it as essential that France have secure sources of energy, Jeanneney was pleased that the ESC accepted Allais's proposal that such considerations should not increase energy prices by more than 10%.[10] Since Jeanneney opposed giving any "absolute priority" to French coal mining if it placed coal-burning French industries at an international competitive disadvantage, he also viewed any talk of a protectionist fuel policy as contrary to French national interests.[11]

While the likes of Maurice Allais in the Economic and Social Council were effectively conducting a cost-benefit analysis of the broad social costs of fuel imports, this rationality of French fuel policy-making was subsequently distorted by wider, political and security considerations. In general, France, and Jean-Marcel Jeanneney, pursued an energy policy within the European Coal and Steel Community and the European Economic Community which was designed to maintain fuel prices at a high level to all Community members.[12] More particularly, in pursuing a fuel policy favouring oil imports, there was a distinctly French aspect to the sourcing of these imports. France had long sought *le pétrole franc* and *l'indépendance pétrolière* and during the 1960s this carried over into favouring oil imports from Algeria.[13] Yet, supplies of Algerian oil came at a rising cost to France during the 1960s. During the 1970s French companies were to lose most of their oil assets in Algeria, while the French government was forced to stand by as Algeria became a member of OPEC and encouraged the organisation's moves to increase prices. Throughout the early 1970s, the Algerian government steadily

---

9   FONT 920430/42, CES, Energy Section, "Étude des problèmes posés par la coordination des diverses formes d'énergie; projet de rapport", presented by E. Mayolle, President of the Section, 13 October 1959, p. 12.

10   M. Allais, "Les aspects essentiels de la politique de l'énergie (suite)", *Annales des Mines*, 1961, IX, pp. 249-88, para. 94.

11   JMJ (Archive of Jean-Marcel Jeanneney, Sciences Po, Paris) French Senate, "Situation de l'industrie chabonnière française; d'une question orale avec débat", pp. 1119-20, col. 443, 21 June 1960.

12   M. Chick, *Energy Policy in Britain, France and the United States*, Edward Elgar, 2007, chap. 3.

13   M. Adelman, *World Petroleum Market*, 1972, p. 237.

    A. Giraud, P. Guillaumat and O. Guichard, "Trois documents définissant la politique pétrolière française", *Revue Pétrolière*, (Nov. 1967), pp. 21-27.

raised the per-barrel tax payable by French companies. Since to boycott Algerian oil would hurt mainly the French companies, France found itself committed to paying an expensive price for such security of oil supply.[14] At the same time, Algeria also supported Libya in pushing OPEC prices upwards.[15] With three quarters of France's energy requirements being met by oil in 1973, even such a supposedly "friendly" source of oil as Algeria was not looking particularly "secure" or reliable. Economically rational at home in its calculation of the national fuel mix and playing down the national security benefits of domestic coal production, French fuel policy was overwhelmed by the political rationale affecting French governments' relations with Algeria. Ironically, the political instinct to nurture a "special relationship" with a particular oil producer only heightened the security risk to France of importing oil and provided little evidence that such political arrangements were any more "secure" than striking contracts in the market.

What then of the United States which enjoyed a much richer fuel endowment than France? As argued above, the possession of significant domestic fuel reserves, while reducing the vulnerability of oil imports, did not reduce the opposition to them. Just as France with its fuel import vulnerability was prepared to increase its fuel imports, so equally was the United States comparatively resistant to such fuel imports. Again, the protectionist arguments were usually cloaked in the language of national security, and often illogically so. In lobbying for protection, US oil producers groups such as the Independent Petroleum Association of America were always happy to point up the security dangers of importing from the Middle East whose oilfields "were only six hours bombing time from Russia".[16] This fear that the Soviets would destroy the means of production, or that they would encourage Middle East producers to halt production, was dramatic but not likely. It was not in the commercial interests of Middle East producers to halt production, and, even if they had wished to, that they were sufficiently organised to do so simultaneously seemed barely credible.[17] They also had little to gain from breaking relations with the American and British oil companies, since they used the vast marketing organisations of the oil companies in order

---

[14] J. Hartshorn, *Oil Companies and Governments*, London, Faber & Faber, 1967, p. 263.

[15] F. Parra, *Oil Politics*, pp. 125, 132.

[16] R. Vietor, *Energy Policy*, p. 96.

[17] C. LaCasse, and A. Plourde, "On the renewal of concern for the security of oil supply", *The Energy Journal*, 1995, 16 (2), 1-23, p. 4.

to best sell their oil.[18] As for the influence of the Soviets, it is true that towards the end of the Second World War, the Soviet Union had demanded an oil concession in Iran, and that Soviet troops had only withdrawn from Azerbaijan in Northern Iran in 1946 under intense pressure from the United States and Britain. Yet it was never entirely clear what the Soviet Union would have done had it acquired greater influence in Iran.

Where the influence of the Soviets in the Middle East was most suspected during the early post-war period was in the events leading up to the seizure of the refineries at Abadan in Iran in 1951. The Soviet Union was assumed both to have encouraged the Tudeh Party's organisation of demonstrations at Anglo-Iranian's Abadan refinery complex and to have been happy at the eventual seizure of the refineries. Clearly oil-producing companies had no wish to see their refineries appropriated, but this risk of appropriation did not necessarily imply any wish of nationalist governments to stop selling oil. Although the seizure of assets occasioned much political agitation, it was not clear that the long-run security implications were so serious. The obvious response to the seizure of refineries in the Middle East was to exploit the growing capability of oil tankers to ship Middle East crude oil to refineries located outside of the Middle East. This is what happened. While before the war, the UK with little domestic refinery capacity had annually imported 2.5 million tons of crude oil, exported 600,000 tons of oil, and met most of its requirements by importing about 9.5 million tons of refined products, by 1958, while refined oil imports remained at their pre-war level, crude oil imports had soared to 29 million tons and exports were of the order of 7.5 million tons.[19] The loss of refineries in the Middle East could therefore be regarded as specific one-off losses which by definition could not be repeated.

While it was always easy to conjure up the frightening prospect of Soviet or Arab nationalist moves against oil fields and oil-producing capacity, much of the response to this fear was irrational. If it really was the case that the sources of oil imports risked being sabotaged and taken over by enemy forces, then there was all the more reason to safeguard domestic fuel supplies during times of peace by maximising fuel imports. So, the greater the Soviet or other threat to fuel supplies, the more need to import as much as possible for as long as possible. As the US Special Committee Investigating Petroleum Resources concluded in a

---

[18] TNA (The National Archives, London) CAB 134/1680, E.A.(58)86, Cabinet, Economic Policy Committee, "Fuel Problems", memorandum by the Minister of Power, 17 November 1958, para. 9.

[19] TNA CAB 134/1680, E.A. (58)86, Cabinet, Economic Policy Committee, "Fuel Problems", memorandum by the Minister of Power, 17 November 1958, para. 5.

report in January 1947: "the reserves within our own borders are more likely than not to constitute the citadel of our defence".[20] This argument was reiterated by many experts in the United States in 1948, including Yale's Eugene Rostow in his book, *A National Policy for the Oil Industry*[21] as well as by the National Security Resources Board. In a draft position paper, the Board reckoned that restricting oil production in the United States as well as in a co-operative Venezuela, Mexico and Canada, and presumably then importing large amounts of Middle Eastern oil, would allow a million barrels per day of Western Hemisphere production to be shut in, in effect creating a military stockpile in the ground – "the ideal storage place for petroleum". In 1958, Clarence Randall, chairman of the Council on Foreign Economic Policy, was still making similar arguments to Secretary of State Dulles and in 1960 the US National Security Council viewed American shut-in production as "Europe's principal safety factor in the event of denial of Middle East oil".[22] Yet such a use of imports in the interests of national security was not what domestic oil and coal producers were seeking. Tellingly perhaps, the National Security Resources Board's 1948 paper was never published because domestic producers "were appalled by its financial and political implications".[23]

That national restrictions on fuel imports should both be illogical in their rationale and almost perversely correlated to the economy's dependence on fuel imports formed but two of the puzzles at the core of national fuel import policy. Further curiosity arose from the perception of risk and the response to it. As seen, much of the perception of the risk of oil imports was based on the perceived risk that the source of oil and its production capacity would be seized by Soviet and other enemy forces, and/or would be appropriated by the governments of the host countries. The assumption was that any such action would result in a immediate and presumably long-term cessation of supplies. Yet, there was little reason to think that this would be the case. Even if it were to occur, other sources of oil were available, and stocks of oil could be accumulated in advance. Given that refineries that refineries were always likely to be an obvious target for nationalist groups in the Middle East, then, as the oil expert Peter Odell argued, there was a case for relinquishing ownership of such Middle-East-based assets. In 1967, following calls at a Pan-Arab economic conference in Baghdad for the "gradual nationalisation of the companies", Odell suggested to the

---

[20] R. Vietor, *Energy Policy*, p. 93.

[21] E. Rostow, *A National Policy for the Oil Industry*, New Haven, Yale University Press, 1948.

[22] D. Yergin, *The Prize*, pp. 428, 537-8, 557.

[23] R. Vietor, *Energy Policy*, p. 93.

Labour Party that: "the time is opportune for the implementation of a little more socialism in our international and national oil supplies. Pragmatism and principle both indicate the desirability of our terminating the empire of British Petroleum (BP)".[24] That in short, BP might be better off selling its assets to the national companies of Iraq, Kuwait, Libya and elsewhere in the Middle East. BP's earnings from the operations were only likely to be increasingly squeezed by the producing countries, and by selling the assets the countries would gain a strong incentive to abandon boycotts while providing BP with greater freedom as to where it bought supplies. Since relinquishing their fixed assets in oil-producing countries and states would give the oil companies greater scope as to where they sourced oil, any increased diversification of supply would bring further security enhancements. The UK Treasury was always mindful that the size of BP's presence in the Middle East carried associated defence costs, although the Treasury was alive to the balance of payments implications of operating in dollar areas.[25] Nonetheless, it was not uncommon for BP to be encouraged to reduce its presence in the Middle East. Yet it was always easier to list alternative or additional areas for exploration and development, such as the American shale oil deposits, the Arctic, the Athabasca and Venezuelan tar sands, Libya and Nigeria, than to demonstrate commercially how these areas, none of which were free of technical or political problems or both, were more attractive than continuing to operate in the Middle East.[26] For most of the post-war period, it was difficult to beat the low development costs of Middle East oil, and any "security" concerns encouraging diversification away from the Middle East would need to demonstrate why such a high security premium was worth paying.[27]

While concern with the vulnerability of oil sources easily resonated in the geopolitical minds of politicians, in fact the second category, that of transportation, was inherently much riskier. Essentially, the risk was

---

[24] LPA (Labour Party Archive, Manchester) Re. 209, Fuel Study Group, "Is British Petroleum compatible with British Socialism?", paper by Peter Odell, November 1967, p. 2.

[25] LPA Re. 393 Fuel Study Group, "Where is the BP group headed?", paper by A. A. Grennard, December 1968, p. 5.

TNA CAB 134/1680, E.A.(58)86, Cabinet, Economic Policy Committee, "Fuel Problems", memorandum by the Minister of Power, 17 November 1958, para. 6.

TNA T312/710, UK Energy Policy, meeting, 31 December 1963, para. 2.

[26] TNA POWE 58/70, SOS(67)28, "Security of Oil Supplies: Transport", paper, Ministry of Power, 16 November 1967, para. 1.

TNA T312/710, UK Energy Policy, meeting, 31 December 1963, para. 2.

[27] LPA Re. 393 Fuel Study Group, "Where is the BP group headed?", paper by A. A. Grennard, December 1968, p. 4.

higher because the transportation of oil involved its passing through third countries which were neither its producer nor its consumer. This was as true of oil passing in tankers through the Suez Canal as it was of oil moving through the 1,040 mile-long Tapline running across Syria from Saudi Arabia to the Mediterranean. Indeed, it was not unusual, as in 1967, for the closure of the Suez Canal and sabotage to the Tapline in Syria to coincide.[28] Even so, despite the psychological shock for the French and the British in 1956 of Nasser's closure of the hundred-mile long Suez Canal linking the Red Sea to the Mediterranean, what was noticeable was the speed, about six months, with which the effects of the crisis were overcome.[29] Similarly in 1967, the effects of the Canal's closure proved to be less severe than expected, with the major losers being those countries foregoing revenue by imposing ineffective embargoes.[30] As had become evident during the Second World War, the essential fungibility of oil gave this, the largest item moving in international trade (10% by value, 55% by volume), an important basis of security.[31] In 1956, as in 1967, the main constraint on oil mobility was the availability, capacity and capability of oil tankers as the closure of the Suez Canal forced shipping to make the longer journey around the Cape of Good Hope, lengthening the journey of Persian oil to Southampton from 6,500 miles to 11,000 miles.[32] Longer journeys increased the demand for tankers as companies like BP embarked upon "the biggest charter operation ever".[33] Access to transport was still the principal problem when the Canal was closed again in 1967 when there was

---

[28] D. Yergin, *The Prize*, pp. 425-7, 488.

[29] M. A. Malterre, "L'influence de la crise de Suez sur l'évolution de l'économie française durant le premier semestre 1957: extracts from a report by M. A. Malterre to Economic Council", *Revue française de l'Énergie*, December 1956, pp. 118-126.

A. Viala, "L'importation charbonnière", *Revue française de l'Énergie*, December 1960, Vol. 124, pp. 116-126.

TNA CAB 134/1675, EA(57)37, National Oil Reserve, Report of Sub-Committee on a National Oil Reserve, 12 April 1957, para. 1, 2.

[30] D. Yergin, *The Prize*, pp. 557-8.

W. Laqueur, *The Struggle for the Middle East: The Soviet Union and the Middle East, 1958-1968*, Harmondsworth, Penguin, 1942, p. 153.

H. Maull, "Oil and influence: The oil weapon examined", in G. Treverton (ed.), *Energy and Security*, 1980, Farnborough: Gower, pp. 3-39; Maull, 1980, p. 4.

[31] M. Chick, "Sécurité nationale, conflit et ravitaillement en carburant et en énergie électrique dans la Grande-Bretagne en guerre", in D. Varaschin (ed.), *Les entreprises du secteur de l'énergie sous l'Occupation*, Arras, Artois Presses Université, 2006, pp. 235-247.

[32] D. Yergin, *The Prize*, pp. 480, 493.

[33] LPA, Re. 393 Fuel Study Group, "Where is the BP group headed?", paper by A. A. Grennard, December 1968, p. 6.

another spate of new tanker ordering. With orders placed, the oil crisis eased and excess tanker capacity emerged. Shipbuilders, coping with the feast and famine fluctuations in demand, found that tankers ordered between 1967 and 1975 were no longer required as oil demand fell after 1973, and in 1974-75 tankers rolled down the slip-way and straight into mothballs.[34]

Yet what was evident from the closure of the Suez canal was that given the mobility of the international oil tanker fleets, providing sufficient tanker capacity could be found, cutting off transport oil arteries, while undoubtedly inconvenient, was unlikely to create insuperable problems for the West. Indeed, as tankers developed in size and technological capability, so the importance of the Canal, and the disruptive effects of its future closure, were likely to diminish. Exploiting economies of scale and associated improvements in welding, propulsion, loading, and navigation, as well as increases in the size of refineries, markets, storage facilities, canals, channels, and harbours, the largest vessels in operation increased from 105,000 deadweight tons (DWT) in 1959 to 546,000 DWT in 1979, and the long-run cost of transporting oil in a 475,000 DWT vessel in 1986 was only 41% of that of a 75,000 DWT (the "optimal" vessel of 1958) and only 23% of the cost of a 30,000 DWT vessel. Indeed, when the Suez Canal was closed in 1973, the largest tankers which were often simply too big to go through the Canal except in ballast were more able than in 1956 to make the longer journey around the Cape although again forcing ships around the Cape did contribute to a tanker shortage.[35]

That the economic impact of the closure of the Suez Canal in 1956 and 1967 was short-lived, did not prevent it from having a large psychological impact on the geo-political mindset of politicians. Now, in addition to perceived, often Soviet, threats to the initial production of oil, there could be added the additional threat to its subsequent transpor-

---

[34] TNA POWE 58/70, SOS(67)28, "Security of Oil Supplies: Transport", paper, Ministry of Power, 16 November 1967, para. 1.

Zannetos, Z., *The Theory of Oil Tankship Rates: An Economic Analysis of Tankship Operations*, Cambridge, Mass., The MIT Press, 1966, pp. 235-257.

Zannetos, Z., "Oil tanker markets: continuity amidst change" in R. Gordon, H. Jacoby and M. Zimmerman (eds.), *Energy: Markets and Regulation: Essays in Honor of M. A. Adelman*, Cambridge, Mass. and London, The MIT Press, 1987.

[35] TNA POWE 58/70, SOS(67)28, "Security of Oil Supplies: Transport", paper, Ministry of Power, 16 November 1967, para. 1.

T. Koopmans, *Tanker Freight Rates and Tankship Building*, Amsterdam, Haarlem Publishing Company, 1939.

J. Tinbergen, "Tonnage and freight", *De Nederlandsche Conjunctur*, reprinted in L. Klaasen *et al.* (eds.), *Jan Tinbergen: Selected Papers*, Amsterdam, North-Holland Publishing Company, Tinbergen, 1959.

tation. The 1956 Suez "crisis" only seemed to confirm to politicians the insecurity of oil imports. In the United States, the crisis could be seen as initiating the run-up to the 1959 sanctioning of the mandatory oil import programme. Either side of the Suez crisis Congress gave the President the power to restrict oil imports through a "National Security Amendment" to the 1955 trade act, should he regard the nation's security or its economic well-being as threatened.[36] In France, EDF were able to use the crisis to persuade ministers to accept their new marginalist tariff structures for the electricity industry. In the UK, not only did the Suez crisis cause the Prime Minister Eden to resign on medical grounds, but the crisis was interpreted by his successor Macmillan as highlighting the insecurity of an increasing use of oil imports. Infamously, one of Macmillan's responses to the crisis was to sanction in 1957 a trebling of the essentially militarily-designed civil nuclear power programme of 1955 which had provided for the installation of between 1,500-2,000 MW of nuclear capacity by 1965.[37]

If politicians were concerned by the impact of short-term interruptions to oil supply caused by such events as the closure of the Suez canal, then one obvious safeguard was to provide for a stockpile of oil for use during an emergency. The holding of stocks and the size of those stocks was a response to a perceived risk of interruption of supply. In insurance terms, the risk of importing oil involved an assessment of the probability, length and cost of an interruption or embargo of supply. Unsurprisingly, given that two-third of Europe's oil supply passed through the Canal, in 1957 the UK government, as chair of the OEEC Oil Committee in 1957, cajoled Western European countries into expanding their oil stocks and storage facilities, as well as supporting schemes for OEEC/OECD countries to share supplies equitably between member countries in an emergency.[38] By 1958, France was stocking the equivalent of 3 months of oil imports and in January 1961, the UK Economic Policy Committee reaffirmed previous moves to increase

---

[36] D. Yergin, *The Prize*, p. 536.

[37] Cmd. 9389, *A Programme of Nuclear Power*, London, H.M.S.O., 1955.

TNA CAB 134/2269, N.P.(63)1, Report of the Working Party on Choice of Investment in Generating Stations, March 1963.

[38] TNA CAB 134/1675, EA(57)37, National Oil Reserve, Report of Sub-Committee on a National Oil Reserve, 12 April 1957.

TNA CAB 134/1675, Cabinet, Economic Policy Committee, "Effects of the oil shortage", 22 March 1957.

TNA POWE 58/38, FPR 4(Final), *Fuel Policy Review*, memo, on fuel policy, 14 July 1965, ch. 5, para. 13.

civil oil stocks to 4 months.[39] The difficult issue was of who was to cover the cost of providing the tankage and holding stocks at this level. Governments inclined to pushing the charges onto the oil companies, an inclination not viewed favourably by oil companies, especially when as in Britain, a duty on heavy oils had just been introduced in the 1961 Budget.[40] Aggrieved by the heavy oil duty, with oil and tankers plentiful, and with claims that their profit margins were under pressure, companies were reluctant to tie up more capital unproductively in stocks.[41] In 1965, the policy in the UK was still to aim at an average level of stocks equivalent to at least 4 months consumption. At this level, assuming increased supplies from USA and other sources mainly in the Western Hemisphere, it was thought possible without serious dislocation and with some degree of rationing to survive a crisis involving the complete cessation of imports from the Middle East for several months.[42]

Stocks also had a potentially useful role in mitigating a further category of risk, that of sudden increases in the price of oil such as occurred during the 1970s.[43] While between the start of 1970 and 1974, the price per barrel of Arabian light crude rose from 1.39 dollars to 10.46 dollars, the single largest jump of over 130% occurred between December 1973 and January 1974 during the Arab-Israeli war. Between 1 January 1973 and 1 January 1975 the price rose by over 475%. What made these 1973 prices increases (and those of 1979-81) disruptive in the short- and medium-term was not so much their size but the abruptness with which they were introduced. OPEC had learnt to exploit a fortuitous rise in prices and, united in part by the anger of its Arab members, hold the price up. It was not capable of spontaneously engineering cuts in production and price rises; only of exploiting for a while a price rise which had occurred for other reasons. Even so, OPEC often struggled to maintain oil prices at a high level for long. While between 1 January

---

[39] FONT (1961) 80AJ206/930275/46, Commissariat Général du Plan, Quatrième Plan (1962-1965), *Rapport Général de la Commission de l'Énergie*, Paris, Imprimerie nationale, p. 20.

[40] TNA CAB 134/1677, EA(57)102, Economic Policy Committee, "National Oil Reserve", memorandum by Minister of Power, 26 July 1957, para. 4.

[41] TNA CAB 134/1695, EA(62)49, Economic Policy Committee, "National Oil Reserve", memorandum by Minister of Power, 29 March 1962, para. 4.

E. Krapels, "Oil and security: problems and prospects of importing countries", in G. Treverton (ed.), *Energy and Security*, Farnborough and Montclair, N.J., Gower, 1980, pp. 40-73, p. 47.

[42] TNA POWE 58/38, FPR 4(Final), Fuel Policy Review, memo, on fuel policy, 14 July 1965, para. V. 13.

[43] T. Randall Curlee and A. Wright, "Spinning Wheels: A Review Article", *The Energy Journal*, 1988, 9 (2), pp. 3-16.

1979 and 10 January 1981, the oil price rose by 134% from 14.55 dollars per barrel to 34.00 dollars per barrel, this followed a period when oil prices had fallen in real terms.[44]

What was striking about the price hikes of the 1970s was that they often appeared to be driven by proportionately small reductions in oil supply. Both in 1973 and again in 1978-79 with the fall of the Shah of Iran and a temporary loss of Iranian oil production, while it was political crises which drove traders to the spot market, the actual loss of oil output was not that large. Even in the heat of the 1973 crisis, the amount of oil production lost was only around 5 million barrels per day (mbd), as available Arab oil fell from 20.8 mbd in the first part of October to 15.8 mbd in December. While importantly there was no longer spare productive capacity in the United States, other producers like Iran were able to increase their throughput by a total of 600,000 mbd. At its worst, in December 1973, there was a net loss of supplies of 4.4 mbd, or about 9% of the total 50.8 mbd that had been available in the "free world" two months earlier. This amounted to 14% of internationally traded oil, in a world whose oil consumption had been growing 7.5% per year. Yet the dimensions of the loss of oil were less well-known at the time.[45] Given uncertainty, panic buying and speculation almost certainly occurred, not least because of the impact which a lack of fuel could have for users.[46] Given short-term price inelasticity, the purchase of oil on the spot market reflected in part the speculative hope of higher prices in the future and with the cancellation of contracts by oil exporters so as to sell into the higher priced spot market, the price hikes could be sudden and steep.[47] Yet in the longer-term there remained large reserves of oil and higher price elasticities as consumers reduced demand.

While governments did move to increase their oil stocks during the 1970s, they envisaged them more as an ultimate source of security than as a means of trading down the oil price. In 1971, prior to the OPEC crisis, the OECD and the European Community regarded oil stocks equivalent to around 65 days of consumption as constituting a commercially reasonable level. In fact, stocks in the UK (72-99 days) and France (120 days) were often higher than this, while in Japan (45 days) and West Germany they were lower. The formal level was also low in the USA, but there "stocks" were held in the ground in the form of reserve production capacity. After the first OPEC crisis, most OECD

---

[44] T. Weyman-Jones, *Energy in Europe*, London and New York, Methuen, 1986, p. 20.

[45] D. Yergin, *The Prize*, p. 615.

[46] M. Adelman, "The 1990 oil shock is like the others", *The Energy Journal*, 1990, 11 (4), pp. 1-13.

[47] M. Adelman, "Coping with supply insecurity", *The Energy Journal*, 1982, 3 (2), pp. 1-17.

and European Community countries with the notable exception of France moved to subsume their stock-holding policy (now around 90 days) into the International Energy Agency's (IEA) emergency oil allocation scheme which was established in 1974 with the strong encouragement of Henry Kissinger.[48] France did not join for fear of upsetting Arab oil producers, French foreign policy being markedly pro-Arab at this time.[49] In the United States, the long-advocated Strategic Petroleum Reserve (SPR) was established in 1975.

In the United States and in the IEA there was little inclination to use these oil stocks as a means of acting on prices. Indeed it has been suggested that high prices, but not wild fluctuations, may have suited Kissinger's wider foreign policy aims, not least as high oil prices provide a means of providing finance to Iran without the need to ask Congress for funds. Instead such funding was provided by high oil prices financed by Japanese and European purchasers of Middle Eastern oil. This also accorded with the general political response of western governments and the IEA which was to try to foster "special", or at least, better relations with oil producers based on the mutual benefits of co-operation. In Paris in 1976, under the leadership of the fuel-poor French, but without support from the relatively fuel-rich UK and USA, the principal oil-consuming nations, OPEC and the non-oil developing countries met for a Conference on International Economic Cooperation in which the greater benefits of such co-operation were contrasted with the general losses resulting from conflict and sharp oil price movements. In the United States President Carter was to pursue a similarly co-operative approach in his dealings with Saudi Arabia, even to the point of agreeing in late 1978 to stop buying oil for the SPR in return for Saudi assurances that it would maintain a high rate of oil output. Whether emanating from Paris or Washington, such vaunting of the benefits of mutual co-operation looked distinctly jejune as oil prices shot up in 1979 and Saudi Arabia reduced oil output on 20 January 1979, from over 10 mbd to 8 mbd. As prices settled at a higher level, and excess capacity began to emerge by March 1979, Saudi Arabia cut output again in April-June 1979 and continued to withhold capacity during much of 1979 and 1980 as prices experienced what Sheikh Yamani referred to as "another corrective action" like that of 1973-74. Nonetheless Carter kept to his side of the 1978 agreement with the Saudis for over two more

---

[48] TNA CAB 164/870, Interdepartmental Working Group on International Oil Questions, October 1971, para. 40-41.

[49] E. Krapels, "Oil and security: problems and prospects of importing countries", in G. Treverton (ed.), *Energy and Security*, Farnborough and Montclair, N.J., Gower, 1980, pp. 40-73.

years, until Congress overrode him and required that the SPR fill be resumed.[50]

Even after the turbulent seventies, considerable differences persisted concerning the nature and use of oil stockholdings. In 1984 the IEA emergency oil allocation scheme averaged about 17% of annual consumption for EEC members, but it was never entirely clear as to how, in the event of a further embargo, such a strategic stock would be shared out given that the IEA members had differing fuel endowments. Countries like the UK and Norway with indigenous oil supplies might well have differing views from non-oil producers as to the timing and extent of any stock draw-down, while within countries there could well be a clash between the interests of private oil stock-holding companies and the national government. In the United States, as with the EEC, IEA and post-Suez schemes before it, the main issues of dispute affecting the SPR continued to concern to its size, financing and operation. The level of the stockpile remained at only around half of the 1 and 2 billion barrels favoured by economists. As with the IEA stockpile, there were also differences between economists and politicians as to when the stockpile should be drawn down. The political tendency of politicians was to wait for the wettest of wet days to arrive. The IEA's emergency allocation scheme was not used in 1978-79 and the OPEC cartel was able to push through the second oil shock. At the heart of the problem of when to release stocks lay the choice of trigger mechanism. The SPR and IEA stockpiles were released by a quantitative trigger mechanism, whereas economists argued for a price trigger to be used. Initially, the SPR would only fire when the "shortfall" reached 7%, although this was later changed to 3%. During the 1979-80 crisis, it never went that high, and nothing was done. Yet the price nearly trebled. In 1990 the Bush administration was again to sit on the SPR waiting for a "real physical shortage" to emerge. Waiting for a large quantitative shortfall or "shortage" was likely to be a long wait. Any "shortfall" trigger mechanism was unlikely to fire, because the level of physical supply shortfall experienced during oil "crises" tended to be small, as price rises dampened demand and encourage the bringing on-stream of previously shut-in production wells in non-disrupted producing countries, as happened in 1979-80 and 1990. Equally with the IEA programme, the stock release trigger point was much higher than any net shortage that had been encountered since the formation of the IEA, and the concern was that the IEA programme might never be activated. Conversely, these comparatively small shortfalls provoked rapid price increases in spot prices, which rose sevenfold in late 1973, threefold in 1979 and roughly

---

[50] M. Adelman, "Coping with supply insecurity", *The Energy Journal*, 1982, 3 (2), pp. 1-17.

2.5 times in 1990. Since a small shortfall could provoke a large price rise, not least as uncertainty and speculative activities began to drive the market, there was a case for governments releasing oil from the SPR and IEA stocks so as to reduce the rate of price increase by increasing supply. The stockpile could then be used to offset the short-term price inelasticity of demand and to lower expectations of future price increases so as to discourage hoarding.[51]

The periodic oil crises of the 1970s had two particular effects on the political formulation of national fuel policies. Firstly, the sharp price movements were interpreted by politicians as indicating the insecurity and unpredictability of oil imports, especially when oil price rises were also commonly and erroneously interpreted at the time as indicative of the steady depletion of oil resources. While obviously geologically finite, the economic availability of oil in the future was to be a function of its marginal cost compared with other fuels. The second effect of the oil price rises was to improve the attraction of competing fuels, if comparisons were made with oil at its higher prices. High oil prices improved the comparative attraction of nuclear power, and in the UK they encouraged the development of oil exploration and production in the North Sea. Previously marginal fields could be developed and, depending on the discount rate used alongside anticipated future oil price increases, existing fields could be exploited. From the mid-1960s, the UK Treasury had long been aware that "substantial discoveries of oil or gas in the North Sea would of course shift radically the balance of our security" and by the early 1970s there were hopes that North Sea oil would enable Britain to be self-sufficient in oil in 1980, while Norway, an insignificant consumer of oil, could be exporting close to one million b/d. Obviously, this affected the "security" fuel concerns of oil producers like Britain and Norway, just as previously had the discovery of major oil and gas fields onshore in the Netherlands, but as well as improving world oil security by further diversifying sources of supply, this same diversification created new complications for those attempting to construct a European energy policy.

What was striking was that there was no substantial return in any of our three economies to a substantial use of coal. In part this was because many pits were closed, as the industry was run down during the 1960s. Clean air legislation also limited the types of coal which could be burnt, and the perceptions of the security benefits of a domestic fuel industry were severely damaged in Britain by the role of the National Union of Mineworkers in the fall of the Heath government in 1974. It appeared

---

[51] B. Okogu, "What use the IEA emergency stockpiles? A price-based model of oil stock management", *The Energy Journal*, 1992, 13 (1), pp. 79-96.

that a monopoly supplier of coal at home offered no more security than a cartelised oil supplier abroad, especially when politicians and their appointed nationalised industry chairmen began to demonise miners and other unionised workers as "The Enemies Within".[52] Natural gas now succeeded coal and then oil as the growth fuel, although any interruption to the flow of gas through pipelines was likely to have greater security implications than the interruptions to the movement of oil in tankers.

The importation of fuel involves risks which can be weighed against the benefits of cheaper fuel. As a risk whose probability and cost can be estimated, contingency measures and insurance provision can be organised in advance to cover the worst effects should the feared event occur. In insurance terms, a premium in the form of an import tax could be applied to imports. This premium could then help finance whatever contingency measures were put in place. Such measures usually included building up stocks. These can be used in the event of an embargo to provide a period of cover during which alternative sources of fuel are sought. Essentially this is the use of stock as a store of time. Such stocks can also be used during the more likely interruption to the transport, usually shipment, of fuel. By definition as this is a blocking of a particular route such as the Suez canal, then other routes can be found to carry a mobile, fungible, cargo. Blocking the movement of fuel down a pipeline is potentially more serious, since alternative pipeline routes are not as easily found. If there is only one pipeline leaving the source of production, then this is effectively more an interruption to supply than to transportation. In this case, reversion may be had to building sufficient stocks to provide time to find alternative sources of fuel.

As well as providing time in which to find alternative sources of, and routes for, fuel imports, a stock of fuel also provides a means of countering the risk of sudden hikes in the price of fuel. This is effectively the conversion of a stock into a flow so as to increase supply and dampen expectations of future excess demand. Just as a stock acts as a store of time, so a flow represents the conversion of that stored time into current time. Stored time in the form of accumulated output is released at a moment in time, which is what the market is, and has the added advantage of acting on perceptions of future time. In a sense, such a conversion of a stock into a flow offends common sense. It has been difficult, for example, to persuade politicians that the correct response to a price hike is to release stocks, rather than store them up for the worse days to come. That reflects the dominant political concern with security of supply, although in fact the risk of ever being completely deprived of

---

[52] I. MacGregor, *The Enemies Within: The Story of the Miners' Strike, 1984-5*, London, Collins, 1986.

all fuel is amongst the lowest of risks. Nonetheless, fuel policy is peculiarly vulnerable to political envisioning of nightmares which can result in expensive programmes such as nuclear power which bear little relation to the economic efficiency of fuel supply.

Political considerations also distort fuel policy inasmuch as they reflect local concerns with such domestic issues as making profits and safeguarding jobs. That such considerations should be close to the heart of politicians is proper and unsurprising. That they should intrude into fuel policy to the extent of protecting inefficient domestic industries and denying consumers an essentially cheaper supply of fuel is much more questionable. That the protection of employment and income should be cloaked in the flag of national security is scurrilous, not least in its lack of logic. That ultimately all politicians have favoured policies which maintained high fuel prices so as to protect failing industries such as coal, or to favour pet projects such as nuclear, is of interest as a constant in fuel policy. Even if the French followed a more rational approach to the sourcing of fuel, and had a heightened sense of the security implications of low economic growth, their treatment of Algeria remained strongly political. Again, politicians were willing to use established practices in the domestic refining and distribution system to maintain high prices to domestic consumers, and the subsequent substantial shift towards nuclear power was at least as much driven by considerations of security as of economics. As ever the consumer voice in fuel policy decisions is the weakest and least organised, and seems quiescent so long as price levels remain steady. Consumer interest groups only seemed to raise their voices when fuel prices rose towards the end of the 1960s, seemingly less concerned at having overpaid for most of the preceding decade. Their interests had not been well served by their political representatives, whose dominant concern was with their local producer groups. There was a certain irony in the fact that it took the cartelised operations of OPEC to render the US import control and prorationing schemes irrelevant, although politicians continued to distort the domestic market with price controls. Security issues necessarily bulk large in political approaches towards energy issues, but often in a context in which inadequate efforts are made to specify the probabilities and costs of risks, and the cost and benefits of precautionary measures. To an important extent, some of these political tendencies could be corrected by adopting a marginalist approach towards the making of energy policy, as occurred in discussions of the future of coal-mining in France. Yet even then, while the economic benefits of oil imports were admitted in theory, they were reduced in practiced by political preferences as to the sourcing of those imports.

PART III

WESTERN COUNTRIES FACING
NEAR AND MIDDLE EAST

Research Subject

The Presence of Compagnie Française des Pétroles in the Emirate of Abu Dhabi between 1936 and 1975

Nicolas CHIGOT

Paris-Sorbonne University, France

This study aims at showing why Total Group is still so firmly established in the Emirate, and has been for decades. To that end, it will analyse the development of relationships between Abu Dhabi and the company operating on its territory and in which CFP holds significant portions of the capital. This work relies to a great extent on the records of the IPC (holding 92.36), on the CFP records made available by Total Group, as well as on the boxes concerning the Persian Gulf kept at the Ministry of Foreign Affairs.

CFP was present in the emirate, for the bulk of the period of concern to us, by way of two companies: the Petroleum Development Trucial Coast (PDTC), a subsidiary of Irak Petroleum Company, which evolved in 1962 into the Abu Dhabi Petroleum Company (ADPC), in which it held 23.75% of the capital, and the Abu Dhabi Marine Areas (ADMA) association with British Petroleum, in which it held 33.3% of the capital. Hence in an initial phase, we will consider the relationships between the emirate and those companies.

Let us remind you that Compagnie Française des Pétroles was established in 1924 in response to France's desire to avoid future dependence on foreign companies for its supplies. Actually, we must emphasise the fact that before 1914, France was completely dependent on other countries, since neither the French State nor French companies had indicated any desire to adopt a focused policy on behalf of exploration for and exploitation of that resource, as the United Kingdom and the United States had done as of the end of the nineteenth century.

The First World War and the oil shortage encountered in 1917, at a crucial time during the conflict, made France realise that this strategic sector could no longer be neglected. Thus in 1920, by virtue of the

San Remo agreements that divided the remainder of the Ottoman Empire among the Allies, France inherited shares (23.75% of the capital) of Deutsche Bank in the consortium of the Turkish Petroleum Company (TPC), which in 1928 became the Iraq Petroleum Company (IPC). That consortium, inaugurated at the end of the nineteenth century, consisted – in addition to Deutsche Bank – of Royal Dutch Shell, and of Anglo Persian (British Petroleum), later joined by the most important American companies associated in the Near East Development.

Hence the CFP was created in 1924 by the French State, represented by Raymond Poincaré and by Ernest Mercier, a great French industrialist specialising in energy. He was given the task of managing the French share of the IPC capital. Hence the company received the task of seeing to the country's supply by operating stable and substantial deposits.

Thus as of the end of the 1920s and at the start of 1930, the initial supplies that France owed to its new company came from Iraq. However, it could already be seen that the French company was fragile because it depended on a single source that gradually proved itself to be rather unstable, as well as due to its minority position within the IPC *vis-à-vis* the major companies from English-speaking countries, which were more experienced and pursued different objectives.

We will see how, under those circumstances, the CFP was led to turn to the emirates, particularly to Abu Dhabi, where it gradually acquired a substantial mining portfolio of excellent quality, simultaneously asserting its position in the Middle East, a key sector for oil operations.

The emirate of Abu Dhabi is one of the seven emirates on the Trucial Coast (formerly Pirates' Coast), in the south-eastern part of the Arabian Peninsula. Great Britain acquired a leading position in the region during the nineteenth century by evicting all of its rivals, including France. In 1820, it concluded a General Peace Treaty with the 7 sheikhs. In 1853 that evolved into a Treaty of Perpetual Peace under which the sheikhs undertook to stop waging war at sea. Finally, in 1892 the sheikh signed the Exclusive Treaties by which they undertook not to establish relationships with any other power, and not to dispose of any part of their territory without Great Britain's approval. Thus they delivered all of the attributes of their external sovereignty to the British, but nevertheless retained internal autonomy.

That region, which now displays its wealth in very modern cities and huge touristic constructions, had the reputation at the time of being one of the world's poorest and most inhospitable areas. As an indication, in the 1950s the emirate's population was only 20,000 (against almost a million in the year 2000), living from fishing and growing dates in the rare oases that existed. The political system and the living conditions were almost feudal, and the emir was a village leader at most.

Hence we will consider how the CFP, by way of the IPC, arrived in that emirate. We will see how the CFP maintained its relationships with Abu Dhabi, and gradually developed its presence, and we will consider whether the French company was able to display original behaviour by comparison with its fellows from the English-speaking countries.

We will also see how it assisted and took part in the colossal development that took place in the emirate, both from the viewpoint of infrastructure and living conditions and in the political sphere, and in particular the behaviour of the Abu Dhabi "government" *vis-à-vis* the companies operating on its soil.

I. IPC's Installation in the Emirates

In this initial part we will see how the IPC consortium was led to take an interest in the Persian Gulf Emirates. We will try to show that the CFP was able to play an important role in this initiative. The fact is that, limited to arrivals coming from Iraq, the French company tried to diversify its supply sources. Not yet having enough experience to become an operator itself in a third party country, the CFP undertook to convince its IPC's partners to extend, to the entire mining domain held by the consortium, possible exploration for and production from other sources of oil. We will see that this persuasion work was not simple to implement, and that the French Group found itself exposed to the diverging objectives of the companies from English-speaking countries.

That will lead us to consider the strategy deployed by the French company within the IPC, in which its situation *vis-à-vis* its purchasers was a fragile one.

A. The CFP Wanted to Extend the IPC Activities in the Persian Gulf

In the 1930s the CFP was completely dependent on oil shipments coming from Iraq. To carry out the task with which the government had entrusted it, and pushed in that direction by the National Office of Liquid Fuels (ONCL) headed by Louis Pineau, at the time it wanted to diversity its supply sources. Since access to petroleum sources was its main objective, it took part in several exploration projects, particularly in Russia as of 1924, in Morocco and in Colombia in 1925, and then in 1929 in Venezuela, Tunisia and Madagascar – and finally in 1933 in Gabon. In all of those initiatives, the CFP was supported – if not pushed – by the ONCL, which was eager for a multiplication of the country's oil supply sources, and which, itself, took the initiative of undertaking exploration in the French colonies or protectorates. However, a good number of those attempts bore no or little fruit, and the CFP was led to concentrate its activity within the IPC framework.

In particular, it displayed great interest in the initial prospecting efforts carried out in the southern part of the Persian Gulf, and it adopted a double policy within the consortium.

In an initial phase, the CFP attempted to increase production in Iraq, an effort bringing it up against its signatory partners in connection with the *Achnacarry* agreements, called *As is*, of 1928, by which they had agreed – prices being particularly low – to take steps aimed at limiting production. In a second phase, it wanted to make investigations in the IPC mining field, which, we remind you, covered a large part of the former Ottoman empire (a unit whose borders, as established in 1928, included the island of Cyprus, Syria, Lebanon, Iraq, Palestine, Transjordan, and the entire Arabian Peninsula except for the Sinai and Kuwait). The fact is that by the *Red Line* agreement of 1928, that mining domain was supposed to be increased, particularly toward the Persian Gulf. Even if it seems that the CFP had difficulty in carrying its point with respect to the first aspect of its policy, on the other hand, it turned out that the extension of the mining domain presented fewer problems, the companies from English-speaking countries understanding the need for locking up that part of the Persian Gulf *vis-à-vis* the competition.

The d'Arcy Exploration Company, a BP subsidiary, like the CFP displayed great interest in the prospects offered by the Persian Gulf, and as of 1936 it obtained the initial exploration permits in the emirates, particularly in Abu Dhabi. That led on 11 January 1939 to a concession agreement concluded between the Petroleum Development Trucial Coast, an IPC subsidiary newly established for the occasion, and the Emirate of Abu Dhabi. Under that concession agreement, Emir Shakhbut of Abu Dhabi granted a concession for a period of 75 years to that company, in exchange for which he received 100,000 Rupees (equivalent to 25,000 dollars) as an annual fee. The concession agreement also provided for payment of a royalty of 3 Rupees per tonne, a very low figure.

A study of that initial concession agreement, which in the final analysis constituted the basis for relationships between the PDTC and the emir, makes it possible to bring out the nature of the relationships between the oil companies and the producing countries in the 1930s. One notes that the balance of power was definitively in those companies' favour. The region was still under British control, and the majority of the time it was the Political Resident or the Political Agent who supervised the Emir's actions. As that presentation proceeds, we will try to show the direction of changes in the concession agreements.

Thus The CFP set foot for the first time in Abu Dhabi, where its mining portfolio would develop constantly.

In this way it managed to completely honour its commitments to the country while diversifying its supply sources, and moreover this took place right in the heart of the Persian Gulf, a crucial and greatly coveted area and one that was going to display much greater stability than the other producing countries in the region, except when it comes to border problems – which, as we are going to see in the following part, soon came to interfere with the company's activities.

B. The Initial Prospecting Efforts Ran into Border Problems

The company's activities were interrupted during the war and did not resume until after it. Starting in 1949, the first exploratory wells were drilled, and in 1952 the company finally discovered traces of oil in the Murban wells. However, in 1954 a violent oil eruption took place, a gas pocket caught fire, and the deflagration caused the death of an engineer. The decision was made to abandon the well, all the more so in that the drilling was taking place in an area whose sovereignty was disputed by the Saudis. The fact is that it turned out that starting in 1949, King Ibn Saudi Arabia informed the British authorities about claims bearing on almost the entire territory of the Emirates. Long negotiations concerning delimitation of the borders got underway, the most decisive episode of which was certainly the arrival of Saudi soldiers in ARAMCO trucks to besiege the oasis of Bureimi, traditionally considered as part of the emirates. Thus Abu Dhabi found itself at the centre of the rivalry between the American and English oil companies, a fact that did not facilitate the company's activities. The fact is that on the basis of a recommendation by the Foreign Office, it was forced to limit its prospecting to the southern part of the Emirate so as to avoid worsening the situation, and so as not to compromise the negotiations. Here we are in the field of geopolitics and the challenges to the presence and the influence of the two major powers, Great Britain and the United States, in the Middle East and the Persian Gulf. Generally speaking, one can see, during the period in question, that the American influence acquired ascendency over the interests of Great Britain, which found it ever more difficult to maintain itself in the region. The fact is that we must remind you that in addition to the Americans' aggressive moves, the British also suffered from the incessant attacks by Nasserian Egypt, violently struggling against Western imperialism.

It can be noted, in those disturbed circumstances, that within the IPC the CFP was the company most eager to defend Abu Dhabi's interests, intervening with French diplomacy to get it to support the English in negotiations. The fact is that the CFP records contain the correspondence exchanged between the company management and the Quai d'Orsay (the French Foreign Office). It discloses close collaboration between the two parties in order to resist the Saudi claims and maintain France's opportunities for accessing possible oil fields included in the Emirates. The Quai d'Orsay even developed a dossier at the request of the CFP president to show that the emirates did indeed enjoy an independent status *vis-à-vis* Saudi Arabia.

Such border conflicts were a constant marking the efforts and the activities of the companies operating in Abu Dhabi, but not preventing performance of the essential parts of their activities. They certainly gave rise to an additional risk borne by the IPC companies that was added to the rather risky nature of oil expiration in that region. This would tend to prove that by adopting the role of the main support for the emirat's claims, the CFP wanted to show its attachment to maintenance, at any price, of a diversity of IPC sources in the Gulf.

Those border problems also had some rather significant consequences for relationships between the companies and Emir Shakhbut of Abu Dhabi.

II. The Age of Upheavals for Abu Dhabi

One tricky issue that the companies had to deal with in the emirates was the lack of qualified interlocutors with whom to deal.

A. The Tense Relationships with Emir Shakhbut

We have already mentioned the fact that the emir was represented with respect to a certain number of questions (particularly with respect to all aspects of foreign policy) by the English Political Agent dealing with Abu Dhabi. At the end of the Second World War, he was also assisted by an advisor who was also English: Mr Clarke. But rather often the relationships among those various persons were rather poor. Hence the company had to deal with the fact that the emir constituted its only interlocutor really representing the State of Abu Dhabi, if one can really talk of a state.

But since the emir was a rather special character, it was a tricky matter for the company to maintain good relationships with him.

Those relationships deteriorated gradually because of the mixed results of the initial exploration efforts in the Emirate. Between 1949 and 1957, the company drilled 7 wells, and only the Murban one indicated the presence of oil.

Sheik Shakhbut, who had a rather complex personality, had the reputation of being the greatest miser in the Middle East, and, as we have seen, the company was entirely dependent on his rather special character, not to guarantee proper performance of his activities, but rather to attempt to maintain good relationships with him. The emir's personality gave rise to sharp criticism, and even to mockery throughout the Middle East. The descriptions of him contained in the records section of the Ministry of Foreign Affairs and in the Total records are also rather unflattering. To be sure, his character can be explained by the fact that his seven predecessors were all assassinated, often by someone close to them. The fact is that such an approach to settling succession issues in the emirates was rather common.

The company's supposed inability to develop the emirate initially caused a feeling of impatience in him, which was gradually transformed into quasi-paranoiac mistrust. He displayed a great lack of understanding of the company's decision to withdraw from Murban, and wound up accusing it of hiding discoveries from him or else of intentionally failing in its search for oil. Even if those accusations, which were rather common in relationships between companies and producing countries, proved to be unfounded, it remains true all the same that at the beginning of the 1950s the discovery of oil in the emirates was not a priority for the IPC groups, even for the CFP, which turned to the Sahara.

B. The Dispute Concerning Territorial Waters and the Creation of Abu Dhabi Marine Areas by BP and CFP

Let us return to the consequences of the border conflict that we mentioned above. The review of the borders in the South-eastern part of the Persian Gulf offered an opportunity, for the sheikhs on the Trucial Coast, to proclaim their sovereignty by agreement with the British authorities (Persian Gulf and Abu Dhabi proclamation) over the territorial waters and the continental shelf adjoining their territory. However, PDTC company and, in the case of Abu Dhabi, the Emir took advantage of this to grant a concession in 1950 for the territorial waters and the continental shelf to Superior Oil, an American company. The PDTC, which considered itself injured, began an open conflict with the Emir, rather impairing relationships between the two parties. Arbitration took place in 1952, headed by Lord Asquith of Bishopstone, who ruled partly in favour of the company with respect to the territorial waters, but found for the Emir in connection with the continental shelf. Since Superior Oil has limited possibilities, it tried to resell its concession to the IPC. The company did not display any interest, but added that since the continental shelf was outside the Red Line agreements, the groups could display interest on an individual basis.

The d'Arcy Exploration Company agreed to repurchase the rights to that concession, and asked the CFP to create an association for operating that concession. Hence the company Abu Dhabi Marine Areas (ADMA) was created in 1953. It is interesting to note that the new concession agreement concluded between the Emir and that company illustrates certain developments appearing in the Middle East. The fact is that the provisions of that agreement are generally more favourable to the emirate than the ones contained in the 1939 deal. They also include a royalty increased to 20% of the crude oil produced as well as provisions relating to development of the emirate, among which we may mention the obligation incumbent on the company to hire only local staff and to undertake its training, as well as a supply of oil for the emirate to meet its own needs at preferential prices (25% cheaper than the market price).

C. The CFP Strategy in the Middle East

Hence we have seen that the CFP found itself involved in the two companies exploiting oil in Abu Dhabi. The French company's strategy, as expressed by its president, Victor de Metz, in that position since 1945, consisted in moderate penetration of the Middle East. Victor de Metz, taking the CFP heritage and its very long-standing presence in the Middle East into account, testified on numerous occasions to his attachment to the region. He felt that CFP's presence alongside the Majors in that oil province remained the basis for a real national oil policy. That strategy was fully applied in Abu Dhabi, whence the acceptance of the partnership with BP. Victor de Metz, interested in the development prospects in Abu Dhabi, conceived the idea of having CFP play an active role in the ADMA. He sounded out the BP president to obtain the operator's role for the CFP within the association. But he ran up against a categorical refusal, the BP president being unable to tolerate the idea that the French flag would float over the ADMA. Nevertheless, the CFP obtained an agreement with BP calling for supplying staff and equipment from France as well as from England. That deal enabled the French company to train its engineers in offshore work techniques.

III. The Emirate of Abu Dhabi Becomes the 5th-ranking Producer in the Middle East

A. The Discovery of Oil in Abu Dhabi

The ADMA, which lost no time, contrary to the PDTC, discovered the Umm Shaif deposit in 1958. That discovery put the Abu Dhabi Petroleum Company (ADPC), the new name in 1962 of the PDTC following the decision to abandon the concessions in the other emirates, in a tricky position. The fact is that the emir, whose criticisms were becoming ever more violent, was on the point of initiating proceedings to put the company into default. Under the pressure of events, in 1960, under rather obscure circumstances, it announced the discovery of oil in the Murban field, to which it had returned in 1958.

The world economic conditions were very favourable to discovery of oil in Abu Dhabi. The fact is that the oil companies, particularly the cartel of the seven sisters, were in difficulty in the major producing countries. Those countries became aware of their importance and demanded a production increase as well as a revision of the concession system to the benefit of 50/50 agreements, like the one concluded between Aramco and Saudi Arabia. In Iran first of all, in 1951, when the Anglo-Iranian assets were nationalised, and in Iraq in 1961, when the Law 80 was adopted nationalising almost the entire IPC concession. In addition, the 1956 Suez crisis impaired the image of certain Western Countries in the Middle East, further complicating relationships between the oil companies and the producing States. Those events contributed to bringing out the less prominent position of the Persian Gulf, where the companies henceforth focused their activities.

Hence oil production in Abu Dhabi developed very rapidly. As an indication, we may mention the fact that in 1962, the first year of exploitation, it came to 760,000 tons. In 1972, it rose to 50 million tons, 60% of that due to ADPC and 40% to ADMA, lifting Abu Dhabi to the rank of 5th-largest producing country in the Middle East, behind Iran, Saudi Arabia, Kuwait and Iraq.

B. Developments in the Emirate of Abu Dhabi in the 1970s

The exponential increase in production triggered numerous changes in Abu Dhabi, representing stern tests for Sheikh Shakhbut. Faithful to his reputation as a miser, he distributed the money resulting from oil exploitation only reluctantly, and episodically. He experienced pressures from the population, from his brother, Sheik Zayed, who held views that were definitively more progressive, as well as from the English authorities pressing him to modernise the Emirate.

The fact is that the Emir's rather special character, as the 1960s got underway, gave a certain originality to the Emirate of Abu Dhabi, as it stubbornly refused to enter into negotiations on adoption of a 50/50 agreement. The relationships between the company and the Emir were then characterised by such mistrust that Shakhbut was very reluctant to accept the company's proposals. He suspected the firm of again wanting to deceive him. It was necessary to await the appointment of Dr Pachachi as advisor on oil affairs to see a change in this situation. A 50/50 agreement was finally concluded in 1965, negotiations having lasted for five years all the same.

There were criticisms all over the Middle East accusing the Emir of being the Westerners' "puppet", which was said to explain the belatedness of the 50/50 agreement. In a situation in which the British presence in the Gulf came in for attacks by Nasserian propaganda, the British authorities were greatly bothered by the Emir's behaviour. Hence it seems that they promoted his overthrow in 1966 to the benefit of his younger brother, Zayed, whose views were more compatible with development of the Emirate. With the advent of this new Emir, relationships were normalised between the company and the Emirate Authorities. The 50/50 agreement was revised, and it insisted particularly on the zones that had to be abandoned by the company and be returned to the Emirate, which would thus be able to grant new concessions. Abu Dhabi became a producer company, like the others, in which the changes obtained by the OPEC were applied.

Numerous efforts were made to constitute an administration and a government, in which a large number of *émigrés* were to be found, particularly Iraqis. Those efforts took concrete form, in particular, in creation of an oil affairs department in 1969. Through that department, Sheikh Zayed began negotiations with the companies to obtain a stake in their capital, which amounted in an initial phase to 25%, a production increase, and an increase in royalties. The 25% interest was entrusted to a national company newly created in 1973, the ADNOC (Abu Dhabi National Oil Company).

In 1974, the emirate indicated that it wanted to increase its holding in the capital of the ADMA and of the ADPC to 60%, and then to 100% in 1975.

In addition, in the 1970s Abu Dhabi constituted the Federation of United Arab Emirates along with its neighbours, at Sheikh Zayed's initiative. The creation of an organised state enabled Great Britain to withdraw from the region, and all external sovereignty was returned to the Sheikh of the Trucail Coast. That enabled CFP/TOTAL group to finally become an operator in the emirate. It seems to have deployed its cultural action policy with that in mind.

C. Total Group Diversifies its Presence in the Emirate and Establishes a Relationship of Loyalty

Some symposia had been organised in 1957 and 1958 in London and Oxford and at Harvard, at which members of the main oil companies were present, in order to develop a concerted response by those companies to the deterioration of the relationship with the Middle Eastern countries. The CFP indicated its great interest in that initiative and followed the discussions closely. It drew the lessons from the numerous proposals made to improve the oil companies' image in the Middle East, and was thus able to develop its own public relations policy, which was christened "cultural action policy". Thus as of 1959, study grants were made to citizens of the Middle Eastern countries in which the group was established, and in particular Abu Dhabi. That first initiative was supplemented by creation of an experimental agricultural centre in the Principality, one of the CFP's biggest sponsorship projects, inaugurated in 1972. That policy is probably not unrelated to the fact that in that same year, TOTAL Group finally obtained an offshore concession for a field near the one operated by the ADMA.

Thus TOTAL continued Victor de Metz's policy by intensifying its presence in the Emirate, which took concrete form – in addition to creation of TOTAL ABK, the company that was to exploit the said new offshore concession – by acquisition of holdings in exploitation of the Abu Dhabi gas. Thus the CFP had a strong presence in the Emirate, which represented, at the end of the period, almost 20% of its oil liftings. While there were nationalisations in Abu Dhabi as well as in the majority of the Middle Eastern countries following the first oil shock in 1973, it is interesting to note that the company that was not nationalised in the Emirate was, precisely, TOTAL ABK, the company in which CFP held a majority stake.

In conclusion, one can say that in Abu Dhabi one witnessed a reversal of the balance of power characterising developments in relationships between the oil companies and the producing states. There was a shift from the past concessionaire regime concluded with a feudal principality to an almost complete appropriation of the oil resource by a modern state (or a state undergoing ultra rapid modernisation).

As far as Total's presence in the Emirate is concerned, one can distinguish two main phases. The first one is characterised by the indirect relationships between the CFP and the Emirate, this from 1936 until 1969. During that phase the CFP seemed to communicate with the Emirate only by way of the two companies, ADPC and ADMA. However, during that time the company developed a certain strategy concerning its presence in the Middle East, which emerged mainly in Abu Dhabi.

In a second phase, more direct relationships existed between CFP/Total group and the Abu Dhabi emirate. One can date the transition between those two phases to the end of the 1960s, while agreeing that the circumstances leading to that change are still rather vague. Nevertheless, one can offer a few hypotheses, including the British withdrawal from the region, which left the road free for firms not carrying on their activity under the British flag. The more direct relationships of the CFP with Sheikh Zayed came into being, on one hand, when in 1969 the French company asked him to authorise construction of an experimental agricultural centre at Al Aïn, and on the other hand by the diversification of Total group's acquisitions of interests in the Emirate: exploitation of the oil as an operator in Total ABK, but also of gas. It will also probably be possible to establish a correlation between the diversification of the French company's presence and the presence of the Quai d'Orsay's diplomacy.

We have tried to bring out the special features of Total Group by comparison with oil groups from the English-speaking countries carrying on their activity in the region, particularly within the framework of the association within the IPC and of its subsidiaries. We saw that the CFP was distinguished by the fact that it received a national mission aimed at supplying the country with oil. To do that, it had to diversify its supply sources to the greatest possible extent, and hence was led to display special understanding of the needs of the producing countries, which took concrete form in particular in the cultural action programme intended for Abu Dhabi (the Al Aïn experimental agricultural centre and study grants).

Finally, one can say that during the years of its presence in the emirate, Total Group managed to establish relationships of loyalty that could help explain the fact that the Group is still as present now in Abu Dhabi.

The Compagnie Française de Pétroles Faces off against the Producer Countries between 1945 and 1975

Constance HUBIN

Paris-Ouest University, France

The Compagnie Française des Pétroles (CFP) is a special oil company in many respects. It was born following the San Remo agreements of 1920, by which the Deutsche Bank shares in the Turkish Petroleum Company were offered to France. In 1928, the Turkish Petroleum Company became the Irak Petroleum Company, and, thanks to the "Group Agreements", the French obtained a right of access to the resources. The French Government established a company, the Compagnie Française des Pétroles (CFP), responsible, as Raymond Poincaré put it, for "developing oil production under French control".

This history accounts for three of the CFP's most essential characteristics:

First of all, it was part of a very limited group of companies enjoying access to the Middle East's fabulous deposits.

But the position it held in that group was somewhat special: it was the only company from a non-English-speaking country present in the Middle East in 1945, and moreover, it very definitely remained a minority shareholder in the IPC (holding 23.75% of its capital). It was of very modest size compared with its partners in the Irak Petroleum Company. The fact is that the Royal Dutch Shell, the Anglo Iranian Oil Company, Standard Oil of New Jersey and Socony controlled a large part of the world's oil production and market. Hence it was subject to its partners' will to a great extent, even though its interests sometimes diverged from theirs.

Finally, 30% of its capital belonged to the State, so CFP was very closely linked with it and with French diplomacy, both of which supported it. It constituted one component of the French policy aimed at energy independence.

As we will see during this presentation, the CFP was far from adopting the same attitude and strategy *vis-à-vis* the producing countries as the other oil companies present in Iraq, as well as in Algeria. Can the characteristics of the company explain the original nature of these relationships?

In an initial phase we will see how, between 1945 and 1954, the CFP managed the feat of winning status as a full-fledged member of the oil cartel. Its experience with those difficult negotiations was crucial for the firm. That experience was quickly exploited during the 1960s, when the CFP had to deal with rising nationalism in Algeria and in Iraq. We will study those two countries in succession to see in what respect and why the CFP pursued an original strategy differing from the other oil companies' policy.

I. Between 1945 and 1954, the CFP Won Status as a Partner of the Majors in the Middle East

In 1945, the CFP held a tricky position within the Irak Petroleum Company (IPC). Because of the "Trading with the Enemy Act", passed in 1939, no oil deliveries between the IPC and the CFP were allowed during the war. The French company's assets were also frozen, and even though that move was canceled relatively quickly (on 9 February 1945), the CFP remained quite marginalized within the IPC.

By indicating that the "Trading with the Enemy Act" had caused the pre-war contracts to lapse, the American companies wanted to denounce the "Group Agreements". But those accords, established in 1928, governed the shareout of oil among the IPC members.

Hence there was a real risk that the CFP would become a dormant partner – or, even worse, would be evicted from the association. If the "Group Agreements" were actually denounced, the CFP could become a mere minority shareholder, and could be the object of collusion aimed at it. This would mean that it would no longer receive crude at cost price, but rather at the market price, collecting whatever dividends the IPC would be kind enough to approve …

While the Americans, during the period between the two World Wars, called on the open door doctrine to join the IPC, between 1945 and 1948 the CFP had to adopt the tactic of keeping its foot in the door so as to stay.

The threats of denunciation of the "Group Agreements" were serious. The American companies present in the IPC strongly desired to take part in ARAMCO (a company operating in Saudi Arabia). But a clause known as the "Red line" prevented such association. When an IPC member wanted to develop a concession within the red line, it had to propose participation in the deal to its partners. Even though Saudi Arabia was inside that famous red line, the Americans wanted to be the only ones to enter ARAMCO, since they had no desire to share those fabulous deposits with the English or the French.

There was then a twin danger weighing on the CFP: on one hand, it might lose access to crude at cost price, and on the other hand it feared that the IPC output would be stifled by the development of the Saudi concession. That fear was all the more justified in that, during the inter-war period, Venezuelan production had doubled, while the IPC output was stagnating. Moreover, for the AIOC (Anglo Iranian Oil Company), which held gigantic concessions in Iran and in Kuwait, Iraq also seemed to lack priority.

An initial indication of this disaffection came quickly: the construction of a large pipeline linking the Iraqi fields with the Mediterranean, insistently requested by the Americans before the war, was deferred. As of January 1945, Victor de Metz, then CFP President, decided to alert the Iraqi Government so as to put pressure on its partners. He had an excellent ally on this in the person of Calouste Gulbenkian. That businessman was responsible for creation of the company, and naturally intended to defend the 5% he still held. He knew the Iraqi leaders well and, in January 1945, expressed his concerns to the Minister of Industry, Finance and Foreign Affairs. That was a rather original attitude at that time, since the shareout of the Middle East's resources among the seven sisters took place in an utterly opaque way *vis-à-vis* the producing countries.

The CFP's fears quickly became a concrete reality: on 9 December, the American companies denounced the "Group Agreements", and on 11 December 1946 they joined ARAMCO.

The CFP then took twin steps:

– First of all, it informed the *Quai d'Orsay* (the French Foreign Office), which took energetic diplomatic steps *vis-à-vis* the English and American governments. The diplomats denounced the sidelining of France in the recent dealing, and the attack by the Americans on the international agreements signed on the occasion of their entry into the IPC. In a letter from the French ambassador to the Minister of Foreign Affairs, the French diplomat refers to the American companies' cynicism as they used "tricks and brutality to attain their ends".[1]

– Then a law suit in the High Court of Justice in London got underway on 20 December 1946. It was aimed at proving the validity of the

---

[1] Item 81.1/80: Jean d'Espaigne inventory. Letter from the French Ambassador to the United States to the Minister of Foreign Affairs in December 1946.

"Group Agreements". Those two suits were aimed at publicizing the case by bringing up the legal problems represented by the association between the American companies belonging to IPC and ARAMCO. The pressure exerted by the CFP was all the stronger in that, while the legal proceedings were in progress, the Americans could not take part in ARAMCO. Thus one month later, in January 1947, they indicated that they were ready to negotiate.

Some marathon negotiations then got underway for the CFP, and in November 1948 they resulted in the "Heads of Agreement".

In exchange for abrogation of the red line, the CFP received several assurances. It waived any claims to the Saudi concessions and, in exchange, assured itself of status as a full-fledged partner within the IPC. In spite of its weak role (23.75% of the capital), it was able to obtain an increase of production in Iraq corresponding to its needs, the IPC's total production henceforth being defined by the sum of the programs desired by the association members.

To guarantee such development of the concession, the Americans also promised to build a large 30-inch link pipeline linking Iraq with the Mediterranean. The output increases would then no longer be prevented by the bottleneck constituted by the shortage of transport capacity. That line represented a colossal investment, especially in the post-war years, when steel as well as foreign currencies were rare commodities.

While construction of the pipeline had been decided on, the CFP's worries were not over, all the same, since the Americans took their time in carrying out that project.

In a letter dated May 1948, Victor de Metz described the situation for a close collaborator, De Montaigu: "The Americans went round and round for 6 months with the IPC to obtain agreement on the specific features of the pipeline, the plant, ... and in the meantime, Gulf (operating in Kuwait) appropriated all of the orders. That wound up with a scandalous delay of one year."[2] In fact, according to the calculations made by Mr Guillaumat, who then headed the Fuels Department (DICA), that corresponded to a foreign currency loss of 8 M£ for France.[3]

Moreover, the CFP was impatiently awaiting that pipeline, since its financial position was a delicate one. It had taken out some very substantial loans with a view to taking part in the investments requested by the IPC and it had to cope with a sudden reduction of crude deliveries:

---

[2] Item sc88/42: Records that arrived or were recovered in 1988. Letter from V. de Metz to R. de Montaigu dated May 1948.

[3] Item 81.1/80: Jean d'Espaigne inventory. Note from Mr Guillaumat for the Minister of Industrial Production dated 28 February 1947.

the invasion of Palestine by the Israelis resulted in the shutdown of an IPC line linking the Kirkuk fields with Haifa. Iraq warranted that no single drop of Iraqi oil would transit by way of Israel.

According to Victor de Metz, the Americans' slowness in constructing the pipeline was far from innocent. He stated in the letter mentioned above that the IPC oil should cost 20 cents less than the Aramco crude. The Americans again granted the first fruits to Saudi Arabia, but also to the Iran-Mediterranean pipeline, since they had to market a good part of that oil.

In the face of the Americans' calculated passivity in building the IPC pipeline, Victor de Metz reacted: he alerted the Iraqi authorities to the risks of development being considerably delayed by comparison with the competing concessions. In an interview with me in 2006, Mr Dalemont, a former CFP senior executive, said that the French oil company had convinced the Iraqis that they should also put pressure on the Americans by rejecting the concession for construction of the Iranian pipeline, which was to cross its territory, before the commissioning of the IPC pipeline.

The orders for the big IPC pipeline were finally put in a little bit later, in 1949. Construction got underway in November 1950 and was completed in April 1952.

CFP's entry into the Iranian consortium in 1954 further strengthened the company's position as the eighth of the seven sisters. The cheap tonnages coming from the Middle East resulted in impressive profits for the CFP. They enabled the company to implement a worldwide refining and distribution strategy.

Hence those agreements are of basic importance for more than one reason if we are to understand the relationships between the CFP and the producing countries.

Above all it is essential to note that the canvas of relationships between producing countries, oil companies and consumer nations is eminently complex. It is more like a game of chess with multiple players than a mere confrontation between producers and consumers. The alliance between the Iraqi Government and the CFP against the concessions and competing companies is highly revelatory in this connection.

The fact is that for the entire period, the CFP maintained a special relationship with Iraq. In spite of its efforts to diversify its supply sources, and the successes scored – as in Algeria, for instance – it remained much more dependent on Iraq than its IPC partners. It then adopted a more conciliatory approach to that country than the Majors. It was also much more mindful than the companies from English-speaking countries of production development there.

Finally, during the immediate post-war period, the CFP accumulated crucial experience with difficult international negotiations. One necessarily thinks of David and Goliath in referring to the disputes between the Majors and the CFP. But the senior managers were able to call on some effective weapons to force the Americans into negotiations, and they were able to cope with the unpleasant surprises, reverses and other attempts at intimidation. That know-how proved to be essential in settling future crises, such as, in particular, the one arising from Algerian nationalization.

II. In Algeria, the CFP Adopted a Pragmatic Attitude *vis-à-vis* Nationalization

This experience with the art of carrying on tricky negotiations seems a decisive factor to us in explaining a somewhat paradoxical situation in Algeria.

How was it that the CFP succeeded better than the French national oil companies in managing nationalization? This is a legitimate question, since the those State-owned companies were established to discover and exploit, and then even distribute, the oil discovered in the French Union and payable in francs, the CFP being considered as too compromised with the interests in English-speaking countries to properly carry out such a mission. Nevertheless, it lifted more franc oil, coming from Algeria after 1971, than the national oil companies.

But in our quest for illumination, let us return to the actual facts that, between the Evian agreements and nationalization, led the French companies presented in Algeria, to adopt divergent attitudes.

Soon after the Evian agreements, the Algerians indicated their desire to eventually control the operating companies. In the face of those demands, the CFP advised "no concessions on the oil already discovered, but help for the Algerian Government in producing and controlling the oil on its territory. The point is to get the Algerian Government to acknowledge that the oil output belongs to the party that found and developed it. Under those circumstances, one can provide for an association".[4] This policy advocated by the CFP is very close to the Majors' stance. Moreover, it was applied in Iran by the consortium, for the main purpose of defending the principle of the concession and obtaining a return to the producing countries of parcels considered unpromising or about which nothing was known, so as to "give them something to think about".

---

[4] Item 82.5/8: 1965 Algerian negotiations. Note dated 4 May 1965 delivered to Mr Pompidou: critical remarks concerning the Algerian memorandum.

The 1965 association that gave rise to the ASCOOP was in line with that policy. The fact is that the Oil Code was not much modified. In exchange the Algerians received 40% of the SN-REPAL, which in turn possessed 50% of the Hassi Messaoud deposit. The tax paid was 2.08 dollars per barrel for the French. In addition, a perimeter of 180,000 km^2 was awarded to the ASCOOP. The exploration work was handled by the French companies, but reimbursement was provided for in case of a discovery. The oil exploited in this way was to be shared among the members of the association at the cost price. Moreover, the French undertook to participate in development of the Algerian industry by way of a loan of 160 million francs at the rate of 3%, repayable over a period of 20 years.

That 1965 association, concluded between States, was considered exemplary by the French Government. At the CFP, the feelings were more mitigated as to the State aspect of those agreements. Mr Labouret, a diplomat seconded from the Quai d'Orsay to the CFP, expressed his fears as follows: "With this agreement between States, all of the economic problems in dispute, in the oil domain, are going to become political problems. It was precisely to avoid that trap that the CFP was established following the San Remo Treaty."[5] As we will see, his fears were unfortunately largely justified.

The CFP then adopted an ambivalent attitude. On one hand, it wanted to put an end to the rumors in the press and in the streets of Algiers to the effect that "the oil companies are blood-suckers looting the country's resources". On the other hand, it was quite aware of the fact that nationalization was highly possible in the immediate future. Thus it attempted to make its investments profitable and to repatriate its funds: in 1960, the fixed assets held in Algeria by the *Compagnie Française des Pétroles d'Algérie* (CFP-A) amounted to 74% of total assets, against only 47% 5 years later, in 1965.[6] In 1967 it refused to form an association with ERAP in the SOMALGAZ (a company that was to market the Algerian gas), the deal requiring a substantial investment that could pay off only in the medium term.

On the other hand, it granted loans to Algerian companies that seemed certain to be profitable quickly.

At the same time, the CFP-A adopted an original policy in Algeria of aiding the local populations. For instance, it established an ophthalmological clinic in Ouargala, which opened in January 1961, because

---

[5]   Item 92.26/1: Mr Labouret's records. Letter dated 18 January 1965 concerning the ASCOOP project.

[6]   Mr B. Desjuzeur, Compagnie des Pétroles in Algeria between 1950 and 1971, master's thesis supervised by J. Marseille, Paris I, 1992.

drought and heat meant that the inhabitants were subject to endemic suffering from eye problems. Already as of 31 March 1961, 120 operations had been carried out and 1,800 appointments held.

Thus, even if it was getting ready for the possibility of a departure, it seems that the partnership within the ASCOOP worked rather well on the CFP side. Resort to arbitration was much more frequent between the French national oil companies and the Algerians, and resulted in tenser working conditions.[7] At the CFP-A, people preferred to engage in negotiation to smooth out difficulties. Mr R. Goetz, who headed the SN REPAL, also remembers perceptible tensions in the association. He stated that "Mr Guillaumat, the BRP boss, was also Armed Forces Minister in 1958. One can understand the fact that contacts with the Algerians were not characterized by maximum cordiality."[8]

The French authorities behaved as if Algeria had not won its independence. When it comes to oil, they displayed astonishing blindness. Thus in a letter dated 24 January 1963 from the DICA director, Mr Leblonc, to the CFP president, one reads the following: "The DICA director wants CFP to obtain more national oil". Similarly, in the minutes concerning a meeting on 19 September 1963, between Mr Perrin (CFP director), Mr de Metz and Mr Leblonc, the latter asserted that "increasing the Saharan production to the greatest possible extent is the only way of retaining the French Sahara".

The fact that the Mining Code was not thoroughly modified, either at the time of the Evian agreements or in 1965, probably strengthened this French illusion.

It was no doubt this colonialist vision of a Sahara remaining under French control that made it very difficult to take the Algerian positions and requests into account in the ASCOOP.

And we note that at the time of the negotiations that got underway in Algiers in November 1969 in connection with a review of the taxation conditions of the 1965 oil agreement, the relationships between the partners deteriorated markedly. In December 1968, *El Moudjahid* contained some sharp criticism of the French oil companies, reproaching them, in particular, for the insufficiency of their investments in Algeria. The taxation policy is also criticized, since the fees collected by the Algerian Government were established on the basis of the export price, which, in those days of relative overproduction, tended to decline. Thus the Algerian taxation was markedly more favorable to the French com-

---

[7] Interview granted by Mr Labouret in July 2006.

[8] N. Carré de Malberg, Talks with Roger Goetze, a senior financial civil servant 1937-1958; Committee for the Economic and Financial History of France, 1997.

panies than the terms negotiated by the other producing countries in OPEC.

In June 1970, no agreement having been reached, the Algerian Minister of Industry and Energy increased taxation unilaterally and then barely a month later, in July, he required the French companies to keep a substantial part of their turnover in Algeria, thus blocking transfers of foreign currencies to France.

The latter decision resulted in the initiation in Paris of intergovernmental negotiations between Mr Ortoli, the French Industry Minister, and Mr Bouteflika, bearing not only on oil questions, but also on many different aspects of Franco-Algerian relationships. The general nature of those exchanges was certainly a disservice to resolution of the oil problem. The fact is that during those talks, the French again brought up the thorny issue of the French property nationalized in Algeria, and particularly the land possessed by the colonists.

In this connection the CFP seemed to be less inflexible than the ministry. Since 1963, Victor de Metz had been preaching the need for increased taxation to the DICA executives – particularly including the institution of a posted price so that the level of Algerian taxation would not be subject to fluctuations in crude prices.

On 1 July 1970, in a letter to the Ministry of Industry, the CFP-A chief, Mr Bénézit, again asked the authorities to increase the reference price for taxation purposes in exchange for a more flexible Algerian position on foreign currency transfers. In addition, he wanted the ministry to be able to "draw the consequences from Algeria's joining OPEC".[9]

Mr Deny, who was then the group's Managing Director for operations, refers to Mr de Metz's disgust at CFP's being sidelined from the intergovernmental negotiations. He commented at that time that the ministry was responsible for the losses that would be suffered by the CFP shareholders, and stated that he was going to request an indemnity from the State.[10]

Those talks between the two governments took 13 months to fail. In February, President Boumedienne announced that Algeria was taking control of the French companies operating in Algeria. On 15 April 1971, the French State withdrew and "henceforth leaves it up to the competent Algerian authorities and to the companies to draw the practical consequences regarding continuation of the companies' activity in Algeria".

---

[9] Item 82.5/8: Algerian negotiations.

[10] Proceedings of the Pierre Guillaumat colloquium, the passion for major industrial projects, headed by G.H. Soutou and A. Beltran, Éditions rive droite, 1995.

The situation did indeed seem to be blocked. The French companies stopped obtaining supplies in the Algerian ports and, on 26 April 1971, sent a warning letter. In the face of the Algerian nationalization weapon, the French companies brandished the blockade threat to pressure the local authorities. The solidarity among the oil companies was fully operational, resulting in the freezing of two-thirds of Algerian output.

The discussions between the CFP and SONATRACH resumed on 3 June 1971. After one month of fruitless negotiations, Mr de Metz sent Mr Berbigier and Mr de Montaigu to Algeria with a question for the Algerians: "You want to nationalize us. Does that mean you want us to stay, or you want to nationalize 100%?"[11] Both of those two CFP envoys had strong experience in international negotiations. Mr Berbigier had led the 1954 negotiations in Iran on behalf of the company, and Mr de Montaigu on his part participated in all phases of the tough negotiations between the IPC and the CFP from 1945 to 1948. They were accompanied by Mr Castellani, "a very shrewd 'pied noir' who knew the Algerians very well".[12] Mr Dalemont also says that the latter's presence played an essential role in the success of the undertaking: "When it comes to such difficult negotiations, personal relationships are very important". Actually the CFP managed to sign an agreement on 10 June 1971, whereas ELF did not reach an understanding with the Algerians before 15 December 1971.

The results of those negotiations were also much more favorable to the CFP.

It could lift 7 million tons of crude, namely half of its production before 1971, whereas the deliveries to ELF were cut by two-thirds, being reduced to 5.5 million tons. When it came to the issue of nationalization indemnities, the CFP, here again, was more successful: it agreed to pay 150 million francs in tax arrears in exchange for a 7-year indemnification amounting to 330 million francs. On the other hand, ELF got almost no nationalization indemnity.

How can one explain such a great difference between the two French groups? It seems that nationalization was understood in very different ways by the two groups.

The CFP considered it as a difficult and sudden reverse, to be sure, but once the impact receded, it was able to negotiate without bitterness. For the ELF senior managers, and particularly for Mr Guillaumat, that nationalization was almost more emotional than economic. It represented treason to France. According to Mr Dalemont, "he felt that it was

---

[11]   Talk with Mr Deny in June 2006.

[12]   Talk with Mr Dalemont in June 2006.

insulting to France". As the State's representative, he made this a point of honor and took refuge in an offended attitude. At the time of the intergovernmental negotiations, Mr Guillaumat wrote to Mr Ortoli to inform him that he authorized him to tell the Algerians that "if need be, ELF Erap will leave Algeria".[13] During the negotiations after June 1971, the national oil companies fought over points considered as preliminaries that were indispensable to the Algerians. Thus they lost precious time, enabling the Americans to sign gas marketing agreements. Thus Algeria had already placed a good part of its production, and was less responsive to the pressure exerted by ELF.

Hence in Algeria, the CFP defended – as far as possible – the concession principle, basing itself on the rules established by the international companies. In the face of an announced nationalization, the CFP applied a prudent policy of withdrawal as of 1965. But during that post-colonial period, in which the relationships between France and Algeria were far from calm, it demonstrated great pragmatism in order to retain what was essential and keep a substantial supply in Algeria on economically acceptable terms. The Algerians themselves emphasized this CFP posture. In a statement dated 30 June 1971, some SONATRACH senior managers indicated: "The CFP has been appreciated, since it presented itself to us as an industry."[14] The Algerians welcomed the said agreement all the more in that the CFP committed itself to providing technical assistance, which they still lacked in part. Moreover, the SONATRACH was delighted to have the CFP as a shareholder since it resulted in substantial credibility for it at international level.

As we have just seen, the fact of being closely associated with the French State was far from always being an advantage in the negotiations with the producing countries. At the end of the 1950s, the French foreign policy in Algeria made waves as far as Iraq, and created a tricky situation for the CFP.

III. In Iraq, in spite of Pursuing Different Objectives, the CFP Did Not Break Away from the Cartel

The war in Algeria actually caused indignation and brought disapproval in the Arab world.

In Iraq, where Nasser's voice was widely listened to in 1958, some Iraqi parliamentarians demanded nationalization of the French shares of the IPC. The Foreign Office warned the CFP about that in a letter dated

---

[13] Letter mentioned by Mr Deny during an interview in 1993.

[14] Item 82.5/8: 1971 Algerian negotiations.

January 1958.[15] That threat was taken seriously, and two possibilities for action were contemplated. The first one, of a collective nature, would entail calling on the solidarity among the groups while getting the IPC members accept the fact that "French nationalization would necessarily be only one stage, soon followed by others".[16] The second one, of an individual nature, would be aimed at convincing the Iraqis of the potential offered by the French market. The note recommended a trip by Mr Victor de Metz to Iraq to clearly indicate the importance attached to that country by the CFP.

The threat quickly dissipated with the advent of General Charles de Gaulle as French president, the Arab world hoping for liberalization, thanks to him, of the policy in North Africa.

This case is of interest to us, because it clearly indicates the relationships that the CFP was able to maintain with Iraq and the double strategy that it applied: as we have seen, on one hand it relied on the other cartel members. It was vital for the CFP to maintain good relationships with the Majors, the defense of the concession principle entailing perfect solidarity among the club members. But in addition, the CFP was also able to indicate its differences to make its own voice heard by the Iraqi authorities.

Similarly, at the time of institution of Law 80 in December 1961, the CFP was less intransigent *vis-à-vis* Iraq than its partners from English-speaking countries. That meant that it could act as an intermediary for renewed contacts. It is interesting to point out here that there was an important difference in viewpoint among the cartel members.

When General Kassem took power in 1958, he was relatively conciliatory *vis-à-vis* the IPC. For instance, he did not question the 50/50 principle (pursuant to which profits were shared equally: 50% for the producing States and 50% for the oil companies). But in October 1958, he demanded 20% of the IPC shares and some large concessions. The IPC members refused. General Kassem then won approval for Law 80, which reduced the operating companies' concession to less than 2,000 km². Only the producing deposits remained in the IPC's hands, with the exception of the one in Rumaila-North and Ratawi, which were just beginning to be equipped. In addition, the port duties in Fao (an important port on the Persian Gulf) were increased very substantially, a fact that gave rise to a little more tension between Iraq and the IPC.

The negotiations began to mark time very quickly and the situation seemed to be blocked.

---

[15] Item 82.7/4: Unstable situation in Iraq because of Algerian policy.

[16] Item 82.7/4: Unstable situation in Iraq because of Algerian policy. Note concerning nationalization of the French holding in Iraq, 24 February 1958.

The English-speaking countries did not agree to any such question-ing of the international conventions in a unilateral way. To them, the defense of international law was what was mainly at stake in this matter. The most important thing was to defend the concession principle, and hence not to accept any reconsideration that might have a snowball effect in the Middle East. Hence the IPC members decided to sanction Iraq by freezing output at the 1961 level. And the fact is that the coeffi-cient by which Iran's exports were increased was twice Iraq's for the years 1960-63.

In a report to the Board of Directors in March 1962, Victor de Metz, returning from a trip to New York, where he sounded out his partners with respect to their intentions, reached this conclusion: "the IPC mem-bers think that time is working for the company".[17] The Americans felt that the Iraqis would be more conciliatory once they saw that the OPEC members negotiating with the companies obtained more than Iraq did.

But that idea disregarded the importance of Iraqi national feeling. Once the Law 80 was approved, it quickly became a symbol of the Iraqi revolution and of the country's economic independence. The Kassem regime could not go back on that law without risking any overthrow by its left wing.

But even if certain IPC members persisted in this wait-and-see atti-tude, it was probably because it was also very compatible with their economic interests.

It was a time of relative petroleum overproduction, and there was se-vere competition among the producing countries in the Middle East. The regular decline of crude prices in Rotterdam was a good indicator of that oil surplus. In 1948, the per-barrel price stood at 3.49 dollars, whereas in 1964 it was only 2.52 dollars. Such companies as Standard Oil or British Petroleum had numerous concessions in the Middle East. They found it difficult to cope with all of the producing countries' requests for an increase while maintaining a price level that protected their margins. The fact is that at that time, a production increase was the only way the producing countries could increase their revenue. It is easier to under-stand why the stagnation of Iraqi output did not seem to be a major worry for the companies, since this meant that they could more easily accept the Iranian or Saudi requests.

But the CFP, on its part, was in an utterly different position. Until the end of the 1960s it was very dependent on Iraq for its supplies. In 1966, for instance, that country still accounted for 46% of its liftings. Mainte-nance of a production increase, at a time when consumption of oil

---

[17] Item 92.10/8: Minutes concerning the Board of Directors' meeting, March 1962.

products was increasing in France at a rate of about 8% per year, was utterly essential for it.

That is why *Française des Pétroles* worked throughout that period on calming the tensions between Iraq and the IPC, and tried to have the dialogue resume. Similarly, it told the IPC members that they should adopt a more conciliatory position.

Actually, it seems that the big trusts were aware of their omnipotence and that they adopted behavior that was sometimes arrogant *vis-à-vis* the Iraqis. In its internal notes, the Middle East Department – DMO (the CFP division responsible for relationships between the company and the IPC) was far from always being laudatory of the IPC staff present in Iraq. Thus one of the negotiators, Sir Herbert Todd, was characterized as a "catastrophic imbecile and probably out to harm the French interests".[18] Similarly, the CFP members traveling in Iraq found a colonialist state of mind reigning in the circle of the IPC expatriates. They wrote that "at the receptions given by the IPC, there was great surprise when people saw that there was not a single Iraqi".[19]

The French desire to calm the tensions was no doubt heard, as of 1963, by Mr Wattari, who was then Iraqi Oil Minister. During an interview in Paris, he assured Mr de Metz that the Iraqis again wanted to have IPC take part in development of the reservoirs that were discovered and in the exploration activities. In the light of those good intentions, Mr de Metz sent Mr Duroc-Danner to Baghdad, and the latter managed to obtain – along with Mr Sutcliff from BP – elimination of the tax surplus in the port of Fao and the resumption of negotiations. Thus the French acted as intermediaries in the resumption of the negotiations in Iraq, which, after two years of effort, would have succeeded except that some important changes occurred in July 1965 in the Iraqi Government, throwing its signature into doubt.

In 1966, the conflict concerning the trans-Syrian oil pipeline complicated the negotiations between Iraq and the IPC a little bit more: the fees paid to Syria by the IPC were, as in the case of the crude liftings calculated since 1955, on the basis of the 50/50 model. But in September 1966 the Syrians demanded an upward revision of the transit rate. The IPC did not give way. Casting doubt on the principle of a 50/50 sharing of the profits with Syria would mean being subject *vis-à-vis* the other producing countries to the same kind of demands. To defend the profitability of the other concessions, the participants therefore preferred to reject the Syrian demand.

---

[18] Item 82.7/4: Unstable situation in Iraq because of Algerian policy. Internal note from the Middle East Department dated 24 February 1958.

[19] *Id.*

But the Syrians did not content themselves with making mere claims. In December 1966 Syria interrupted the loadings from Iraq. Iraq was strongly affected by that measure. Since the oil was no longer lifted, the oil companies no longer paid fees, and in a few months the Iraqi Public Treasury lost 100 million £. In the face of a unilateral measure that broke the international agreements signed between Syria and the IPC, the English-speaking countries again called for absolute firmness.

Victor de Metz, on his part, was greatly worried. He knew that the Iraqi State absolutely needed its oil revenue and that a worsening of the situation could lead it to make far-reaching decisions, such as actually questioning the IPC concession.

The CFP asserted in a letter sent to its four partners that it felt excluded from the decision-making. It also stated that "if the interests of all of the other companies is the impasse, the CFP is greatly concerned by the problem".[20] One must realize that for the CFP, the halt to loadings in Syria resulted in a sharp drop of its supplies. If that situation lasted for a year, the CFP liftings would decline from 67 to 40 million tons. Moreover, since the winter that year was a rough one, there was a real risk of heating oil shortages in France. It is interesting to point out here that the CFP interests were more in line with Iraq's than with those of the Majors.

In the same letter, the CFP also asked its partners to help it find replacement supplies, particularly for light products in the Mediterranean. It partners provided contrasting responses. Mobil offered help, but Shell said it could not do anything. BP, on its part, offered the oil of Kuwait, a fact that obviously raised the problem of chartering. As to Standard Oil, it asserted that it had only heavy oil. Even if the companies did not rule out the CFP request, we can also see that the support was not full-fledged. Hence one may once again qualify the idea of unconditional solidarity among the oil groups.

One month later, at the start of January, the situation was identical. The CFP was still trying to convince the groups that negotiation was better than breaking off relations. It even offered to negotiate with Damascus itself and to propose a new price on behalf of the IPC. That was wasted breath, as its partners rejected its proposals. No doubt outraged by the Majors' rigidity and wait-and-see attitude, Victor de Metz called on the French Minister of Foreign Affairs. He told the minister that there was a risk of losing the Iraq concessions if no solution was found in Syria in the near future. Diplomatic steps were quickly taken in London and in Washington, and at the beginning of February,

---

[20]   Item 91.8 /74: Correspondence between the CFP and the IPC four Majors during the Iraqo-Syrian crisis in 1967.

the Majors finally agreed to resume the negotiations, and an agreement was reached in March between Damascus and the IPC.

Thus, in spite of its weak influence within the IPC, but thanks to the unwavering support provided by French diplomacy, the CFP managed to make its voice heard. Once again it displayed the greatest possible pragmatism and a more open stance toward dialogue with the producing countries than the Majors.

This support provided by French diplomacy also constituted an advantage for the CFP following the Six-Day War. The fact that it was a French company, strongly linked with the government, a point that was a handicap in 1958, became a definite advantage in the negotiations with Baghdad. The resentment of the English-speaking countries, considered responsible for the Arab defeat, was very strong in the Middle East at that time, and Iraq decided to slap an embargo on the Majors. The CFP, thanks to its French nature, was spared. The Iraqi Government even said that it wanted new cooperation in the petroleum field with a French company. Victor de Metz thought that the circumstances were finally favorable to resolving the situation that arose from the Law 80.

Thanks to Baghdad's benevolent attitude *vis-à-vis* the CFP, it could negotiate, in the IPC's name, thus reaching an agreement finally making it possible to develop the North Rumaila field. The reserves that deposit were estimated by geologist W. Bruderer at 2 billion tons.

But Mr de Metz had not anticipated that ERAP would also be in the race. The fact is that the Élysée (the French President's office) felt it would be opportune to send the national company to negotiate some new concessions in Iraq. The Majors were furious, and hence viewed the CFP's action no longer as a step in their favor, but rather as negotiations competing with the IPC's. The English even called the negotiations led by Mr de Metz "Joan of Arc". As if the CFP boss were only an emissary of General de Gaulle, having a single objective: getting the English out of Iraq. The CFP's position was so delicate that Victor de Metz tried first of all to reassure his partners, and he managed to get them to agree to having the CFP act as mediator between Baghdad and the IPC.

Contacts resumed between the CFP negotiators and the Iraqi authorities. But all of the proposals resulting from those conversations were rejected by the IPC. The CFP then constantly warned its partners of the possibility that the Iraqis would conclude a deal with a third party for exploitation of a deposit discovered by the IPC. The fact was that the American independents, ENI and even ERAP – in the hope of getting into Iraq – offered much more advantageous terms than the ones suggested by the IPC. Moreover, in 1968 ERAP signed an agency contract with Iraq. It provided that the mining titles as well as the production system belonged to the company of the producer country. The financial risks involved in exploration were for the oil company's account. The oil discovered in this way was shared with the national company. But in spite of those new contracts, the IPC limited itself to a strict defense of the concession right.

Actually, the chances that the IPC could develop the Rumaila deposit were fading. In May 1968, Iraq assigned development of North Rumaila to the INOC, its national company. Moreover, following General Bakr's access to power in July, the visits to Moscow became more frequent. In that same summer of 1969, the Soviets promised operational assistance for developing Rumaila. In June 1972, the break was consummated and Iraq nationalized the IPC concessions.

It seemed during those interminable negotiations that none of the contending partners felt any real desire to reach an agreement.

The Majors had numerous concessions and were awash in crude. They found it ever more difficult to maintain prices in Europe guaranteeing their profit margins. Hence they were not in any hurry to see new production coming onto that market.

On their part, the successive Iraqi governments were quite aware of the fact that the Law 80 was untouchable, and that reaching an agreement with the IPC would be tantamount to political suicide.

The CFP strategy on its part continued to focus mainly on the alliance with the Majors. While Baghdad encouraged it, by its proposals, to bring about a dislocation of the IPC, the CFP refused to sign a bilateral agreement with Iraq. Even after the Iraqi nationalization, and even though a particularly favorable fate was reserved for it, it continued to stick with the Majors.

Unlike the companies from English-speaking countries, following nationalization, the CFP was able to continue its liftings in the Mediterranean, as was indicated by an AFP dispatch dated 29 July: "The contract was concluded in execution of the Franco-Iraqi Agreement of Paris in June 1972. That provided for sale, for a duration of 10 years, of Iraqi oil to France."[21] Thus the CFP benefited from the good relations between Paris and Baghdad to escape the embargo. But even if the French foreign policy unquestionably helped the CFP in its relationships with Iraq, let us not neglect Baghdad's favorable judgement of the CFP attitude during those years of negotiations. Within the IPC, the CFP was always the one looking for an agreement aimed at increasing production. It was also able to appear less arrogant and more understanding than its partners with respect to the Iraqi demands.

---

[21]   Item 82.7/216: Iraq, negotiations from July to December 1972 concerning indemnification after nationalization.

For all that, Mr Granier de Lilliac did not jettison the solidarity with his IPC partners, and he told the Board of Directors in October 1972 that he was "looking for an overall solution for the members of the IPC before signing a 10-year contract for France".

The conversations continued in fact until February. That same month the ten-year contract with France was signed as well as the settlement of accounts between the IPC and Iraq.

If one tries to determine the essential elements of the relationships between producing countries and oil companies between 1945 and 1975, the first thing to note is no doubt the new position in the oil economy acquired by the producing countries in 1975: the Iraqi Government was absent from the negotiations, and it was even unaware of certain clauses in the Heads of Agreements. It did not determine either the rate of production or crude prices. After 1975, everything was no longer decided among cartel members, but rather in a direct dialogue between the oil companies and the producing countries.

However, one must qualify the idea of brutal and systematic opposition between those two protagonists. There were rivalries between producing countries that sometimes served a company's interests. For instance, by playing on the rivalries between Iran and Iraq, the CFP was able to speed up construction of the IPC pipeline at the beginning of the 1950s.

But one also notes rivalries between the oil companies that serve the producing countries' interests. Again in Iraq, ERAP, ENI and the American independents, by proposing agency contracts, made the Iraqis aware of the fact that the concession procedure was no longer the only possibility.

There were also particular cases of hostility between producing countries and consumer countries connected with colonial history and which could therefore help a company representing another country. Thus the English had more painful relationships with the Iraqis, and as of 1963 the CFP benefited from the difficult diplomatic relations between those two countries.

But one must always keep in mind the political and diplomatic component of the agreements concluded between producing countries and an oil company, a fact that must not make us forget that their basic content is economic.

Actually, it was commercial interest above all that underlay the CFP strategy *vis-à-vis* the producing countries. If the CFP remained in Algeria, it was first of all because the Algerian crude – light, with little sulfur and close to the French coasts – remained highly competitive at the price negotiated in 1971 by comparison with crude coming from the

Persian Gulf. Similarly, the CFP attitude in Iraq was also dictated by economic considerations diverging from the Majors' interests.

But one must also note that the CFP had rather little room for maneuvering in Iraq. Its position as the eighth of the seven sisters precluded it from running the risk of slamming the cartel's door. In the face of the power of the big oil groups present on all markets, and in all of the major production areas, the CFP could not break with them without creating a very delicate situation for itself.

Hence pragmatism seems to us to have been the Ariane's thread of the CFP policy. The following statement by Mr Berbigier, in an interview granted in February 1970, is a good indication of that state of mind: "What counts is not the legal form taken by the contracts between producing countries and oil companies, but rather success in amortizing the gigantic investments within sufficiently short periods."[22]

---

[22] Item 92 AA091/151: Statement by the presidents and other directors, interview with Mr Berbigier in February 1970: the CFP in the national and international oil context.

Before "Mattei's Formula"
AGIP-ENI's Foreign Policy, 1926-1957

Daniele POZZI

University of Milan, Italy

While the American independents were eating into some of the market of the seven (sisters), a more far-reaching threat was emerging from a man who, at first, seemed merely comic: the head of the Italian State Oil Company, Enrico Mattei. He was combative, aggressive and exasperating; but the oil companies soon had to take him seriously, for he hit them on all their most vulnerable points. He was a nationalist, claiming that Italy had been done down by the 'oil cartel'. He was the ally of the producing countries, persuading them that they had been cheated[1].

When Anthony Sampson portrayed the founder and chairman of Ente Nazionale Idrocarburi (ENI) in his popular book, *The Seven Sisters* (1976), Mattei's image as a lone rebel was already well established. Back in the Sixties, both supporters and detractors alike pictured ENI's attempts to gain a position in the international oil market like the struggle of a single extraordinary individual, both supporters and detractors pictured ENI's attempt to gain a position into the international oil market like a struggle of a single extraordinary individual, who was driven whether from his personal commitment to Italian energy independence or from his obsession against oil majors. According to Pierre Fontaine[2] – who indicated ENI as an example to influence French public opinion –, Mattei was a sort of "Jean d'Arc du pétrole italien", while in Don Votaw's view, he acted as a "Socialist robber baron", greedy for power[3]. However, whether authors loved Mattei or they detested him – it seems that intermediate options were out of the question – the literature

---

[1] Sampson, A. *The Seven Sisters. The great oil companies and the world they made.* Coronet, London, 1976, p. 161-162.

[2] Fontaine, P. *La Nouvelle Course au Pétrole.* Les Sept Couleurs, Paris, 1957, p. 107.

[3] Votaw, D. *The Six-legged Dog. Mattei and ENI. A study in power.* University of California Press, Berkeley, 1964, p. 17

usually describes ENI's internationalisation during the late Fifties as a project which started and ended with Mattei's chairmanship (1953-62). In fact, every aspect of the peculiar approach of the Italian company to its operations abroad and – besides – its original deals with oil producing countries, is usually explained as a result of Mattei's entrepreneurship, without any influence from other dimensions of the firm (its previous history, the context in which it operated, and other capabilities involved in its operations).

This paper focuses on the origins of the 1957 agreement between ENI and Iran's National that went down in history as "Mattei's formula". This contract – which allowed the producer a 75% profit share and, besides, a partnership on an equal basis – was a turning point in ENI's experience and marked a new attitude of the company toward developing countries.

This essay, instead, aims to offer an insight into the history of the Italian oil company abroad, before 'Mattei's Formula' and, besides, before the creation of ENI itself. I would like to argue that the strategy of the company during Mattei's years can be fully understood only by taking into account its previous experiences abroad and, most of all, the first efforts of AGIP – the State-owned oil company which gave birth to ENI in 1953 – before the Second World War. AGIP's successes (few) and failures (many) during the inter-war period could contribute to explaining both the pool of capabilities available for the internationalisation of the Fifties and the weaknesses which limited the performance of the company.

AGIP's Origins between Russia and Romania

The oil business begun in Europe during the first years of the Twentieth Century, driven mainly by the rising demand of the most advanced economies of the Continent, rather than by the availability of domestic oil as was the case in the US European oil companies therefore had been created with an international scope[4]. Furthermore, in the European oil industry, as in other kinds of European big businesses, there was a strong presence of the State, both as a regulator and through the creation of State-owned enterprises (SOEs).

---

[4] De Goey, F. "Henri Deterding, Royal Dutch/Shell and the Dutch market for petrol, 1902-46". *Business History* (44), 2002, p. 55-84.

Jones, G. *Multinationals and Global Capitalism from the Nineteenth to the Twenty-first Century.* Oxford University Press, New York, 2005, p. 48.

In fact, the creation of AGIP, in 1926, could be associated with other cases of public intervention in the oil business which followed WWI[5]. In other words, both the concerns about the risk of an 'oil famine' and the eagerness to obtain a favourable position in the area previously under the control of the Central Empires (Mesopotamia, Caucasus, Galicia) led to the creation of new legislative instruments or to the direct participation of States in the share capital of a variety of forms of oil companies (APOC 1914, CFP 1924, CAMPSA 1927).

At the moment of its constitution, however, AGIP was neither endowed with a significant supply of crude oil (in Italy or in some satellite area) nor was it legitimized as a monopolistic refiner or distributor on the domestic market. Also at first CFP had at its disposal insufficient financial resources, no supplies of oil, and was burdened with the interdiction to refine or sell oil directly and with a weak position inside the Iraqi international consortium (TPC, then IPC). Nevertheless, the French company had representatives among its private shareholders, almost all the companies already operating in France (even the branches of the foreign majors). Furthermore, in the following year, the State never denied its diplomatic and financial support when it came to improving the position of the company[6].

AGIP was created as a company under the private corporation law, even thought its share capital was completely owned by the State. The first president was, for instance, Ettore Conti, one of the most prominent Italian electrical industrialists and the deputy president of the main universal bank of the country, Banca Commerciale Italiana. Its deputy was Piero Pirelli, owner of the Pirelli tyre company. However AGIP was very far from the efficiency and independence from politics that its flavour of private business would suggest.

Besides, Conti was part of a network of relationships that embraced finance and politically-supported big business[7] and he was close to the powerful Minister of Finance, Giuseppe Volpi. The latter – at the same time a member of the government, a financier and an electric industry tycoon – was a significant example of how the borderline between business and politics was blurred, both in pre-fascist Italy and during the

---

[5] For a reconstruction of AGIP/ENI's history from 1926 to 1965, and for complete archival references, see Pozzi D. *Dai Gatti Selvaggi al Cane a Sei Zampe. Tecnologia, conoscenza e organizzazione nell'AGIP e nell'ENI di Enrico Mattei*. Marsilio, Venezia, 2009.

[6] Nouschi, A. *La France et le pétrole de 1924 à nos jours*. Picard, Paris, 2001.

[7] Amatori, F. "Italy: the tormented rise of organizational capabilities between government and families". In: Chandler, A. D., Amatori, F. & Takashi, H. (eds.), *Big Business and the Wealth of Nations*, Cambridge University Press, Cambridge, 1997, p. 247-275

Regime. Very often some of the most relevant decisions were taken directly by Volpi before the board of the company met, just to rubber-stamp the decision taken by the Ministry. When Volpi left office, in the summer of 1928, Conti's position weakened as a result and he had to resign after an unsuccessful attempt at agreement with APOC[8].

Due to this origin, AGIP's first attempts abroad were more an offspring of Italian foreign policy than the result of a coherent strategy of internationalisation.

For instance, during its first years, AGIP suffered from the swinging objectives of the Italian 'ostpolitik'. During the 1920s, in fact, Italian diplomacy tried to gain a position of regional power with regard to the Balkans and Eastern Europe, backing, in turn, the aspirations of the Caucasian Republics, the USSR, Romania and other countries (Volpi was one of the main supporters of the attempt to build an Italian sphere of influence towards the East[9]). Oil interests were often involved in this complex web of relationships and AGIP was often affected by the consequences of the choices of the Government.

The creation of AGIP itself was related to the aim of sustaining better relations with the USSR, as its first achievement was to save the Società Nazionale Oli Minerali (SNOM). SNOM had been created in 1920 by some influential private entrepreneurs (among them, Pirelli, Agnelli, and electric power producers very close to Conti and Volpi...) to import oil products at a competitive price, relying on the purchase of large stocks from dealers that were independent from the majors. After the re-opening of diplomatic relations between Italy and the Soviet Union – Italy recognised *de facto* USSR with an Italian-Soviet commercial agreement in the 1923-24 –, SNOM shifted its core business from industrial fuels to petrol and oriented itself toward a long-term exclusive deal with the Soviet oil syndicate that would make the company a valuable asset for Italian foreign policy.

Also due to the good relationship with the government, by the mid-1920s, SNOM owned a small retail network but the agreement with the Nephtesyndacat was very unfavourable for the Italian company and, furthermore, SNOM's commercial competences were scarce, and by 1926 the company was on the verge of bankruptcy.

---

[8]   Meetings 26/09/1928 and 15/10/1928 Cda AGIP (1926-28), f.11/b.1/Exploration & Power (E&P)/Archivio Storico ENI (AS ENI); see Bamberg, J. H. *The History of the British Petroleum Company: the Anglo-Iranian years, 1928-1954.* Cambridge University Press, Cambridge, 1994, p. 115-116.

[9]   Webster, R. A. "Una speranza rinviata. L'espansione industriale italiana e il problema del petrolio dopo la prima guerra mondiale", *Storia Contemporanea* (XI): 1980, p. 219-281.

The company was acquired by AGIP just after the creation of the SOE, with the idea of keeping alive a business, judged as strategic, under the umbrella of the State. The SNOM acquisition appears thus in the line with the Italian idea of 'supported' capitalism, and it could be seen also as an attempt on the part of the State to free private industrialists from the burden of a business they were not able to manage.

Conti organised AGIP as a holding, thus the parent company did not exert any activity on its own, but was the centre of financial coordination between SNOM and ROMSA (a small refining company acquired by AGIP in the Italian enclave of Fiume). As a matter of fact, the operative branches were not really accountable to AGIP. They kept their own management and there was no effective integration among them[10].

The subsequent evolution of AGIP's commercial business showed the weakness of the position of the company facing the Italian subsidiaries of the majors, and its complete lack of experience of the SOE. Besides, AGIP was incapable of re-negotiating the long term agreement with the USSR to adapt the deal to the unforeseen conditions under which the company had to operate during the 1920s and the 1930s. In fact, AGIP was set up with an expectation of a scarcity of oil and rising prices. Consequently, supplies from the USSR at fixed prices, SNOM's retail facilities and some help from the government (e.g. easier authorisations to open new petrol stations) were considered advantages sufficient to guarantee AGIP a place alongside Standard and Shell. Nevertheless, after the First World War, the international oil market reversed its trend and competitors answered AGIP's attempts to erode their market share with a price war that the SOE could not sustain[11].

Similar pitfalls were noticeable also in AGIP's effort to enter the Romanian oil business.

After the First World War, Italian diplomacy and the business world regarded Romania as a possible satellite, due to the economic, cultural and political bonds between the two countries[12]. Besides, Romanian oil production was rising and, in 1925, Romania supplied 7% of the Italian imports of oil products (62,000 tons) and some Italian-participating companies had operated in Romania since the beginning of the century[13]. The possibility of involving a national oil company in Romania was

[10]   Meeting 19/06/1926, Cda AGIP (1926–1928), f.11/b.1/E&P/AS ENI.
[11]   Difficulties are reported, for instance, in meetings 16/05/1927, 19/09/1927, 29/11/1927, 28/3/1928 Direttivo SNOM (1925-28), f.2a43/b.38/E&P/AS ENI; meetings 22/09/1927, 01/02/1928 Cda CUN (1920-29), f.1b9/b.38/E&P/AS ENI.
[12]   Stângaciu, A *Investitii si Investitori Italieni în România (1919-1925)*. Editura EFES, 2006, Cluj-Napoca. Other information are in doc. 28248/sc. 315/Scatole Rosse/E&P/AS ENI.
[13]   Calcan, G. "Aspect of Romanian petroleum industry in the inter-war period". *Annual*

indeed envisaged by Italian politicians even before the creation of AGIP, to take advantage by the withdrawal of the Central Powers[14].

The decision to enter Romania, therefore, was not taken by AGIP's management to reduce the dependency of the company on Soviet oil, approaching the standards of the integrated competitors. It was, indeed, the result of the role assigned to AGIP as a tool of Italian diplomacy, so the investment was undertaken without a real evaluation of its effectiveness.

Following the structure that Conti gave to its activities in Italy, AGIP's participation in the Rumanian oil business took the form of financial control over pre-existing activities, rather than to cause the company to adopt an integrated multinational structure. This solution was contrary to the will of the Italian government and overcame the limits imposed by the Romanian mining law of 1924 which discriminated against direct foreign investment in the oil business[15].

In Autumn 1926, AGIP purchased a major share in the Romanian company, Prahova, which gave to the state-owned company rights to over around 50 hectares of oil fields, and a production of almost 15,000 tons/year (in 1925). In addition, AGIP took control over Prahova's subsidiaries, with a share of 54% in the refining company Petrolul Bucaresti, and 66% of the retail company Atlas Petrol[16].

In October 1926, Conti presented the acquisition in Romania to the board of directors as an outstanding success: in fact the situation was a little less bright. Through Prahova, AGIP controlled a mere 0.6% of Romanian crude, and the Romanian products were mostly sold locally.

In addition, although there was a very unlikely possibility that AGIP could import Prahova's products in a future they could only account for a tiny share of the company's needs (the Russians supplied AGIP with around 300,000 tons/year of products, versus the 60,000 tons/year produced by Petrolul Bucaresti's plant). To achieve this limited result, AGIP tied up around 40% of its own capital share for the acquisition of Prahova, drying up any possibility of investing seriously in Italy, to improve the pool of activities inherited by SNOM.

---

of the University of Mining and Geology "St. Ivan Rilski" (XLVIII): 2005, p. 37-40.

[14] See 1925-1926 correspondence between the Ministries and Mussolini, doc. 6071 and 6075/sc. 92/Scatole Rosse/E&P/AS ENI.

[15] Pearton, M. *Oil and the Romanian State*. Clarendon Press, Oxford, 1971, p. 112 and ff.

[16] Prahova owned around 15 wells in Călinot, Bustenari, Runcu, Gropi and Grausor (32.2 ha). It was waiting for the success of applications for other fields (20 ha) in the region of Ochiuri. See doc. 28248/sc. 315/Scatole Rosse/E&P/AS ENI.

As a result of these structural weaknesses, and due to many mis-judgements on the part of its top management, AGIP could not develop a coherent and autonomous strategy, but had to follow political direc-tions and the choices taken by its powerful competitors (for instance, a price reduction below AGIP's profit level). Conti was forced to leave the company in 1928, after the failure of an attempt to reach a more sustainable pattern of activities, substituting the dependence on the Russian with a possibly even more restrictive deal with the APOC.

From Iraq to the Empire

The new chairman strengthened the bonds between the company and the administration and, at the same time, ended the subordination of AGIP to the interests of external economic groups. Partially this trans-formation depended on the evolution of Fascist economic policy toward a State-entrepreneurial model (that officially was born only some years after the 1929 crisis) but the change of strategy in AGIP was also due to the personal commitment of its new president, Alfredo Giarratana, a 39 year-old engineer from Brescia (a large Northern industrial city). Giarratana belonged to a generation of young enthusiasts of Fascism that considered the Regime a device to modernize the country by pur-suing an idea of technical rationality and nationalistic aims, against the old elitist capitalism inherited from the Liberal era. During the 1920s, he emerged in the Fascist movement of its home town and chaired the utility company owned by the municipality[17]. As a publicist and as a member of the municipal concerns' national association, he promoted the idea of a public owned company managed with the same efficiency as private competitors[18]

In the pursuit of a structure which could give AGIP better possibili-ties to tackle the business, Giarratana abandoned 'holding form' for a better integration among the different branches of activities. For ins-tance, SNOM disappeared, merged into the parent company as its commercial department. In a similar way, Romanian activities were subject to better control and a stronger integration among them was established[19].

---

[17] Zane, M. (2001). *Alfredo Giarratana. Un manager dell'energia nelle vicende sociali ed economiche di Brescia e dell'Italia del Novecento*. Grafo, Brescia, 2001.

[18] It could be useful to make a comparison with the achievements of the technocrats during the same period in a completely different national context like the French oil industry. See Sassi, M. "Le Rôle du Technocrate: Ernest Mercier et la mise en place d'une industrie française entre les deux guerres", *Bulletin de l'IHTP* (2004).

[19] Meetings 17/01/1929, 31/01/1929, 20/02/1929 and 10/06/1929, Cda AGIP (1929-31), f.12/b.1/E&P/AS ENI.

For Prahova this meant – in December 1928 – the dismissal of the previous management and the development, inside the company, of Italian managers such as the Italian engineer, Mario Amico, who led the technical department[20]. Besides, the integration between Prahova and the downstream subsidiaries was improved, and, by the summer of 1929, AGIP had begun to plan a future integration with regard to its Romanian and Italian activities.

Under Giarratana's leadership, Prahova updated its technical skills, introducing – from 1929 to 1930 – rotary rigs instead that the traditional percussion drilling. At the end of the 1920s, rotary was becoming a standard for the major companies in Romania – where it was introduced from the USA in at the middle of the decade – but it was a completely unknown novelty for the Italian oil company. During the winter of 1929-1930, AGIP started negotiations with some American companies (National Supply Company and Oil Well Supply Company) to buy new rotary rigs for Prahova[21].

In the following years, Romania became a training field for the Italian technicians who were sent there to practice rotary drilling with Prahova before the new technique could be introduced into Italy. In fact, AGIP could find very few possibilities to put to work its personnel in producing oil fields in Italy, and the lack of direct experience gathered 'on the job' was one of the causes of the low efficiency of the company's upstream units. Romanian subsidiaries offered the possibility of breaking this vicious circle, and supplied the parent company – more than with crude or refined products – with the possibility to experiment in the oil business and to bring into AGIP a first core of competence around which to build a strong mining branch[22].

Unfortunately, Giarrana's reforms were just begun when the 1929 crisis hit the international oil business, bringing to a halt the Romanian oil boom and nullifying the profitability of AGIP's investments in that country. Prices collapsed suddenly in 1930 while production reached a peak in the mid-1930s. Then the whole Romanian oil industry began to come apart, as the exploited fields were not replaced by new finds (low prices discouraged the investment needed in a long run perspective).

---

[20] Meeting 10/06/1929, Cda AGIP (1929-31), f.12/b.1/E&P/AS ENI; doc. 28229/sc. 314 and doc. 1573, 1576/sc. 17/Scatole Rosse/E&P/AS ENI.

[21] Doc. 116-119/sc. 2/Scatole Rosse/E&P/AS ENI.

[22] Among the technicians trained in Romania were: Italo Veneziani, Alberto Zanmatti, Piero Chiapponi, Giovanni Chiura, Bionaz. See Pissard M. G., *La Leggenda del Pionere. Diario Mazzini Garibaldi Pissard (1929/1983)*, ENI, Roma, 2008, p. 37, 46 and 50.

Prahova's fields reached their production record – 578,000 tons/year – in 1934 and then declined at a faster pace than the Romanian average[23].

In a situation of falling demand, the total dependence on the old agreement with the Soviet Union undermined the possibility for AGIP to react effectively to the changing environment. Consequently, Giarratana made the first steps toward better control over the supply and even backward integration, also in a scenario wider than the Romanian frame.

On a medium to long perspective, in fact, AGIP pursued direct control on crude by entering into an international combine, the British Oil Development Co. (BOD), created in 1929 by businessmen of the City of London, to gain some research permission by taking advantage of the difficulties between IPC and the Iraqi government[24]. In addition, to improve the position of AGIP in the short run, Giarratana tried to re-negotiate the contract with the Soviet oil syndicate. The new agreement had to develop as a real alliance between AGIP and the Soviets: however the behaviour of the Russian partner, the opposition of the majors, which started a press campaign against the agreement, and internal rivalries inside the Fascist party, undermined the project and forced Giarratana to resign in February, 1932[25]. The young engineer succeeded, at least, to put in charge some of the managers who would direct the company until the war, maintaining some continuity after the end of his chairmanship (e.g. Ettore Carafa d'Andria, Oreste Jacobini).

Under Giarratana's successors – usually retired Ministers, without any experience in the oil business – AGIP operated in a context characterised more and more by the international isolation of Italy and by growing political control over the economy; as a result, external conditionings progressively prevailed on the possibility of building a coherent development path for the company.

BOD's agreement was, for instance, the more crushing failure of the Italian company. After exhausting negotiations, in 1932 BOD was allowed to start exploration in Mossul. The first results were encouraging, but the Iraqi government required the payment of high dead rents to maintain the rights. In contrast, the balance among BOD's shareholders was very unstable: AGIP acquired a major share in the combine by 1934, but very soon had to reduce its participation because the Italian

---

[23] Production fell to 246,000 tons in 1942, a 57% reduction. In the same period, Romanian production fell by around 34%.

[24] Longrigg, S. H. *Iraq, 1900 to 1950. A political, social and economic history.* Oxford University Press, Oxford, 1953, p. 210-211.

[25] Meeting 30/06/1931, 10/12/1931, Cda AGIP (1931-35), f.13/b.1/E&P/AS ENI; see also Pizzigallo M., *L'AGIP degli anni ruggenti (1926/1932)*, Giuffrè, Milano, 1984, p. 238 and ff.

government did not provide the company with the needed resources – in hard currency – to maintain its position[26]. More important than the complex evolution of BOD's ownership was the fact that, since 1934, AGIP's technicians had begun to lead the exploration in Iraq as operative officers, earning relevant experience in the management of operations abroad. In the meanwhile also, the top management improved its negotiation capabilities, thanks to the continuous bargaining with the other owners, and some managers – e.g. Carafa d'Andria – developed very strong relations inside the British oil industry.

A first finding of oil occurred in 1935, but AGIP had to leave BOD the following year since Mussolini's imperial obsession required the company to divert all its resources toward the exploration of the recently acquired colonies in East Africa.

Italy had peacefully acquired its first tiny African colony – Eritrea – in the 1880s, but since then East Africa had had almost no relevance for the motherland's economy. The government asked AGIP to evaluate the possibility of beginning some activities in Eritrea in 1927, but the option was rejected as economically worthless. By 1934, however, East Africa had become a paramount issue for the Regime and AGIP was forced to build some facilities in Eritrea, to offer a bridgehead for the aggression towards Ethiopia, planned for October 1935[27].

After the creation of the so-called Italian Empire, AGIP was rewarded with the monopoly of the Italian East African market, a privilege AGIP could not manage without relying on the help of some foreign companies. Besides, AGIP was engaged in the effort to retrieve and exploit the rich reservoirs of raw materials which, in the opinion of the Italian leaders (and theirs alone), existed in the recently-conquered colony. In fact, the exploration run by AGIP from 1936 to 1940 did not achieve any results, in spite of a small finding in the Dahalak Islands, part of the Eritrea colony.

The unfortunate exploration campaigns in Ethiopia, Somalia and Eritrea, thus diverted a main part of AGIP's resources from other, more promising, fields of operation, such as Iraq and Libya, another Italian colony, where exploration started in 1936[28]. However, the investment

---

[26] Meeting 10/01/1935, Cda AGIP (1931–1935), f.13/b.1/E&P/AS ENI; meeting 25/01/1936, Cda AGIP (1935-40), f.14/b.1/E&P/AS ENI.

[27] Meeting 15/10/1934, Cda AGIP (1931–1935), f.13/b.1/E&P/AS ENI. About Italian colonialism, see Del Boca A., *Gli Italiani in Africa Orientale. La conquista dell'Impero*, Mondadori, Milano, 1992.

[28] Pizzigallo, M. *La 'politica estera' dell'AGIP (1933-1940)*. Giuffrè, Milano, 1992, p. 75 and ff.
Del Boca, A. *Gli Italiani in Libia. Dal fascismo a Gheddafi*. Mondadori, Milano, 1994, p. 271-272. In the 1930s it was impossible to foresee the real potential of Libya

made to exploit the hypothetical East African oil, reveal themselves to be useful in an unpredictable way: the needs for the African exploration, for instance, caused AGIP to hire directly a new generation of geologists and young technicians (among them the geologist Giancarlo Facca and Dante Jaboli), who, during the war, found effective employment in the Northern Italy's fields, becoming a key resources for the finding of natural gas which has taken place here since 1944.

Coming back to the Domestic Industry: Natural Gas

After the war, the evolution of the economic policy of the European countries and the transformation of the international oil industry led to the overcoming of the old models of oil that SOE had adopted, to a context of crisis and 'autartic' economy.

For instance, from 1945 onwards, France re-organised its regulatory system around the Bureau de Recherches de Pétrole (BRP), a public concern entrusted with the coordination of research and development of the industry in the motherland and in the colonies[29]. On the other hand, oil became a part of the development planning also in Spain, since INI (the public concern created on the model of the Italian IRI in 1941) substituted CAMPSA as the main player in the hydrocarbon national industry[30].

AGIP too evolved toward new forms of business and toward a new role within post-war national economic planning. In 1953, this process took the form of the creation of Ente Nazionale Idrocarburi (ENI), a new public concern merging AGIP and other minor SOEs as its operative subsidiaries.

It is impossible here to present the details of the development of ENI from AGIP's roots. However, it is important to stress some points related to the national/international scope of the company. The creation of ENI was made possible by the finding of natural gas in the Po Valley, when the first reservoir was discovered 30 km south of Milan during the war. This allowed the company to recognize other similar geological structures near Piacenza and Ravenna by the early 1950s.

Previously, during autarchy, methane was used mostly as a petrol surrogate: this was almost the only suitable use for the small amount of

---

as an oil producer because there was not yet available a geophysical technique suitable for 'reading' the desert (where surface geology is impossible, due to the thick layer of sand).

[29] Grayson, L. E. *National Oil Companies*. John Wiley and Sons, Chichester, 1981, p. 26 and ff.

[30] Tortella, G., Ballestro A., & Díaz Fernández J. L. *Del Monopolio al Libre Mercado. La historia de la industria petrolera española*. LID, Madrid, 2003, p. 223 and ff.

gas retrieved during the 1930s, mostly from small, shallow fields in the Po Delta area. New findings, in contrast, shifted the scale of the business, since its large output could be used more profitably as industrial fuel, substituting for coal in the northern Italy factories. This implied a complete re-thinking of the business: AGIP needed to reach large consumers (Dalmine, Fiat, Edison, etc.) to gain a stable base of consumption. In addition, a network of pipelines had to be built in order to reach the main industrial cities of Northern Italy. Consequently, the company had to find a balance between huge fixed investment (in mining and transport facilities) and large – but delayed – profits[31].

It would be useful to make a comparison with the French gas industry developed by the public concerns ERAP and SNPA since the find of the St. Marcet gas field in 1939. At the beginning of the 1950s, French production was smaller than the Italian. Besides, ERAP was still relying more than AGIP on the traditional use of methane as a petrol surrogate[32]. To better understand the differences between the two industries, it is also important to highlight that AGIP found its first reservoir only a few kilometres from the most industrialized Italian city, while the French fields were situated in the South-West, the most economically backward region of the country. This could hardly represent a profitable market such as Lombardy.

As a result of the advantages given by the new natural gas business, at the end of the 1940s, AGIP already owned a base of activities and resources that allowed the company to make profits, then re-invest these for growth. While oil products in the post-war market were rebuilt by the Anglo-Saxon majors, methane became AGIP's new core business. The cooperation between the entrepreneurial leadership of Enrico Mattei and the capabilities of the technicians of the mining branch during the 1950s (many of them reached executive position inside the company) allowed the company's re-birth on this new basis. This meant a drastic shift of the strategic focus from the import-refining-selling activities toward the mining business – which Mattei supervised personally – and, thus, as natural gas was strictly a domestic business, AGIP concentrated its best resources on its activities in Italy.

The image of AGIP – and ENI since the mid-1950s – as a 'domestic-only' company, has to be balanced by a correct understanding of the international relationship the company enjoyed during the development of the natural gas business. In fact, the hydrocarbons industry always

---

[31] See documents in CEDI. *Archivio storico. Verbali Comitato tecnico ricerche e produzioni (1948-1949).* Centro stampa AGIP, San Donato Milanese, 1991.

[32] Brunet, C. "Le gaz naturel en France". In: *Atti del VII Convegno nazionale del metano e del petrolio*, IRES, Palermo, 1952, p. 871-880.

had a very internationally-open configuration, and during the 1940s and 1950s, AGIP's technical management was committed to catching up with international standards in mining activity. Sometimes, the updating process had some point of connection with the pre-war international experience.

For instance, alongside new links with the American oil industry, AGIP maintained some connection with the British oil world: Italo Veneziani – who after the war led his own company and worked as contractor for AGIP – exploited the connection established during the BOD venture to facilitate the agreement between the Italian company and the Santa Fé Drilling Company, an American contractor who worked for AGIP from 1949 to 1952[33]. Bonds with Great Britain remained relevant, mainly in the downstream business: for instance, Ettore Carafa d'Andria – who remained in AGIP's top management until 1952 – played an important function in the negotiation with AIOC, which brought about the creation of the joint-stock company IROM, in 1949. AGIP delegated its refining business to this company, receiving from AIOC – which did not have plans or a significant retail network in Italy - the needed supplies of crude, under a fix-terms contract (AGIP was *de facto* the AIOC's reseller for the Italian market)[34].

AGIP did not retain any relationship with the producer countries, but the pool of capabilities developed by some of the technicians during the pre-war experience abroad had a key role also for the exploration of the Po Valley. For instance many experienced drillers had mastered rotary techniques abroad or had been directly trained by specialists with international experience (as Veneziani). Besides, some of the more prominent geologist in the company (such as Giancarlo Facca or Dante Jaboli) had been hired by AGIP to look at the 'colonial adventure'.

In some way, AGIP and then ENI had, in their inheritance, a germ of internationalization.

A New Internationalisation

By 1952 – Parliament was still passing the legislation for the creation of ENI – AGIP technicians started to address Mattei with regard to the problem of the future destination of the exploration personnel and machinery: the Po Valley was entering the exploitation phase and the company needed new plans to fulfil its exploration capabilities.

---

[33] See documents in CEDI [1991], p. 176-181 and 291-292.
[34] Meetings 24/04/1947 and 25/05/1947, Cda AGIP (1946–1947), f.19/b.2/E&P/AS ENI.

One of the possibilities considered by the company was to start some activities abroad again, but AGIP (and then the new-born ENI) was still suffering from the lack of international experience and by the weak position of Italy in the international diplomatic arena. Consequently, it was not easy to identify a realistic opportunity.

During these years, AGIP received different offerings for participation in – not very promising – exploration in Greece, the Yemen and Lebanon, but did not embrace any of these agreements[35]. In fact, the company recognized its best opportunity was the restoration of exploration in East Africa. This area had the unmistakable advantage to be somehow already known to AGIP – which had kept data and samples from the previous exploration missions – although the diplomatic position of Italy after the war undermined almost every possibility to gain some sort of control over the former colonies.

After 1952, the UN settled some of the outstanding matters and AGIP started negotiations with the British authorities, which had to maintain its mandate over Ethiopia and Eritrea until complete independence was achieved (Eritrea was merged into the Ethiopian federal State). The aim of the Italian company was to recover some of its proprieties left in the colonies during the war, and, besides, to achieve some rights to begin new explorations in Eritrea. AGIP reached a deal with the mandatory authorities and with the Eritrean government by the Fall of 1953, but the opposition of the Ethiopian federal government – backed by the American oil company Sinclair – froze the agreement just before AGIP's geologists could take a step in Eritrea[36].

The exploration mission, lead by Giancarlo Facca and by the academic consultant, Professor Giovanni Merla, was diverted toward Somalia: AGIP had very few hopes of the oil potential of this area, but, at least the country was 'diplomatically' friendly, because Somalia was under Italian mandate until 1960.

The correspondence between Facca and Mattei shows that the attitude of the company toward the host country was a mix of colonialist nostalgia and of concern about good relationships with the local elite[37]. Referring to Mattei about his mission, Facca announced that the feeling of the population toward AGIP was so favourably oriented that it was impossible the birth of a "Somali Mossadegh", even after independence. Facca's action, indeed, went beyond the old colonialist approach: the geologist had a good number of meetings with Somali notables, religious authorities and tribal chiefs and the company offered some young

---

[35] Doc. 43069/sc. 478/Scatole Rosse/E&P/AS ENI.

[36] Doc. 14642, 14657, 14695/sc. 186/Scatole Rosse/E&P/AS ENI.

[37] Doc. 3259/sc. 43 and 48843/sc. 632(1997)/Scatole Rosse/E&P/AS ENI.

promising Somalis a scholarship in Italy. These were largely Facca's personal initiatives, outside an organic plan or radical cultural change, but they showed that the company was beginning to consider the relationship with the host communities as a relevant issue, and that it was impossible to define the position of the company in a producing country only through negotiations with other Westerner partners or by force. Unfortunately, all these efforts revealed themselves to be worthless, as no oil was found in Somalia in the following years (ENI left the country in 1963).

It is possible to recognize a similar melange of traditional and innovative attitudes toward producing countries in ENI's first penetration into Egypt, an area that then became one of the main crude suppliers for the company. In some 1953 reports, Dante Jaboli begun to evaluate the possibility to starting some work in this country after the coup during which Gamal Abdul Nasser overthrew King Faruk I[38]. At the end of the year, the geologist led a first mission in Egypt and, the following year, Mahmoud Younes – Nasser's right hand for economic issues – visited Italy, meeting Mattei. However, ENI could not reach a satisfying agreement with the Egyptian authorities, because all the most promising areas had already been granted to other foreign companies.

As the possibility of favourable direct investment was diminishing, ENI's first significant attempt to gain a direct supply of crude had many similarity with the BOD's operation: in fact, in 1955, ENI accepted the offer to participate in the share capital of IEOC, an international combine that operated in Egypt and had as its main shareholder the Belgian oil company Petrofina (jointly with Swiss and American financial investors). ENI brought to IEOC fresh capital – needed to start exploration in new areas – but progressively contributed also with its technical expertise, substituting for IEOC's previous operator, Southern California Petroleum Co. by 1957.

Progressively, ENI acquired a larger share of the capital, and tried to strength its position inside IEOC, while the Belgian partner maintained the larger share of the top management, leaving only the technical direction to ENI[39]. In this situation, the Italians judged the Petrofina proposal to offer the Egyptian government a share in a new subsidiary company, as a potential danger for ENI interests inside IEOC (the first draft of this agreement was presented in 1955).[40]

However, after the Suez crisis in 1956, Egyptian politics took a radical turn, and Nasser's economic policy inclined toward a progressive

---

[38] Doc. 49084/sc. 656(1973)/Scatole Rosse/E&P/AS ENI.

[39] Documentation about Egypt is in b.55, 64 and 91/Direzione Estero/ENI/AS ENI.

[40] Documents in f. 1dff/91/Direzione Estero/ENI/AS ENI.

nationalisation[41]. Following the previous negotiation started by Petrofi-na, in 1957 ENI agreed to create COPE, an operative company of which a 50% share of the capital was owned by the Egyptian government and the remaining 50% by IEOC. In the meanwhile, the weight of the Italian company inside the international combine had grown and, eventually, Petrofina had to leave the venture after Egypt had seized Belgian inte-rests in the country, as a reprisal against colonial policy in the Congo (1960).

From late-1950s onward, therefore, ENI began a strong cooperation with Nasser's regime, not only in upstream business, but also in refining and engineering: the Italian SOE had some ideological similarity with the supporters of a strong public intervention for the Egyptian develop-ment, and Egyptian leaders, Nasser and Mahmoud Younes, felt strong personal affinity with Mattei and his right hand, Eugenio Cefis[42].

Conclusions

The different experiences abroad of AGIP and ENI before 1957 show some interesting elements of continuity, which also influenced the strategy and the performance of the company in the following years.

First of all, since its birth, the company was burdened by a lack of direct control of its raw materials. This referred more to a problem of flexibility and of the predictability of the investment than to a pure issue of the price of crude: often the Italian company had to tackle a context of falling prices while it was still dependent on fixed-term supply agreements, which did not allow any possibility for reducing the cost of the crude in response to the trends in the market. As a consequence, to achieve a vertically integrated structure – necessarily international – became a paramount issue, both before and after the Second World War.

On the other hand, AGIP and, in its first years, ENI, had serious pro-blems caused by the lack of international experience. Conti's AGIP could scarcely manage even its domestic business and had no capability for understanding the complexity of investment abroad, but also under Giarratana the company did not have an effective economic basis to sustain its internationalisation and to defend itself from political inter-ference. During Mattei's chairmanship, on the other hand, ENI could rely on the profits and on the technical capabilities accumulated in the natural gas business. Even so, the company was shy about taking its first

---

[41] Tignor, R. L. *Capitalism and Nationalism at the End of Empire. State and business in decolonizing Egypt, Nigeria and Kenya*. Princeton University Press, Princeton, 1998, p. 144 and ff.

[42] Tonini, A. *Il Sogno Proibito. Mattei, il petrolio arabo e le "sette sorelle»*. Edizioni Polistampa, Firenze, 2003.

steps in the international arena. In fact, ENI's strength was built entirely on a domestic business – even with relevant international links – and its competitive advantage could be adapted to the new context only through a long and complex process of learning by doing.

ENI was able to achieve the international needs for technical skills relatively quickly, thanks to the fact that its core of competence was well established in this field. More difficulties arose, nevertheless, in ensuring the adequate effectiveness of the company in selecting and pursuing strategic aims abroad. In fact, even after the war, the Italian company had to choose between moves on the diplomatic chessboard or just agree to a proposal offered by other operators.

For this reason the company began its 1950s wave of internationalisation, following the path of AGIP's pre-war experience, relying on the means both of a combination with international investors and of a semi-colonial relationship with a producer country. However, ENI became precociously conscious that the post-war context required a renewal of the traditional attitude of the company toward host countries: it is possible to recognise a germ of this acknowledgement in the Somali operation, but it became evident in the evolution of the Egyptian venture.

In the mid-1950s Egypt was still a relatively new producing country. However, older and richer producers began to challenge the existing equilibrium, since ENI and other independent companies offered these governments strong bargaining power against the majors. For example, after the weakening of the most conservative faction inside the Shah's court, some Iranian personalities started to search for allies to call into question the Consortium's hegemony[43]. During the summer of 1956, Ahmed Maybud, one of the Shah's advisers, initiated contact with ENI. Maybud proposed the creation of a joint company between ENI and NIOC (the Iranian national company) which was to take over some research areas freed up by the consortium[44]. The agreement would overwhelm the traditional fifty-fifty basis and the Iranian government would receive 2/3 of the profits as royalties and revenues. The international oil industry was changing forever and 'Mattei's forumula' was born.

---

[43] Karshenas, M. *Oil, State and Industrialization in Iran*. Cambridge University Press, Cambridge, 1990, p. 88 and ff.

[44] About Iran: b.10, 20, 21, 50 and 83/Direzione Estero/ENI/AS ENI.

The Relations between Eni and Iran: 1954-1957

Ilaria TREMOLADA

University of Milan, Italy

The purpose of this essay is to give you an overview of the relation-ships between Eni, the Italian State Oil Company, and National Iranian Oil Company, Nioc, in the period ranging from 1953, year in which Eni was set up, up to August 1957, date on which Eni was authorized, through the signature of an agreement of revolutionary nature, to search for oil in the Persian territory.

The first part of the essay concerns the route of approach between the parties signatory of the agreement, while in the second part the coming into existence of the agreement will be treated, paying particular attention to its characteristics of the same which may be considered to be revolutionary.

Among the most important novelties represented by the Eni-Nioc agreement, one in particular appears to be of paramount importance, since it is the origin of the agreement itself: the agreement was not proposed by Eni, but by the Iranian government.

Up to now historians have always believed, following the recollec-tions of the protagonists of that period and the beliefs rooted in the public opinion at that time, that the Eni-Nioc agreement was created by the then President of Eni, Enrico Mattei. This distortion of the actual facts is based on two elements: the exaggerated consideration of Mattei's skills and personality and, on the other hand, the persistency in leaving out of consideration the will of the Middle-East countries to emancipate themselves.

The dynamism and boldness of Enrico Mattei, who, since the early years of Eni's establishment, was considered an unconventional man with an enormous personal power by the Italian and world public opin-ion, have been considered the source of his success on the international oil market. Though his importance for the growth of Italy in the postwar period cannot be denied, it has increased, also because of his tragic death, up to making him a mythological character. The wish to glorify his activity and achievements has characterized the first reconstructions after his death in a plane crash in 1962, thus severely influencing their contents. In other words, staff and journalists who wrote about Mattei's presidency have dedicated the main part of their works to the description and emphasis of his character which rose to a mythical level; the scientific nature of the reconstruction of the facts therefore very often had to give way to a sensational reconstructions of the events.

On the basis of the researches on the documents of Eni, I can now affirm that, even as far as the Eni-Iran agreement is concerned, the works published until now, to a greater or a lesser degree, give only a simplified and influenced version of the facts. It can generally be said that the mistake which recurs most often is that of thinking that Enrico Mattei has acted on his own. It is clear that such a belief leads to completely ignoring the environment, which instead was of vital importance.

Two equally strong wishes became true with the signature of the contract with Iran: the Persian determination to quit a situation in which its oil resources were under foreign control, and the Italian wish of international acknowledgment. Without either of these two factors the agreement would not have come to exist. The world immediately perceived the Mattei factor, thanks also to a certain boasting by Eni's president, whereas it took the Iranian aim less into consideration. The fact that the all the circles concerned tended to consider Mattei as the sole maker of the new contract helps to understand how stubborn was the attitude of the Atlantic Powers. The international diplomacy, so very engaged in challenging the desire of self determination of the Middle East countries, denied to itself the reality of the facts: the Middle East countries were growing up and were ready to compete on the international market, in certain economic fields. Steady in the purpose of defending at all costs the economic subordination imposed upon the Middle East countries after the fall of the Ottoman Empire, the Western Countries however were still tied to a policy of domination which, though that period was still showing a relevant power of control and conditioning, was experiencing troubles due to the will of self determination by the populations which were so far under colonial domination.

The field which first had to realize that times were changing was the same which had caused the creation of ideal conditions of total economic subordination of the Middle East countries: the oil field.

That this subordination was dangerous and harmful for the oil manufacturing countries was clear to the respective local governments in the 1940s. After the Second World War several attempts to change the situation were made, by forcing multinational oil companies, and the governments supporting them, to recognize that exactly when the subordination of the Arab region appeared to be consolidated, the very Arab countries were becoming aware that this unfair mechanism was choking them.

The first result of such recognition was the request to change and to improve the relationship between the oil manufacturing countries and the oil companies. The anglo-american multinational companies, which were already part of the Persian international consortium created after the nationalization of the Iranian oil industry undertaken by Mossadegh in April 1951, were reluctant to meet Teheran's expectations and to improve the situation. This attitude led the Iranian government to seek new partners to make business with, on the basis of conditions favourable for both parties.

The quality of the relationship between Italy and Iran, bound since a few years by close friendship, gave Rome a leading role in the Persian come back.

When the oil industry was nationalized by Mossadegh, leader of the National Front, with the purpose of withdrawing it from the control of the Anglo-Iranian company, holder of all oil research concessions, a serious diplomatic crisis broke out; the crisis was resolved in 1954 with the removal of the leader of the rebels from the government and with the set up of an international consortium which substantially readmitted the British company to the oil operations in Iran, but with the difference that the company would not hold all the oil concessions, which had to be shared with the major US oil companies.

In the course of the first phase of the crisis, Mossadegh asked Agip, the former Italian state oil company before the set up of Eni, to send consultants to Teheran to support the activities of the new born national industry. The Italian government sent some delegates supervised by Earl Carafa D'Andria, vice president of the Italian company. Later on, some privately held oil companies agreed to purchase from the Iranian company part of the oil which the latter company with difficulty had managed to produce, in the absence of the British technicians who had taken care up to then of the working and maintenance of the oil extraction plants.

Some oil stocks left Abadan despite the prohibition to export oil imposed by the Anglo-Iranian company at the time of the nationalization of the oil industry. The British company believed to own the oil extracted from its own plants, and therefore prohibited the Iranian government from exporting and selling oil.

Mossadegh, ignoring the prohibition imposed by whom he considered enemies, tried to market the oil in an attempt to show that his country was able to manage the oil industry even without the British support.

Some Italian entrepreneurs, believing that the Iranian market, no longer under British control, was a good opportunity of expanding their activities, joined up to form a company, named SUPOR. SUPOR had to coordinate the Italian companies interested in exporting their products to Iran, receiving oil in exchange. Head of the project was the CEO of the Coal Consortium of Genoa, Franco Mortillaro. The agreement was signed on May 11, 1952, and provided for the supply, in five years, of 12,500,000 tons of oil, in exchange for products of Pirelli, Fiat, Solvay, Lepetit, Galileo, San Giorgio, Olivetti, Ilva, Ansaldo and other companies.

The relevance of the agreement obtained from the Iranian government caused the whole issue to become a political problem: the UK and the US strongly opposed an agreement which, due to its relevance, could have been a good basis for the future Italian commercial success in Iran. As regards the Italian government, it did not take SUPOR's business into any great consideration at first but later on, it showed its interest by defending the agreement from attacks by UK and USA, and then by incorporating said company.

The history of SUPOR is fundamental not only for understanding the Italian politics in the Middle East and its limits, but also because the company, in the brief period between its establishment, 1952, and its ruin in 1955, was able to set up a huge network of relationships, governed with great skills and enthusiasm by the Italian Embassy in Teheran.

These relationships, which included Persian politicians from the prime minister, initially Zaehdi and then Ala, to the chief officers of NIOC, led to a relevant share also from the Italians. From the moment it was clear that the British would have made every effort to oppose the implementation of the agreement signed by SUPOR, the pressure for the government to prohibit the export of the products to the companies parties in the agreement became constant. The Italian Ministry of Foreign Affairs had no constant conduct, sometimes granting licenses to export the products, sometimes refusing them. Also in this case the problem of Italian foreign politics, crushed between loyalty towards its allies and the ambition of power, again came to a head.

After a long wrestle with the Foreign Office, SUPOR began again to transport oil from Iran to Italy, but the obstacles encountered in selling the oil once it reached the Italian coast, were such that they drove the company to ruin. Once the relevance of the agreement signed in 1952 was recognized, even just for its overall value, a state company called Safni acquired SUPOR, putting in fresh capitals. An attempt to save

SUPOR was made also by some banking groups, but without success; due to the lack of future prospects, the company's economic figures were considered irrecoverable.

After the purchase of the SUPOR by the state, in fact, the US oil companies, owners of the biggest refineries in Italy (Livorno and Bari) refused to process the oil imported from Persia, thus blocking any chance of earnings for the company. The Italian government decided not to force any action as it could have done, by obliging refineries to process the oil, as it contemplated by the state's oil law. This took all SUPOR's hopes away. At the end of 1955 the important agreement signed in 1952 was terminated by the Persian government for failure to meet delivery obligations.

Together with the compensation agreements came to fail also a project submitted a few months earlier by the Perisan government to the Supor-Safni company: the project concerned the set up of an Italian-Iranian company for the processing, transport and sale of the Perian oil. Considering that the very bad financial situation did not allow SUPOR to start a new project, its chief officers indicated to the Persian government the name of another company which very likely would have had interest in undertake business with the Shah, that is the STOI of Emanuele Floridia.

STOI had a medium sized refinery plant located near Florence, and was among the privately owned plants which had processed some oil supplies shipped from Persia. The first contacts between Floridia and Teheran date back to May 1955. After one year, in June 1956, a preliminary agreement for the set up of a mixed-capital company was signed: 50% to STOI, and 50% to Persia, for the refinery and sale of oil.

On the way back from his business trip to Teheran, in the course of which the preliminary agreement concerning the setting up of the new company, to be named IRANCO, was signed, Floridia forwarded to Eni a proposal made by the Persian government. Although contacts between Eni and Iran were for some months already underway, they had led to nothing concrete until then. Eni for some time now, according to Agip's tradition, had shown an interest for oil researches in foreign territories. The vitality of the Middle East countries, induced by the desire of freeing themselves from the colonial subordination, was an ideal opportunity of entering a world otherwise dominated by Western giants. For these reasons, in those years Eni threw itself into other projects in other countries belonging of the same area like Egypt and Libya.

Floridia reported to Eni's chief officers that he had been appointed to seek possible partners interested in investing in a mixed-capital company for searching and exploiting Persian oil on an equal basis. Floridia submitted also a resume of the project which already contained the two most innovative proposals: the setting up of a company of mixed capital with equal shares, and a royalty of 50% on the overall production, followed by the equal distribution between the two companies of the remaining 50%; this means that Eni would have received only 25%.

The day after, Eni's chief officers received a generic approval from Mattei and asked Floridia to inform Teheran that Eni would be ready to discuss the draft of the agreement proposed by the Iranian government a few days earlier.

A commission was therefore organized, in which Attilio Jacoboni, for Eni, Sarti and Jaboli, for Agip and Salimbeni for Snam took part. Floridia would have joined them with the sole purpose of introducing them to governmental circles. Talks with the Persian governmental representatives aimed at SAIP, a company of the Eni group, obtaining better fiscal conditions and broader territorial concessions. The commission headed for the Persian capital in early August, together with the CEO of STOI, Floridia. The business trip, which took place between 8 and 22 August, led to the signature of a preliminary agreement the terms of which were discussed in that period.

Once they arrived in Teheran, Jacoboni, Sarti, Jaboli and Salimbeni were introduced by Floridia to Mr S.A. Maybud, representative of the Persian government encharged with handling oil affairs. On 8 August, in the afternoon, a first meeting was held, followed in the next days by meetings with Naficy, Director of NIOC for the Exploration, with Dr Mostofi, CEO and with the Swiss geologist of the company, Augusto Canseer Biaggi.

In the year following this first mission there were several other meetings during which the final agreement was drafted and then signed in Teheran on 3 August 1957.

The agreement set forth the setting up of a mixed capital company to be named SIRIP. This company had a research concession over 25,000 km^2. of territory, for which no rent had to be paid. Research expenses would have been borne by Italy, whereas the handling and the starting of the production in the oil field and the transport of the oil would have been equally shared. Profits would also have been shared, as follows: 50% to Iran, 50% equally divided by the two shareholders.

The historical revolutionary profit sharing system, which from then on shall be called "Mattei's formula" was due to be perceived, in August 1957 when the final agreement was signed, as an unconventional change of the rules until then in force in the oil world. Eni practically received only 24.75% of the profits, but the exemption from the payment of any tax or rent whatsoever tax, or rent, including those on concessions, allowed Eni to initially save the relevant amount of 20 million dollars, and 10 million dollars each year for the rental of the fields, which initially was provided for in the preliminary agreement.

What will be clear to all, will be the abandonment of the *fifty-fifty* rule, which according to a declaration made by the Iranian politicians to the Italian commission would not have been changed, and which was confirmed by the payment of 50% of the profits to the state. The difference with respect to the past was the presence of a national company involved in the research, that forced the parties to a subsequent profit sharing which, together with the sum already due to the state according to the custom, increased Iran's profits by 25%.

The unfair profit sharing, more theoretical than real, had a significant impact and caused an extremely strong reaction in the international oil circles. To understand the reasons for the strong opposition to the agreement signed by Eni, the question of profit sharing must be put aside; and the attention should be focused on the fact that, for the big oil corporations, the worst novelty was another: the sharing of investments and resources of both States. At this stage it must be pointed out that Italy was guilty of paying attention to the Iranian projects thus putting the will of self determination of the country over and above its economic political relationships.

PART IV

SOUTH AMERICA

Petrobrás, New Technologies and Oil Self-sufficiency in Brazil[1]

Armando JOÃO DALLA COSTA[2]

Federal University of Paranà, Brazil

José BENEDITO ORTIZ NETO[3]

State University, London

The economic interest in oil began at the start of the nineteenth century, when it was used as a source of energy, replacing the gas produced by distillation of plant coal, for public lighting, called "lamp oil". That function lasted until the 1870/80 period, when Thomas Edison succeeded in systematising and developing knowledge of electric energy, which did away with all other sources of elimination. Thus the commercial interest of the fossil fuel was substantially reduced, and did not make a comeback until the end of the nineteenth century, and above all in the twentieth century, starting with the time of the invention of petrol and diesel engines. Since then, this factor of production has had sufficient commercial justification to be explored *ad infinitum,* or until exhaustion[4].

In addition, this new use of oil gave birth to one of the planet's richest industries, a new and important growth methodology, and the use of science in factory work. The oil industry, along with the chemical industry, was the pioneer in using science, thanks to R&D programmes, as an instrument of economic growth[5]. Starting at that time, the use of

---

[1] Study presented to the Colloquium called *The relations between oil producing countries and oil companies*, La Défense, 18-19 September 2006.

[2] Doctor in Economic History awarded by the University of Paris III (Sorbonne Nouvelle). Professor in the Department of Economics and Coordinator of the Business Economic Research Centre of the Federal University of Paraná-UFPR (www.empresas.ufpr.br). E-mail: ajdcosta@ufpr.br.

[3] Economist from the State University of London and Master's degree in Economic Development awarded by the UFPR. E-mail: netolon@yahoo.com.br.

[4] Debeir, J.-C. *et al.* "A Expansão do Sistema energético capitalista", *Uma história da energia*, Brasília: Ed. da UnB, 1993, p. 169-206.

[5] The German chemical industry was the first one to use this theme for developing synthetic paints in the 1860-70s, but it found in the ascension of oil – which required

R&D in the various industries is rather conspicuous, because of its essential nature in development of new products and technological processes of organisations. Many authors[6] emphasise the essential nature of this theme in designing technological R&D programmes as a central element in a strategy making possible and promoting the advance of the institution to a leading market position.

The leading country in the process of scientific learning in the oil industry was the United States. Much of the world scientific basis required for use of and exploration for oil comes from the efforts made by that country's researchers. However, that progress did not make it possible to make oil production in Brazil viable. This is because Brazil was to discover years later, at the end of the 1960s, that the majority of oil reserves were under the sea, and not on land, as was the case in the other countries, such as the United States. In the light of that reality, the United States developed a technological path, with respect to extraction of the mineral, that was almost entirely by way of territorial basins, what is called onshore or inland technology. And the insufficient technological knowledge of how to explore for oil at sea at the time did not correspond to Brazilian reality, in view of the average depth of the Brazilian wells, which were deeper than the North American ones.

In the light of this technological stalemate, the Brazilian authorities had to decide between producing a technology reflecting local reality, acquiring such technology under contract with international institutions, or else importing the mineral. Perhaps influenced by the military nationalistic awareness of the strategic importance of the country's natural resources, as well as by the absence of international know-how, the decision was made to locally produce a system of innovations, a fact that made it possible to explore the high seas for oil, the technology known as offshore. Whatever the motivation for that decision may have been, Petrobras, through the intermediary of its Technological Enablement Programme in Deep Waters – PROCAP – established in 1986, made innumerable discoveries that gave the institution the title of international leader in oil exploration in deep waters.

To understand the intrinsic, or even hidden forces in technological expansion in a process of innovations, the present study adopted the neo-Schumpeterian theoretical frame of reference, particularly the ones known as evolutionary, in order to portray the development of offshore

---

chemical discoveries, such as catalysts and more effective refining methods – a major source of reasons for moving forward in the use of science.

[6] Freeman, C., "Networks of innovators: A synthesis of research issues", *Research Policy*, 1991, p. 499-514; Soete, L., *The economics of industrial innovation*, Massachusetts: MIT Press, 3rd ed., 1997, p. 85-105; 265-285.

technology as carried out by Petrobras. This theoretical option consists in the fact that those authors essentially analyse the behaviour of variants that include technical progress, particularly the innovation systems as a function of institutions, and by the conception of the externalities generated by technology during the ex post period of competition, which, in the conception of this work, can reflect the performance of the Brazilian oil company.

In this context, the first section of the work is aimed at reminding you of a few elements contributing to an understanding of the historical path followed by the State-owned company. The second section is aimed at clarifying the theoretical points that are important to the study. The third, in turn, emphasises the particular innovative features of offshore production. Finally, we will describe a few conclusive aspects making a more explicit reference possible between the Petrobras activities and the theoretical precepts.

I. Elements for Understanding the Petrobras History

During more than fifty years of history, in addition to contributing to economic development by production, refining and distribution of oil, Petrobras established itself as a model business with respect to a technological lead, R&D and economic performance. Even if its career began in 1953, in the interest of a better understanding of its history one must mention the context of the Brazilian economy in the first half of the last century[7]. It was at that time that the national economy made the transition from an agricultural-exporting base to an industrial economy, and it was the time of replacement of imports, in an initial phase, to an economy supported by the consumer durables industry and basic products. It was in those circumstances that Petrobras was born and consolidated itself.

The *O petróleo é nosso* (The oil is ours) campaign, intensified shortly after the end of the Second World War, contributed to the State's establishment of the oil monopoly, to be exercised by Petrobras, created by

---

[7] Starting in 1930, there was some significant changes in the sectorial dynamics of Brazilian industry, increasing in accelerated fashion in the "heavy" sectors (intermediate goods) of industry and at a lower rate in the consumer goods sectors (Villela, A. & Suzigan, W. *Política de governo e crescimento da economia brasileira 1889-1945*, Rio de Janeiro: IPEA, 2nd ed., 1975. The growth rate of the demand for oil and for its derivatives, which was 11.3% in 1940, increased to 22.4% in 1950, putting pressure on imports, in a proportion of 7.9% in 1939, 10.4% in 1950, and 17.7% in 1952 (Marinho Junior, I. *Petróleo: Política e Poder*, Rio de Janeiro: José Olympio, 1989, p. 26).

law n° 2.004 of 3 October 1953[8]. That law established Petrobras as a mixed-economy joint stock company, with shareholder controlled by the Federal Government, a monopoly being declared in the Union for all activities involved in the oil chain.

However, creation of a State-owned company was not the first attitude adopted by the government with respect to natural resources and to supplying oil. Since the foundation of the Geological and Mineralogical Service of Brazil (1907) the establishment of the Mining Code (1934) until creation of the National Oil Board – CNP (1938), the discussion focused on Brazilian geological possibilities in terms of hydrocarbons and how to develop refining of imported oil in the country. The perception of the relationship between the two activities and the nationalisation of refining would be the key to financing research/exploration/production – concentrating the risks and the costs of the oil industry – were not unrelated to the State pro-monopoly leadership[9].

Creation of the CNP empowered to regulate and control imports, stocks and distribution, establish or propose changes in prices, taxes and levies, demarcate the exploration concessions and prohibit refining concessions for foreign companies marked an important phase in the career of the national oil industry. By developing the exercise of internal supervision of the oil industry as a whole[10], the CNP bolstered the interpretation viewing the birth and the philosophy of action of that entity as a cautious response, inspired by events that marked nationalisation of Mexican oil.

In that context, Petrobras then appeared, with an initial capital inherited from the CNP of US$ 165 million, a modest amount when compared with the capital of US$ 500 million with which Petróleos Mexicanos – PEMEX began its activities[11]. The original legal authorisations (sources of financial resources and taxation and levy profits) enabled Petrobras to inaugurate a positive approach. Thus, preceded by Mexico and by Italy, Brazil moved into the second of the innovative institutional procedures relating to organisation of the world oil industry – IMP, later

---

[8]   Alveal, Carmen. "A Petrobrás na economia global: desafios e oportunidades de uma estatal de trajetória singular". *Anais do II Congresso Brasileiro de História Econômica e 3ª Conferência Internacional de História de Empresas*. Vol. IV. Niterói: ABPHE/UFF, p. 183-198, 13-16 October 1996, p. 185.

[9]   Carvalho, G. *Do monopólio aos contratos de risco*, Rio de Janeiro: Forense Universitária, 1977 ; Macedo e Silva, A. *Petrobras*: a consolidação do monopólio estatal e a empresa privada (1953-1964). Tese de doutorado, Campinas: IEI/UNICAMP, 1985.

[10]   Martins, L. *Nação e corporação multinacional*, Rio de Janeiro: Paz e Terra, 1975.

[11]   Marinho Junior, I., *op. cit.*, p. 278.

incorporated by the majority of late-capitalism countries: the phase of State oil monopolies[12], sectorially planned.

Establishing and developing a financially dense and technologically complex industry required: i) a commitment relationship with the suppliers of capital goods; ii) an increasing need for imported equipment and foreign technical assistance; iii) and a guaranteed and advantageous flow of crude oil for operating the expanding refinery sector. At that time in its career, Petrobras incorporated the visible experience in evolution of the INP, above all the path followed by the cartel's *major* businesses.

The independent and innovative actions in the supply of resources for its expansion gave birth to the development of two characteristic Petrobras features that helped explain its career performance: i) its function as making national private capital more dynamic, counterbalancing the technical-economic and political strength of international capital, and ii) its performance as a competent entrepreneur.

At the turn of the 1960-1970 decade, the State-owned company had exceeded the expectations of the effective policy followed by the military governments[13]. Already during the first half of the 1970s, it completed the internal "verticalisation" of the industry, advanced so as to become the leader in establishment and growth of the petrochemical sector (Petroquisa's subsidiary), and gave birth to the agglomeration (by its subsidiaries Petrobras Distribuidora, Petrofértil and Petromisa) and to the internationalisation of its activities (by way of Braspetro and Interbrás). In 1975, the Petrobras entrepreneurial group was the leader in Brazil and in Latin America in the ranking established by *Fortune* magazine. In 1982 it ranked twentieth among the world's largest companies. In 1991, it gave indications that its R&D had developed to the point of winning first place from the *Off-Shore Technology Conference* due to its technological pioneering.

Another important point interacting in the recent history of the company was the installation of the Privatisation Plan since 1991, which markedly reduced the strength of the State-owned oil group with the privatisation of the petrochemical and fertiliser divisions (Petroquisa and Petrofértil) and with the extinction/liquidation of the sectors relating to ore extraction and foreign trade (Petromisa and Interbrás). That

---

[12] Among the events inaugurating the process of creation/nationalisation of oil companies, we must mention the acquisition of a majority of the shares of the *Anglo-Persian Company* (now *British Petroleum*, privatised) by the British government in 1914 and the creation of *Yacimientos Petrolíferos Fiscales* in Argentina – YPF, in 1922, followed by the *Compagnie Française de Pétroles* – CFP, in France, in 1924 (Mommer, 1994).

[13] Alveal, *op. cit.*, p. 189.

process reached its peak in 1995, when the National Congress removed the State monopoly from the Constitution.

In spite of this change in the understanding of the economic model and of the State's role in the economy, the discussion concerning the oil industries[14] remained on the agenda in the light of the importance of that sector, which was strategic in international economic development. The oil industry is obviously a function of: i) the level of sales of the IMP holding second place in the global business *ranking* (*Fortune* magazine, 1994); ii) the major conventional markets that revitalised the expansion of the oil industry in the last century (North America, Europe and Japan) are characterised by rhythmic dynamics; iii) the dynamic potential of the oil industry shifted toward the developing regions and countries which, generally speaking, hold hydrocarbon reserves and potentials that are economically advantageous.

These recent business conditions did not affect the investments or the profits of the business. On 17 February 2006, Petrobras reported a record net profit of R$ 23.7 billion in 2005, up 40% by comparison with 2004[15]. The amount is the largest ever recorded by a business with open capital anywhere in Latin America. In discussing that performance, the company attributed the results to the 10% increase in oil production in Brazil and abroad, in addition to the heavy workload handled in the Brazilian refineries. Another positive factor was the reversal of its trade deficit, having recorded net exports of 58 thousand barrels per day in 2005, disregarding natural gas and alcohol.

Finally, there is emphasis on the greatly anticipated Brazilian oil self-sufficiency. Under the title of "*One year for history and for Brazil's future*", the company announced self-sufficiency as being more than a mere certain number of barrels. "It is a great conquest that few countries have made. A reason for pride and motivation for growth with a stronger economy, with more resources and jobs"[16]. Thus in the first half of 2006, the country joined the selected group of nations that are self-sufficient in exploration for and refining of oil, one of the essential raw materials for industrialised, or post-industrial countries.

---

[14] The State-owned oil companies control 91% of oil reserves, 86% of natural gas reserves, and 62% of oil production. The private oil corporations control 73% of the refining capacity and 79% of marketing of oil and natural gas derivatives (Freires, 1995).

[15] Rangel, Juliana, "Petrobras tem lucro histórico de R$ 23,7 bilhões", Revista *Petróleo e Gás*. Available on http://www.oglobo.globo.com.br/petroleo/materias/2006/02/17/191897674.asp. Accessed: 12 April 2006.

[16] "Um ano para a história e para o futuro do Brasil", available on http://www.autosificiencia.com.br/geral/geral.asp. Accessed: 21 April 2006.

II. Technological Innovations, Appropriation by the Firms and Economic Development: Theoretical Aspects

Until the 1960s, a major part of the studies of technology were strictly technical, but economists have always recognised the importance of innovation for increasing productivity as a result, for countries' competitive performance. One of the first persons working in the economic sciences to analyse this theme in greater depth was Joseph Schumpeter. He managed to give technology a central position in the theory of economic growth and development.

As time went by, the intensity of the studies of technology increased. The 1980s were marked by a greater interest in technological knowledge as applied to the industrial sector, since it was the most dynamic (factor) in the economy. According to some authors[17], it became one of the main elements causing the divergence between the growth rates of the developed countries and of the developing countries. According to these principles, when technological advances are undertaken by countries that are still developing, in an amount making it possible to develop competitive advantageous, there would be a convergence tendency vis-à-vis already developed countries. One can say that such innovations appear to be short-cuts to higher levels of income and development.

In Bell's thinking, two of the main factors making innovation possible are: technological capacity and productive capacity of a country/region.

Technological capacity: this refers to the resources needed for managing and administering scientific-technological changes, such as: capacity, knowledge, persons' know-how, and the institutional structure. The constitution of scientific knowledge of human capital, in turn, will be given by formal and tacit learning. The former takes place in a "school" space, and the latter, on its part, will come from experience, from laborious observation, and from the very exercise of activity. Values that have been presented theoretically by Kenneth Arrow in 1962, in the form of the concept *learning by doing*, originally in the *Review of Economic Studies* (June): *"The economic implications of learning by doing"*, and later by Rosenberg[18] by the principle of *learning by interacting*. Indirectly, the two concepts concern the ability to transform knowledge by a different objective.

---

[17] Bell, M.; Ross-Larsen, B.; Westphal, L., "Assessing the performance of infant industries", *Journal of Development Economics*, No.16, p. 101-128, 1984.

[18] Rosenberg, N. *Exploring the black box; technology, economics, and history*, Cambridge: Cambridge University Press, 1994, p. 9-23; 161-189; Rosenberg, N. *Inside the black box*, Cambridge: Cambridge University Press, 1982, p. 81-140.

The process of knowledge formation, which will lead to innovation, must be linked with the fact that knowledge is cumulative, a fact that will have two implications: i) the existence of the technological *gap*, since the countries that have stimulated technological competence for a longer period will have a larger "stock" of knowledge, and hence will be more likely to be in a leadership position; ii) the technological competence of countries is unable to change in such an intense way over a very long period of time, since they cannot progress without having a stock of knowledge. This means that a time dependence on innovative constraints of a technological nature is created, so that "what the firm can expect to do, technologically, in the future is sharply limited by what it has been able to do in the past[19]".

It will then be the technological capacity that will make the greatest possible distribution and absorption of technological knowledge possible, thus creating another stock variant: the Productive Capacity. The addition of technological capacity and of productive capacity will form innovations, or at least provide a technical possibility thereof.

With the combination of capacities, in a technological R&D context, one observes, *inter alia*, a formation of Technological Paradigms. They may be defined as the model for and the example of solutions to selected technological problems, by means of certain principles derived from natural science and the selected technological material. So all of the research and results supplying technological procedures are included in specific knowledge able to resolve and perfect various problems concerning technology and productive techniques, respectively. Finally, it is the technological research process and its establishment as a model to be followed. The paradigm is going to predetermine the technologies to be adopted and the ones to be avoided, as well as the procedures to be used, which chemical properties are to be developed or maintained, and the nature of the tradeoffs involved in the issue, among other particularities.

The development, sophistication and even handling of a paradigm will be "conducted" by technological trajectories carried out within the paradigm. The technological trajectory will be the direction of technological progress in the paradigm, in which it will be influenced directly by technological and economic variants. To quote Giovanni Dosi[20]: "A

---

[19] Dosi, G., "Technological paradigms and technological trajectories", *Research Policy*, Vol. 2, No. 3, p. 147-162, 1982, p. 225; Dosi, G., "The nature of the innovative process", *Technical Change and Economic Theory*, London & New York: Pinter Publisher, 1988, p. 221-238; Rumelt, R.; Teece, D.; Winter, S., "Understanding corporate coherence: theory and evidence", *Innovation, organization and economic dynamics: selected essays*, org. Giovanni Dosi, Massachussets: Edward Elgar Publishing, 2000, p. 264-293.

[20] Dosi, G., *op. cit.*, p. 227.

technological trajectory is the activity of technological progress between the trade-off of the economy and the technology defined by a paradigm".

The choices will often be defined from among several possible paths (trajectories), the stock of knowledge will be the main factor delimiting the border of the paradigm, and learning will have to develop or limit the meaning of the trajectories, as well as detect new investment opportunities that may appear "on the road" of technological change (the spillover effect). One can understand this context as a criticism or as a complement to the neo-classical frame of reference concerning technology, which possesses a less dynamic vision with respect to the effects of technology on the economy.

By comparison with the behaviour of the trajectories, or of the chosen paths, technology will be inherently connected with the innovator's profile – at the level of the risk accepted by companies, and also with the intrinsic uncertainty of the possible distinct results. These limiting factors may be conceptualised as economic, social, institutional and technological factors.

Economic factors: the economic interest of the organisation or the lucrative nature, the market conditions and the availability of R&D expenditures are evident.

Social and institutional factors: the degree of the society's need for the product; the environmental aspects; the political interest in the sense of intended resources, as occurred in the military and space programmes in the USA, after the Second World War, which offered large amounts of money to persons who developed R&D in the semiconductor field, in addition to guaranteeing purchases; or else, in the various import substitution policies, which supposedly, by way of protectionist policies, made it possible for local industry to create better capital accumulation conditions in order subsequently to invest saved own resources.

Technological factors: these consist essentially of knowledge, ability and technical know-how of the persons concerned. The set of these attributes will determine the feasibility of a project of lack thereof, and above all the technological capacity and productive capacity.

In the conjunction of these factors, the technological decisions will be made. However, with respect to exercise of the choices, one must take note of the potential fact that the technological decisions at a given time will be conditioned by the development of past knowledge, and in the same way they will prepare for a few future tendencies, what Rosenberg called "technological imperatives" of research in technology, because technology, in a certain way, will be time-dependent. This path of dependence[21] may be recognised as a factor limiting the firm's skills. It will also be a major generator of an environment in which skills can be applied more productively, because of the routing created in specialisation. The focus of the business will be formed on the basis of this dependent trajectory, with marketing and production.

By increasing the cumulative amount of knowledge, of formal and tacit learning and of dependence of a trajectory on its technological regime, in general, the R&D programmes form the productive and technological capacity of an institution. And the programmes will be carried out by way of various organisational forms. They take place mainly in the Universities, Governments and private laboratories. In their diversity, the institutions will compete with each other and cooperate among themselves in various ways, in addition to differentiating themselves in terms of size, objective and mechanisms of action.

Apparently the evolutionaries generally point out three possibilities for technological development, but always included in an institutional context: one of them is isolated R&D, another is acquisition of the technology of a third organisation, and lastly there is the development of technology in an integrated way. Generally speaking, the first option is the most widely used one for small technological improvements, and not for development of new technologies in the proper sense. The second option has its advantages, but there are also problems, such as of the one of lock in, of high costs and of risks of technological transfer, and of difficulty in reaching a leadership position. The third option is obviously a strong one in industrial research, in which a set of companies will form an alliance, both horizontal and vertical, in connection with a research programme.

With respect to vertical integration, non-observance of this practice may have a reflex that is almost as devastating in the technological dynamics of that industry or sector. *A priori*, the first author to attach more importance to this causal relationship was M. Frankel[22], who, while studying the English economy in the first half of the twentieth century, found a strong correlation between small-scale integration in a few industries, specifically the iron and steel industry and textiles, as a consequence of the relatively non-intensive dissemination of technological innovations. This caused a loss of competitiveness vis-à-vis the German and Japanese counterparts, and greater integration was observed. According to the author, that fact made a greater number of innovations possible, and hence greater market competitiveness. Subse-

---

[21] Theoretically conceptualized by *Path – Dependence.*

[22] Frankel, M., "Obsolesce and technological change in a maturing economy", *American Economic Review*, 1955.

quently, the study by Kindelberger in 1964 (quoted by Teece, 1988) corroborated the maintenance of these principles by the comparison between General Motors' hegemony in the automobile industry, after the 1930s, when it was integrated with an electricity company, whereas its competitors did not do this. The integration was carried out with General Electric, with which they managed to develop the first diesel combustion automobile with electric starting. It is on the basis of that initiative that, in the future, the other automobile companies included electrical engineers in their work teams.

The integration into knowledge, by such conceptualisations, will be considered as the model research infrastructure to be exploited, once there are indications that integration will offer the integrators more sophisticated products, more quickly, than without the Union. This methodology is in keeping with the liberating expansion of international trade, which intensified market competition. For maintenance of the companies, they will have to adapt in real time to the changes determined by the market, or become a leader of such transformations, always in an innovative process. This new reality has become the action of companies in attempting, in isolated fashion, to produce all capital knowledge and to transform it into products and innovative technological processes, a saga that is close to undoable. The strategy based on alliances of companies around research and development soon became a rising manoeuvre.

A few difficulties connected with this trick, such as the dissemination of knowledge among allies, particularly if one of them does not have a technological and productive capacity below what is needed. In the contracts carried out in connection with technological transfers, it is difficult to estimate the costs, the period and other details. To minimise the difficulties and enlarge the results of science, a few authors[23] emphasise the fact that research within or outside the company cannot be considered as replacing, or as competing; on the contrary, the success of companies is often to be found in the success of determining how the in-house aspect must be developed, and how much must be obtained outside the firm.

But whatever the intensity of integration of research into a business may be, having operations emerge and making them profitable will depend on the technical and productive ability to develop and market products that can use – at least in part – the company's already existing costs, such as: logistics, equipment, and human capital, among other things. This means that the accumulative knowledge will be the predom-

---

[23]   Teece, D., "Technological change and the nature of the firm", *Technical Change and Economic Theory*, London & New York: Pinter Publisher, 1988, p. 256-281.

inant variant in the question concerning innovations and R&D programmes.

In the face of these informative variants, the object of the work consists in presenting a product in the oil industry that, by a significant technological advance offered by Petrobras, which, affected several times by integration into research, established a new paradigm concerning the process of exploring for and producing oil in deep waters. And thanks to the technological versatility of the programme, it makes it possible to develop several trajectories and new business opportunities, and above all the durability of the country by comparison with oil supply, a sector in which Brazil reached autonomy in the first half of 2006.

III. Concerning the Availability of Oil under the High Seas for Petrobras' Technological Innovations

A. History of technologies relating to offshore production

The ascension of the world offshore industry took place between the years 1930 and 1950 in Venezuela and in the Gulf of Mexico, respectively. As of then, exploration began to spread to the North Sea and formed the first companies in this segment, including Shell, Exxon, Texaco and AGIP[24]. In Brazil, already at the end of 1950 because of the geographical analyses, there was an awareness of the fact that the company had oil deposits in deep waters, even though still without a precise definition of the locations. Confirmation came in the discovery of the first offshore well in 1968, in the Campo de Guaricema, in the North Eastern part of the country, and the first drilling, also in 1968, in the Campos Basin, in the Garoupa field, in the Southeast. The following year was also marked by more discoveries, with the Campo de São Mateus, and later the Campo de Ubarana, both in the Potiguar Basin, near Rio de Janeiro. Starting with the time of those initial discoveries, Petrobras inaugurated a series of others. However, those discoveries did not have any further effect because the existing technologies did not match up with the Brazilian reality[25].

---

[24] Furtado, A. T.; Freitas, A. G., " Nacionalismo e Aprendizagem no Programa de Águas Profundas da Petrobras", *Revista Brasileira de Inovação*, Vol. 3, No. 1, p. 55-86, Jan./Jul. 2004.

Furtado, A. T.; Freitas, A. G., "La Trayectoria Tecnológica de Petrobras en la producción costa afuera", *Revista Espacios*, Vol. 17, 1996, available on: http://www.revistaespacios.com/a96v17n03/32961703.html. Accessed: 16 May 2005.

[25] "História do petróleo no Brasil", available on: http://www.comciencia.br/reportagens/petroleo/pet06.shtml. Accessed: 18 May 2005.

For marine exploration in a general way, one can synthesise the entire process in the form of three distinct technological sets, which in turn are the objects of research by offshore companies: the platforms, the drilling system and the mechanism for evacuating the oil from the depth to the platform.

The most common type among platforms with fixed support may be the "Tension Leg Platform" (TLP), due to the idea that one leg makes a sure balance possible. Because of its characteristics, the structure may become ineffective in greater depths, a fact that will require a floating mechanism. This effectiveness may be proven before the platform of Shell Oil, an American subsidiary of Royal Dutch Shell, installed at Bullwinkle in the Gulf of Mexico at a depth of 411 meters. That is the world's deepest fixed rig. Its installation, in 1991, demonstrated extremely skilful use of engineering knowledge of the time.

The equipment that carries out the first part of the process of oil extraction is called "Christmas Tree". With the discoveries of more voluminous wells, as well as due to the use of smaller rigs, of the embarkation type, it was necessary to have the least possible weight under the rig, and with that the anticipated production system appeared, in which several equipment items, formally under the rig, were positioned in the water. This system is called subsea abroad. The Christmas Tree is one of those equipment items, and began to be called a Wet Christmas Tree.

As was emphasised before, the drilling technology is another issue to be settled for viability of production of oil from the high seas. This technology is divided into two stages: the oil exploration system (props) and the drilling itself. The initial challenge consisted in construction of mobile maritime probes, for the purpose of making greater potential possible and reducing the costs of effectiveness in detecting oil wells.

The first probes were installed on the boats in the end of the 1930s. Already in the 1940s, in the interest of greater optimisation, the technological trajectory moved toward development of probes, no longer installed but rather adapted to such a mobile function. Thus they became veritable embarkations, called "probe boat" (the system now used). In the 1950s, in addition to the boats, semi-submersible probes were produced, which were installed on the rigs. In the subsequent decade, the important trajectories were by comparison with the drilling technology, which, already at the outset, managed to excavate great depths[26].

Several other complementary technologies were developed in parallel to make offshore production possible. The most important ones were

---

[26] Furtado, *op. cit.*

installation of pipes for evacuation of the production and seismics in a maritime environment.

This collection of technologies made continuous expansion of offshore production possible, including for the North Sea, which, starting with the 1970s, began to rival the Gulf of Mexico in importance order with respect to the volume of investments. However, at the beginning of the 1980s, it became ever clearer than even if there is a seismic and drilling technology for working in deep waters, that did not arrive with the production technology. The technological production system, relying on fixed rigs, established in the Gulf of Mexico will have to be radically reformulated in order to reach greater depth.

To enable Brazil to enter this segment of the oil industry, to have an average depth of its wells exceeding 1 000 meters, the need for developing new technologies was the only option. After the decision was made, Petrobras inaugurated an original technological trajectory, by proposing the floating production system. In the face of the absence of the scientific knowledge required for such a project, the country had to fill that space in international experience, or else, in embryonic fashion, there was knowledge with respect to offshore technology.

As was pointed out, before becoming a producer of offshore technology, the company had to use imported technology that was adapted to the local production conditions, by a process of developed innovations. Thus before initiating major programmes on behalf of technological development, it seemed more consistent with the principle to first look for the knowledge by outside acquisition, with improvements.

Thanks to that effort, the company managed to obtain its first hardware, a submersible probe. After that, the firm concluded an alliance with the national shipyards in order to obtain, in the mid-1980s, the first legitimately Brazilian hardware in connection with offshore technology, which was the reconversion of the probes to make small production rigs. Those attitudes showed as of the offset that the company had opted for partnerships in its R&D activities. Petrobras was able to apply this strategy in its subsequent research programmes.

B. The Development of the Research Programmes Relating to Offshore Technology in Brazil after 1986

In the interest of better development of the technologies for exploring for oil at great depth, and to be able to shake off the outside "limit", Petrobras created an R&D investment programme, isolated from the group's other activities. That programme was known as PROCAP – Programme for Technological Capacitation in Deep Waters – which, because of the prospects of the business by comparison with the likely positive results derived from exploration of the major oil reserves in the marine depth, led the company to invest 1% of its sales in R&D, becoming one of the greatest technological programmes in the country's history[27]. That expense was rewarding for Petrobras, since, according to Carlos Tadeu da Costa Fraga, executive manager of Cenpes – Leopoldo A. Miguez de Mello Research and Development Centre, of Petrobras – the return on investment was 4.3 dollars for each dollar spent at the beginning of the Procap, and in 2004 the return on investment reached 8.2 dollars[28].

A large part of those resources was invested in the Cenpes, created ten years after the foundation of Petrobras, in 1963, now in operation at the Federal University of Rio de Janeiro, at Ilha do Fundão. The first great accomplishment by the Cenpes came in 1968, when, on the basis of its exploration, it found the first oil basin in Brazilian waters, in the Campo de Guaricema (SE)[29]. However, the company, consistently with the positive precepts relating to group research, included the Procap in a research network along with competitors, suppliers and research institutions. The first and perhaps the main ally was the Alberto Luiz Coimbra Institute for third-cycle studies and Research in Engineering of the UFRJ, the Coppe, where a figure of 1,000 projects concluded in partnership with Petrobras was reached, and which gave birth, in 1994, to the Underwater Technology Multidisciplinary Group, which works on different programmes: robotics, welding, hydroacoustics, etc[30]. Another great Petrobras ally in research concerning offshore technology was the Centre for Oil Studies[31], of the School of Mechanical Engineering of the Unicamp, established in 1987 with Petrobras' support. The Centre, in addition to being a research partner, makes a significant contribution to training of skilled labour. Other institutions, such as Poli-USP and the

---

[27] Bruni, P. B., "Petrobras: Estratégia e esforço tecnológico para alavancar competitividade", *Análise da Conjuntura das Indústrias do Petróleo e do Gás*, No. 3, Mar. 2002, available on: http://www.ie.ufrj.br/infopetro/pdfs/petrogas-mar2002.pdf. Accessed: 17 May 2005.

[28] "O desafio dos óleos pesados", available on: http://www.dep.fem.unicamp.br/boletim/BE38/artigo.htm. Accessed: 10 October 2005.

[29] "Centro de Pesquisa da Petrobras: Linha do Tempo", available on: http://www2.petrobras.com.br/tecnologia2/port/centro_pesquisasdapetrobraslinhatempo.asp. Accessed: 10 October 2005.

[30] "Pesquisa petrolífera do Brasil na fronteira do conhecimento", available on: http://www.comciencia.br/reportagens/petroleo/pet07.shtml. Accessed: 19 May 2005.

[31] "Cepetro: Centro de Estudos em Petróleo", available on: http://www.cepetro.unicamp.br/. Accessed: 13 May 2005.

Institute for Technological Research of São Paulo, became of basic importance for maintenance of the Procap[32] throughout all those years.

It is thanks to that conjunction of institutions that research and the results made progress in connection with offshore technology, while improvement resulted from the development of routines.

1. Procap 1: The Beginning of Exploration in the Offshore Segment in 1986-91

This programme was carried out for six years and implemented 109 projects aimed at improving the company's technical skill in production of oil and of natural gas in water up to a depth of 1,000 meters. During those six years of the programme, 80% of the projects were aimed at extension of existing technology, and 20% at technological innovation.

Procap 1 innovation

The consecration of the first Procap was the installation of the floating and early production system in the Marlim Basin, in 1,027 water streak meters, in which the performance of the floating rig was going to crown the future of that system, since it was accompanied, in addition to the technical viability, by greater economic profitability than the other models. To sum up, this new model had a series of advantages over the others, such as: a reduced installation period and the possibility of serving as provisional production units, since, not having any fixed structure, the rig could be removed to move into new spaces. The Marlim I production system, which required construction of a new rig, had a total cost of 1.331 billion dollars for output of 100,000 bpd[33] of oil. The Auger TLP system[34] had a very similar cost: 1.2 billion dollars, but for markedly less production: 46,000 bpd of oil. The major operating companies recognised the fact that the floating production systems are characterised by better costs and more options for development of production fields in deep waters[35].

---

[32] With respect to the availability of resources for R&D, the company receives investments by CTPETRO, the sector's leading fund for scientific and technological development, created in 1998 by the National Plan for Scientific and Technological Development for the Federal Government's purpose of promoting a national system of innovations. The fund receives the royalties from the oil and is jointly supervised by the National Oil Agency – ANP – and the Ministry of Sciences and Technology. It is directed by a management fund, operated by the FINEP, with participation by students and entrepreneurs.

[33] Bpd = Bbl means barrels per day (1 barrel is equivalent to 158.98 litres or 0.159 m³).

[34] Shell Oil rig.

[35] Furtado, *op. cit.*

With its consolidated knowledge, the company adjusted its objective, thinking that the innovations should no longer be incremental to become absolute. That decision was made because the available technology was not consistent with the depth that the Brazilian State wanted to exploit.

2. Procap 2000: Learning and Development of Internal Research in Petrobras between 1993 and 1999

Procap's success encouraged the company to establish PROCAP-2000 in 1993, widening research on exploration at a depth of 2,000 meters. That programme developed 20 projects, with a budget of around 750 million dollars. In addition to the expansion of the exploration limits, the programme also aimed at reducing production costs. With that in mind, 80% of the projects were oriented toward innovations, and 20% toward extension, exactly the opposite of the previous stage.

A great challenge under that programme was the discovery of another deposit in 1996 that was going to become one of Petrobras' most precious possessions, since it was a giant oil field (132 km²), the Roncador field, in the Campos Basin (RJ), at a depth of 1,853 meters with a water streak between 1,500 and 2,000 meters, reserves of 3.3 billion boe[36], a deposit thickness of up to 200 meters and oil between 18° and 31° API[37], considered light for oil at that depth. In addition to the reserves, much of the technology developed for that field was used in other fields, as was indicated by José Fomigli, manager of the Marlim Rig: "Roncador represented a fundamental stage in development of other units[38]" (Petrobras, 2005).

The discovery occurred at a time when the company lacked sufficient equipment for production. But with the objective of guaranteeing control under the reserve, once the market already showed strong tendencies at the opening, which occurred in 1997. The Petrobras management, not having enough time to construct a new rig, had to opt for readaptation of an already existing one, rig 36 (P-36), which was operating in the Marlim field (proving the gain in exploration potential of SPF before the TLP). That field had a smaller depth (1,360 meters), a differ-

---

[36] Barrels of Oil Equivalent – used to express volumes of oil and of natural gas in terms of barrels, by converting 1 m³ of gas oil into 6.289941 barrels of oil.

[37] American Petroleum Institute – is the form of expressing the relative density of an oil or derivative. The less dense the oil, the lighter it will be, which indicates superior quality. The API scale, measured in degrees, vary inversely with the density of the oil, that is, the lightest oil (least dense) will be the one with the highest degree. Pursuant to that scale, when the scale is 0-10, the oil will be extra-heavy; between 11 and 22, heavy; 22 to 30, average; and more than 30, light.

[38] "Petrobras na Vanguarda", available on: http://www.dep.fem.unicamp.br/boletim/be10/Artigo_Petrobrasnavanguarda.htm. Accessed: 16 May 2005.

ent mineral quality (heavier) and smaller quantity, which resulted in a need for readaptating the entire system, as well as the water injection mechanism in the reservoir. The success of that operation gave the national company a reference title and technological leadership in the offshore oil world, confirmed in 2005 by the obtaining in the month of March of the "Distinguished Achievement Award – OTC'2001".

The discovery of the Roncador field, in the Campos Basin (RJ), and of others that occurred had the result that in 2000 "marine oil" accounted for 75% of Brazil's oil and gas reserves. Those products continued to be exploited solely by Petrobras, which experienced a proportional increase in production. In 1987, only 1.7% of production was marine, but in 2000 the percent had increased to 55%.

The quest for economic viability of production in ever larger depth became a challenge to Petrobras, which experienced a market restructuring in 1997, with the creation of the National Oil Agency – ANP – and the related opening of the market to foreign companies.

Procap 2 innovations – Innovations for exploiting the Roncador oil

As a strategy for quick and reliable reconnaissance of the field, Petrobras used an anticipated production system with the ship *Seillean,* an FPSO-DP[39], rented from Reding&Bates, which, thanks to adaptation for the new well, became the world's first dynamic positioning ship to operate in such depths. It uses a set of propellers that maintains its position on the basis of the orientation indicated by sensors installed on the sea bed and by the GPS[40]. Use of the vessel was temporary, until adaptation of the P-36 rig.

With respect to the propellers, the technology used was considered as the technological limit for the period. For operation of those propellers, an original type of underwater technology was used, and in particular a subsea system consisting of a drillpipe riser[41] and a wet Christmas tree – TLD 2000. The drillpipe riser is a new riser system with a composition making more agile and safer assembly possible, in addition to using a kind of screw that makes it possible to descend to ever greater depths. The riser is installed on the Christmas tree, collecting its production.

For the arrival of the 36 rig, some new technologies were developed in partnership with other institutions, among them a new horizontal wet

---

[39] Floating Production Storage and Offloading Systems – Transformation of a super-tanker into an oil production rig (A Parceria, 2005).

[40] A technological instrument making a determination of an exact geographical location possible by satellite.

[41] In which the drillpipe is a drilling system and the risers are the "conduits" through which the oil is brought to the surface.

Christmas tree, the ANMH-2500[42]. Another strong point of the Christmas tree is rapid disconnection, making the project safer, once the entire anticipated system is based on dynamic positioning. It is horizontal because the drilling may not be simply vertical, which increases the drilling dynamics.

Another innovation was the system used for anchoring the rig, the name given to the whole unit: Christmas tree, drillpiper and riser. This is because the unit as a whole determines the place where the rig is located. The new anchoring equipment also came to be constituted by material with a propylene base, a kind of polyester. The plan for this new material was developed by the Petrobras laboratory (Cenpes) and was carried out by the companies Quintas e Quintas of Portugal, and by the São Leopoldo Rope Company, in Rio Grande do Sul. This anchoring system was invented for the Marlim field and it is characterised by being more effective and having a lower cost. The advantage of polyester is that it is lighter and more resistant to traction, so that it requires less energy for oil transport, less flow being lost, and there is also an increase in the production of and receipts from the field. In addition, the installation cost is almost 20% less.

Another important point in the Roncador project was the system of electricity generation of the P-36 and of the P-47, the two being very close. The energy, generated by diesel turbines installed on the P-36, is transmitted to the P-47 by cables installed on the seabed, which may be used up to depth of 2,000 meters. The distance between the two units is about one thousand meters.

In addition to the innovations for exploration of the Roncador field, other technologies were developed during the Procap 2000, such as the SGN – Nitrogen Generation System. This system functions as a heat generator to remove the paraffin that forms on the walls of the risers.

Those technologies were developed on the basis of Petrobras' present need. Moreover the company, anticipating future needs and to take advantage of the knowledge available at the time, developed some technologies for wells not yet discovered, which would require technology applicable to even greater depths. Along these lines the long-range well was developed, making it possible to drain several reservoir locations from one and the same origin. The new technology proved to be necessary a few years later, at the start of 2005, with the drilling of a well in Marlim Sud, with a water streak of 1,500 meters and with 4,400 meters of horizontal distance. In that case, if it were a question only of one point of origin, the production volume would be much less.

---

[42] Made jointly with ABB, FMCICBV, Cooper Cameron and Kvaerner, and an upgrade made in a Drill-Quip tree.

With respect to the limits of 2,000 meters, they were reached, and the Petrobras management raised its sights by creating a new Procap.

3. Procap 3000: the Present Stage and Petrobras Research Projects between 2000 and 2006

Procap 3000 has a duration of six years and an initial budget of 128 million dollars for R&D, including 350 employees. The forecast is that 190 projects will be carried out. The purpose of the programme are: make the production of Marlim Est and Albacora Est viable, in the Campos Basin (RJ), and the next stages of Roncador and Marlim Sud; reduce investments in development of production in terms of water strike exceeding 1,000 meters; and contribute to reducing extraction costs of the producing fields.

Procap 3 innovations

The risers for 3,000 meters. The alternatives studied include use of the hybrid riser, using metal and composite materials such as carbon fibre or other plastic components.

The Procap 3000 team also studies development of a totally electric Christmas tree that would not use the present hydraulic jacks. Marcus Coelho, one of Procap manager, emphasised that "the drilling technology for that depth already exists. In December 1999, we drilled an exploratory well at 2,977 meters. Procap 3000 is oriented toward development of production".

The Cenpes, with the IPT – The Technological Research Institute of São Paulo – developed a laboratory programme used to simulate deformations of rocks over time, very common in the salt rocks, and which can lead to complete destruction of the entire oil prospecting system. That equipment will make exploitation possible of a recently discovered well in the Santos Basin (SP), which begins at 2,000 meters but has a large layer of salt, as far as the bottom of the well, at 6,407 meters[43] (Exploração, 2005). Moreover the equipment represents a new era in offshore exploration, since such deformations are the main obstacle to oil prospecting in several regions of the planet.

The Cenpes, with the SGI, an American supercomputer company, in an operation similar to the above innovation. They are developing a 4D seismic, which makes it possible to display images in 3 dimensions, and then in the fourth, which is time. Thus it will be possible to determine the exact point and the flow of oil, at any depth, a fact that will enlarge the reserves of Brazil and of the world.

---

[43] "Exploração: Petrobrás confirma vestígios de petróleo na Bacia de Campos", newspaper *Gazeta do Povo*, p. 24, 1 September 2005.

With an eye on minimising losses that can occur at the time of development of exploration of oil wells, Petrobras created the Advanced Oil Recovery Programme – PROVAP – which has the following objective: develop the production of fields considered sub-commercial due to technological limitations; produce techniques and models for management of reservoirs making it possible to increase, with economic advantage, the oil field recovery factor; and contribute to revitalising mature fields, without neglecting the issue of preservation of the environment[44].

IV. Final Considerations from Theoretical Support

We will now present the main activities developed by Petrobras, with respect to the process of technological innovations and which can be visualised in a theoretical context, thus demonstrating that, at least in the case of this company, the theoretical principles of the evolutionaries had some very positive results.

A. Characteristic of Knowledge Accumulation

This is a non-exclusive premise of the evolutionary authors, but one that is intrinsically connected with their various principles.

The first discoveries of the submersible oil deposits just showed the production potential, but the status of technological knowledge prevented realisation of the discoveries. To solve this problem, and Brazilian knowledge of offshore exploration being almost nil, the decision-makers decided to acquire technology abroad and to simply make small improvements in it, until the cumulative amount would be sufficient for developing the country's own technology.

After this "initial step", the accumulation of knowledge at a monotonically increasing rate made it possible to successively break through the depth limits of 1,000, 2,000 and 3,000 meters. The formation of knowledge did not make it possible to explore the 3,000 (meter) deposits, without first going by way of 2,000 meters. And now, with sufficient technology for this purpose, the company managers anticipate the technological possibility of exploring at 4,000 meters.

In addition to the question of depths, there have been several technological mechanisms required for exploration of the oil developed by the company, but one important system is still lacking: the rigs. So far,

---

[44] "PROVAP", available on: http://www2.petrobras.com.br/tecnologia/portugues/ programas_tecnologicos/pravap.stm. Accessed: 16 May 2005; Rosenberg, N., "The direction of technological change: inducement mechanism and focusing devices", *Economic Development and Cultural Change*, Vol. 18, p. 1-24, 1969.

Brazil does not have the technology for producing them, but this situation is close to coming to an end since the present technology transfer agreement with Singapore, for production of two rigs, provides for an arrangement between Petrobras and the national shipyards so that the rigs can be produced locally, with Asian technology. With an absorption of knowledge in the future the country will be able to produce the rigs separately, or at least a good part of them.

But generally speaking, because of the different objectives reached by research concerning Petrobras, forming a whole stock of knowledge that the other country do not have, this has created a technological gap by comparison with the others, generating a leadership characteristic for the Brazilian oil company.

B. Trajectories

Pursuant to the description given in the first chapter, the trajectories vary in such a way that one can replace another. An example of this was the change in the structure of the rigs. The first countries used only a fixed support, but in the light of the diseconomies of scale resulting from the increased depth, the design work (trajectories) moved toward another technique, floating support. This trajectory made the offshore paradigm possible for depths exceeding 500 meters.

The probe technology also is marked by the same profile. If, previously, the probes were coupled to the boats in the interest of greater effectiveness, they were transformed into boats, and some of them into small-scale production rigs.

C. Entrepreneurial Alliances in Terms of R&D Projects

The symmetry with the theoretical postulate in question occurred during the initial period of the offshore oil exploration programme when Petrobras established a vertical alliance with the national shipyards for local production of probe boats. Shortly thereafter, Petrobras created a partnership for the R&D programmes with the technological research institutions of the Unicamp (Cepetro) and of the UFRJ (Coppe). In addition to those institutions, many private businesses were developed jointly with Petrobras, generally suppliers, among which we may emphasise the following: the São Leopoldo Rope Works, in creation of the polyester anchoring material; American firm SGI, in the supercomputer sector; and the national and international ship building industry for development of rigs.

D. New Business Opportunity

Another important result of the investments in technological innovation is to be found in the high potential for creating new business opportunities. Such externalities, even in such a specific branch of science as the one concerning offshore technology, are not an exception.

In this context, according to Furtado & Freitas[45], this was one of the main consequences of the first Procap. Actually, what happened is that several of the various technological innovations that appeared during that period could be used in other maritime activities, such as the system for anchoring the entire floating structure of the rigs, which also began to be used in boats, above all submarines, since it makes greater safety possible in the light of the atmospheric pressure at great depth. Underwater robots were another innovation, replacing divers in connecting the rig with the underwater wells, which became a reference for production of robots for operating in great depths. The development of the national shipyards, the great majority of them installed in Rio de Janeiro, contributes greatly to job creation in that State, in order to respond to the Petrobras' requests for boats and boat parks, that being yet another externality of offshore technology.

At the time of the three *Procaps,* there was a substantial impact on the human resources of the institutions concerned by the Petrobras research, above all with respect to the engineering programmes of the Unicamp and of the UFRJ. This spin-off effect of knowledge made it possible to enjoy, not exactly a business opportunity, but rather an externality that was positive for society.

E. Investment in Technology as a Factor Making for Convergence between Countries

Finally, with respect to convergence vis-à-vis developing companies, the technological progress tends to offer, as one of the premises of the "evolutionaries", the possibility of incorporation into the positive consequences resulting from the Petrobras devotion. This can be imagined in the form of a real possibility for self-sufficiency in oil in Brazil, because of the oil prospecting in deep waters, as demonstrated by the 2004 production of 540,717,037 barrels, about 85% coming from the maritime areas (462,084,935 barrels) (2005 production). Income convergence appears when you consider the improvement of the population's well-being due to the fact that the country is less vulnerable to possible supply shocks in connection with the production factor, and hence lower inflationary pressure, improving the country's macroeconomics scenar-

---

[45] *Op. cit.*

io. Another variant lies in the possibility of saving on foreign currency which would be used for oil imports.

A final consequence, which may be used indirectly as an example of convergence, lies in the Petrobras performance. It has created one of the main Brazilian experiments in constituting a national system of innovations, in view of the fact that the country's industrialisation is dominated by the presence of multinationals, and without many examples of original technologies. And the presence of a national system of innovations if they believe in the entire positive dynamic potential based on technical progress, will be more consistent with Brazil's ambition to become an industrialised country.

Supplementary References

"Auto Suficiência", *Revista Eletrônica Petroquímica,* available on: http://www.petroequimica.com.br. Accessed: 18 May 2005.

"Bacia de Campos", *Revista Eletrônica Petroquímica*, available on: http://www.petroequimica.com.br . Accessed: 18 May 2005.

Fraga, O. "A parceria empresa-universidade em alto-mar: o caso das plataformas da Petrobras", *Revista Politécnica On Line*, ed. 246, 2002, available on: http://www.poli.usp.br/RevistaPolitecnica/busca.asp?results=results. Accessed: 10 October 2005.

Mommer, B. "The political role of National Oil Companies in the large exporting countries: The Venezuelan Case", Revista *Economies et Societés*, Série Économie de l'Énergie, EN, No. 6, p. 111-135, 1994.

Mowery, David C.; Rosemberg, Nathan, *Technology and the pursuit of economic upheaval growth*, 2nd ed., Cambridge: Cambridge University Press, 1994.

"O petróleo é nosso", *Revista Eletrônica ComCiência*, available on: http://www.comciencia.br/reportagens/petroleo/pet01.shtml. Accessed: 16 May 2005.

"Produção Nacional de Petróleo", available on: http://www.anp.gov.br/doc/dados_estatisticos/A48. Accessed: 20 July 2005.

UM ano para a história e para o futuro do Brasil, available on: http://www.autosuficiencia.com.br/geral/geral.asp. Accessed: 21 April 2006.

Von Tunzelmann, G. N., *Technology and Industrial Progress: the foundations of economic growth*, England: Edward Elgar Publishing, 1995, p. 1-100; 354-388.

The Case of Petrobrás in Brazil

Juliana BASTOS LOHMANN
Federal University Fluminense Rio de Janeiro, Brazil

George LANDAU
University Tancredo Neves, Sao Paulo, Brazil

Petróleos Brasileiros S.A. (Petrobrás) was conceived over a half-century ago as an expression of state capitalism, with overtones of state interventionism in the economy and national security. It is remarkable that the enterprise has evolved to become a successful example of association between public and private capital, and a competitor among major international oil corporations, with all the dynamism of a private enterprise, Petrobrás was created by law in Brazil in 1953 (Law 2,004) as a mixed-capital enterprise with majority ownership by the federal Union, i.e., the Government, and enjoying a monopoly over every aspect of the petroleum industry (then virtually non-existant in the country), under the guidance and control of the National Petroleum Council (CNP). Subsequent statutes and regulations changed the structure and scope of the company, including a period after 1975, when foreign oil companies were allowed to enter into risk contracts detracting from the monopoly.

In June 1995 a constitutional amendment was enacted which extinguished the state monopoly exercised on behalf of the national government by Petrobrás. Passage of this amendment, led to the enactment in 1997 of a comprehensive Petroleum Law (Law 9,478/97), which regulated the functioning of the industry and created a normative-regulatory body, the National Petroleum Agency (ANP), whose authority Petrobrás was at first most reluctant to acknowledge. With a few subsequent amendments and a collection of resolutions emanating from the Agency, this is the statute now in force, while a polemic law for gas is being reviewed by Congress. The law is polemic because it contrasts two entirely different approaches to the issue of access to gas pipelines, on which Petrobrás still enjoys a virtual monopoly, and more modern market-orientated approaches, which the state company is vigorously opposing.

This paper will focus on the dichotomy between Petrobrás' role as an instrumentality of the government and its place in the global, highly competitive petroleum market. Following an analysis of the legal-institutional framework described above, with a view to illustrating the many significant changes undergone by Petrobrás, the paper dwells on the ambivalent relationship between the company and the Brazilian state, which has gradually evolved over its 53-year existence, and especially during the latter years of the twentieth century. In many respects, Petrobrás used to behave as a state within the state. This tendency has abated in recent years, but still surfaces occasionally.

Indeed – for a variety of reasons which can only be explained with the background of some knowledge of Brazilian politics and psyche – Petrobrás has, since the Petroleum Law (which led to the presence of foreign companies as operators in the oil & gas sector), oscillated between being an instrumentality of the state and a private company answerable to its shareholders, and to this end competing fiercely both domestically and on the world scene. The pricing policy of Petrobrás illustrates this dichotomy, and is explored in the paper, which however goes into greater detail to analyse the new diplomatic configuration which is taking place in Latin America, and particularly in Bolivia, where Petrobrás' relationship to the Brazilian state and government is being severely tested.

Finally, the paper attempts to forecast for the short- and medium-term future what will be Petrobrás' new role *vis-à-vis* the Government, now that Brazil has achieved self-sufficiency in petroleum production and is on the verge of becoming a sustainable exporter of oil and its by-products. The enquiry also focuses on Petrobrás' own diplomacy, as it conquers new markets and competes for oil & gas assets in a variety of countries (22) all over the globe, and may de facto act overseas on behalf of the Brazilian state, but primarily in the pursuit of its own corporate interests.

The Case of Petrobrás

Petróleos Brasileiros S.A. (*Petrobrás*), Brazil's national oil company, is today a synonym of a successful association between government and private enterprise, but it was not always so. At its inception half a century ago, it reflected the then prevalent doctrine of national-capitalism, based on the twin concepts of state interventionism in the economy, and national security, brought by the many military engineers originally entrusted with senior management positions in the state company. But the company has evolved, and is now structured much more like a large private corporation, as will be seen below. It is quite remarkable that, from such origins, Petrobrás should have been able to morph into a dynamic international energy enterprise (beyond petroleum), the 8th in the world ranking, and competing with the majors.

Petrobrás is a mixed-economy enterprise established by Law 2,004, of October 3rd, 1953, sanctioned by President Getúlio Vargas within the spirit of national capitalism then prevalent, and was hailed as a great victory for nationalism ("Petroleum is ours!"), even though at the time Brazil produced virtually no petroleum at all. The company was created to implement the federal monopoly, enshrined in the Constitution, on the ownership of Brazil's petroleum resources and all other aspects related to the petroleum industry, under the guidance and control of the National Petroleum Council (CNP), established in 1938. Subsequent legislation, in 1957 and 1977, regulated the relationship between Petrobrás and CNP; the latter was entrusted with the supervision of the national supply of petroleum products. In 1978, the by-laws of Petrobrás were approved, to adapt the company's structure to the new Corporations Law enacted about one year before.

Under the Constitution of 1946 then in force, Petrobrás was structured as a public corporation governed by a Board of Directors consisting of a maximum of 12 members, of which: (a) a president, appointed by the President of the Republic and subject to dismissal by him *ad nutum*; (b) 3 to 6 Directors appointed by the President for a period of three years; (c) up to 3 counsellors elected by public entities, except the federal Union, for three-year terms; (d) up to 2 counsellors elected by private entities, for three-hear terms. Counsellors are elected by the General Shareholders' General Meeting (AGO), at the rate of one per each 5% of the voting capital. The president of the company and the directors constitute the Executive Board, entrusted with the management of the company; the directors are responsible for specific sectors, ascribed to them by the company's Board. There are five departments, geared to the end-objectives of the company: exploration, production, industrial, transport and commercial. There are also a variety of technical services, and a noted research centre (CENPES), created in 1963, which accounts for the company's many technological break-throughs, including its leading performance at drilling in ultra-deep waters. The company has always been central to Brazil's process of industrialisation, and to this day its procurement policies, emphasising domestic content, have exercised a significant effect on the country's technological advances.

In 1968, the company began to establish a series of subsidiaries. From 1970-71, Petrobrás started to operate overseas, notably in the Middle East. It did so through a subsidiary specifically created for the purpose, *Braspetro*, which in turn originated a trading company, *Interbrás*, both subsequently dissolved. Today, Petrobrás is a giant holding company, constituting a veritable system. There are many subsidiaries, and a number of affiliated or connected enterprises (*empresas coligadas*), i.e. those in which Petrobrás has minority participation; the subsidiaries are active in fields as varied as fuels distribution (BR Distribuidora), transport (Transpetro), petrochemicals (Petroquisa), gas (Gaspetro), fertilisers (Petrofértil), etc.

The first oil shock, in 1973, caught Brazil unaware and with only a small domestic petroleum production. Braspetro had discovered and began to operate the giant Majnoon oil field in Iraq, close to its border with Iran, but when Iraq became aware of its potential it virtually expropriated the field, with only a nominal indemnity. This, and the Iraq-Iran war, caused Petrobrás to leave the Middle East (to which it is just now returning). The oil crisis brought home Brazil's vulnerability to external shocks, and its dependence on OPEC's exorbitant pricing spurred domestic exploration. In this connection, an important bench-mark occurred in 1975, during the Geisel presidency and with Shigeaki Ueki at the helm of the Ministry of Mines & Energy (MME), when Petrobrás initiated risk contracts with a number of foreign oil companies, a polemic decision that, however well-intended, failed to yield the desired results, basically because Petrobrás reserved for itself the most promising areas for E&P, leaving to other oil companies those with the highest risk.

Under the Brazilian federal constitution of 1988, now in force (albeit amended over fifty times), the federal Union, i.e. the national state, has a monopoly on petroleum & gas E&P, refining, import and export, and transport (art. 177). In 1975, under president Cardoso, constitutional amendment No. 9 was enacted on November 11, 1995, which provided the legal underpinnings for the Petroleum Law (Law 9,478 of 1997). The latter greatly liberalised the régime of oil & gas in Brazil, and essentially devolved to the federal Union the monopoly rights that had in practice been enjoyed on its behalf by Petrobrás. The same law established a normative-regulatory agency, ANP (the National Petroleum Agency, subsequently expanded to include also gas and bio-mass based fuels).

During the first few years of its establishment, ANP became embroiled in a veritable power struggle with Petrobrás, which was understandably reluctant to accept the Agency's regulatory primacy, but eventually, with changes in their respective leaderships, the relationship became relatively harmonious. It should be said that after 2003, when the administration of president Luis Inácio Lula da Silva (Lula for short) came to power, the government took steps to curb and downgrade the autonomy previously enjoyed by the normative-regulatory agencies, including ANP, subjecting them to the political control and stewardship of their respective Ministries, in this case the Ministry of Mines & Energy (MME). Today the areas of competence and jurisdiction of enterprises Petrobrás and Eletrobrás on the one hand, and on the other of agencies ANP (for petroleum & gas) and ANEEL (for electric power) are more clearly defined, and a collaborative spirit prevails among them.

In president Cardoso's second term (1999-2002), the presidency of Petrobrás was exercised by Henry Philippe Reichstuhl, a financier who was responsible for a profound restructuring of the company, bringing it to the status of a large multinational oil enterprise. As such, Petrobrás was able to reinforce its finances, specifically to undertake domestic E&P, by borrowing as of 2000 on world capital markets, with privileged status – better than Brazil's sovereign ratings. This occurred and particularly with the New York Stock Exchange, where Petrobrás' ADRs are among the most traded papers. Today, the company's finances are regulated both by the US' Securities and exchange Commission (SEC) and its Brazilian equivalent (CVM), *Comissão de Valores Mobiliários.* Strengthened by this influx of liquidity, Petrobrás could aim at oil self-sufficiency (eventually attained in 2006), diversified growth and high profitability.

On March 24, 1999, a special General Shareholders' Meeting of Petrobrás approved the company's new by-laws, allowing for the first time foreign nationals as shareholders: a major break-through. Reichstuhl's singular merit was to enhance the company's competitiveness and environmental accountability, in marked contrast with the corporatist and paternalistic culture that had prevailedover the first few decades. He in effect changed the company from a national oil company to a highly diversified energy corporation, run as a dynamic private enterprise. To symbolise these changes and reflect the new reality stemming from the Petroleum Law, in 2000 Reichstuhl tried to change the brand name of Petrobrás to Petrobrax, with a new logo, but there was such a popular outcry against any change to this national icon, that the idea had to be dropped. In the year 2000, Reichstuhl succeeded in securing the approval of a new corporate-management model, under which the subsidiary Braspetro was absorbed into the structure of the company proper, under a Board member presiding over the international area – a sure sign that the company was about to expand its international operations, as indeed it did. Today, they cover 22 countries, and are expanding at a dizzying pace.

A. Brazil: an Energy Power-house

The year 2006, in which Brazil attained self-sufficiency in petroleum production – thanks to Petrobrás' extraordinary efforts since the Petroleum Law was enacted in 1997 and eliminated the company's monopoly – is also the year in which Brazil as a whole became an energy power-house, with a notable contribution of Petrobrás in other sectors as well (electricity, bio-fuels, etc). Petrobrás has also become a global leader in certain technological segments, e.g. drilling in ultra deep waters. The company's new strategic plan for 2007-11, approved by the Board on June 30, 2006, calls for investments of 87.1 billion dollars, i.e. an average of 17.4 billion dollars p.a. 86% of which in Brazil (75 billion dollars) and 14% abroad, an increase of 66% over the 2006-10 business plan. As regards petroleum, beyond the national self-sufficiency resulting from a production level of over 1.9 million barrels/day at the end of 2006, the company is investing 49.3 billion dollars in 2007-11 for domestic E&P, and 12.1 billion dollars for exploration overseas, notably in six countries of South America, but also in 16 other countries spread over five continents, focusing on the US side of the Gulf of Mexico and West Africa. Joint production of petroleum, natural gas and LNG should attain 3,493 boe/d in 2011, of which 2,925 boe/d in Brazil. For 2015 the over-all target is production of 4,556 boe/d.

Petrobrás already exports heavy crude (mostly unsuitable for processing by Brazilian refineries), and plans to significantly increase such exports. On the other hand, the company is adapting its refineries at home to process the domestic crude, is building a new one (in partnership with Venezuela's PDVSA) in the northeastern state of Pernambuco, planning for another with a capacity of 500,000 b/d, and is proactively engaged in a programme of acquisition of refineries elsewhere (in the US, Colombia, Europe and Japan).

Petrobrás announced on July 11, 2006 that it had found light oil, as yet unquantified, in the BM-5-11 block in ultra-deep waters in the Santos basin. The company described this find as "a historic bench-mark for Brazilian exploration, because this well is the first to be drilled through a layer of evaporitic salts over 2,000 m deep." Additional investment will be required to evaluate the size and productivity of the deposit, which is still being drilled by Petrobrás as operator (65%) in association with BG (25%) and Petrogal (10%). The discovery, at a depth of 2,140 m, confirms Petrobrás' working hypothesis that, beneath the oil & gas found in the Santos basin, there is, at great depths, another basin with very significant volumes of oil.

Petrobrás intends to double, by 2011, its output of light oil, which currently accounts for 11% of the company's domestic production. Despite the significant (66.2%) increase of its volume of investments in 2007-11 over the preceding period (2006-10), analysts have questioned the relatively small increase (26%) in oil production (from 1,880 million b/d to 2,374 million b/d five years later) – to which should be added the depletion factor, since 1.1 million b/d are simply replacements for deposits nearing exhaustion by 2011 – but Petrobrás explains it by concentrating on the extraction of light oil. The production target for 2015 is 2.812 million b/d.

Petrobrás is likewise vastly expanding its operations in the area of petrochemicals, in which it plans to become a major exporter. Already the largest enterprise in Brazil over-all, the company is also responsible for the largest-ever investment in the country, a 6.5 billion dollarscapital outlay for the construction of a petrochemical complex at Itaboraí, in the state of Rio de Janeiro. Petrobrás new business plan for 2007-11 calls for investments of 23.1 billion dollars in the supplies sector (which includes refining and petrochemicals), a 62% increase over the previous plan.

The Bolivian nationalisation of the gas industry, and the supply risks it entails for Brazil – which depends on Bolivian gas for more than half of its consumption of 48 million m^3/d, which will double by 2011 – has caused Petrobrás to ascribe a high priority to the development of internal production, the construction of the infrastructure required to transport it to consuming centres, and securing reliable supplies from abroad, notably in the form of imported LNG. Petrobrás will invest 17.6 billion dollars over the period on the natural gas chain, and its partners are expected to invest another 4.5 billion dollars, totalling 22.1 billion dollars.

The national electricity shortage of 2001 led Petrobrás to invest heavily in thermo-electric power generation, mostly gas-fired (although the Bolivian crisis may now force a new shift to fuel oil and/or ethanol). Thus, the company finds itself now in control of several such plants. Moreover, the foreseeable scarcity of gas (domestic demand for which, half of its for power generation, is growing at the rate of 17% p.a.) has led Petrobrás to focus on the production, and eventually the export of bio-fuels. As regards, those produced from sugar-cane (which in 2005 accounted for 30.4 million TEP (petroleum-equivalent tons), Petrobrás is heavily involved in this burgeoning sector. Bio-fuels already are the second largest component in the national energy matrix, and tend to grow exponentially.

Petrobrás expects to have available 100 million m^3/d by 2011, of which 30 million m^3/d will come from Bolivia through Gasbol under the contract in force until 2019, with the remainder originating in domestic gas production (from the basins of Campos, Santos, Espírito Santo and Camamu-Almada) and, marginally, through imports of LNG. The Bolivian nationalisation led Petrobrás to suspend further investments in the country and to annul a tender to expand by 50% the current 30 million m^3/d capacity of Gasbol. The company will build more gas pipelines to carry the domestic product to consuming centres. Petrobrás now has, either at the planning phase, under construction or recently-concluded, 3,091 km of new gas pipelines in Brazil, with a carrying capacity of 119 million m³/d and valued at well over 5 billion dollars. The urgency of the task requires the company to pay extra fees, for instance given the logistical difficulties of laying pipelines in Amazonia.

B. A State Instrumentality or a Private Corporation?

Petrobrás has always been in an ambivalent position *vis-à-vis* the dichotomy state enterprise versus private corporation, but this situation became particularly apparent since the company's capital was opened in 2004, when the Brazilian Treasury sold its "surplus" equity, i.e. those shares exceeding the 50% plus one share of voting capital, required by law. The federal Union, both through the Treasury and through BNDESPar (the holding company that is a subsidiary of national development bank BNDES), holds 57.6% in the voting capital (ON) of Petrobrás plus 15.5% of the non-voting capital (preferred shares – PN). Another 20.6% of the equity belongs to Brazilian individuals and corporations. And foreigners own 30.2% of the company's voting capital, of which 27.3% in the form of American Depositary Receipts (ADRs) traded on the New York Stock Exchange (NYSE) and 2.9% in the form of nominal shares traded on the S. Paulo Stock Exchange (Bovespa) and registered in the name of foreign persons and firms.

At the outset of the Cardoso government in 1995, thought was given to the possibility of privatising *Petrobrás*, as part of the country's largest ever programme of privatisation of public enterprises (over 110 billion dollars), but the idea was discarded, given the insurmountable political difficulties in tampering with this national icon. The idea has resurfaced now that the main political parties are preparing their respective platforms for the October 2006 elections. PFL, a relatively conservative (centre-right) party, allied in the presidential campaign with PSDB, has also considered the possibility of including in its programme the privatisation of the Bank of Brazil and Petrobrás, but decided not to, on the grounds that it would take more than four years (the length of a presidential term) to prepare the public for such a decision. It is therefore a foregone conclusion that no such initiative will be taken by the next President of Brazil, whoever he (or she) might be.

However, this is not only a financial question, it is essentially a political one. The truth is that Petrobrás is both an instrumentality of the Brazilian state (and therefore subject to the political vagaries of its government) and a commercial enterprise, accountable to its hundreds of thousands of shareholders, both in Brazil and abroad. The administration of President Luiz Inácio Lula da Silva (2003-06) has politicised Petrobrás as never before, putting the presidential Chief of Staff (currently Minister Dilma Rousseff), a former Minister of Mines & Energy), in the chair of the Board of Directors, staffing the company with (mostly inexperienced) trade unionists, vastly increasing its payroll and generally interfering with its decision-making process, e.g. in the matter of domestic prices for petroleum by-products and gas, where Petrobrás – for electoral purposes – was (and is) obliged to absorb rising international prices for these inputs without passing them on to consumers, for fear of fuelling inflation.

In this election year, 2006, there is increasing evidence that the Lula Administration intends to make political use of *Petrobrás*, Brazil's largest company, as a campaign tool. Not content with staffing with the President's workers' Party (PT) stalwarts the Board and senior positions of the state-owned company – a perhaps undesirable but legitimate corollary of politics in a democratic régime – the government is, alarmingly, preparing to use Petrobrás as a vote-getter. For propaganda purposes, there is nothing better than advertising the country's self-sufficiency in petroleum production. Another element in this effort is the timing and degree of subsidy of Petrobrás' fuels pricing policy. Yet another is the series of agreements with PDVSA, of very questionable benefit to Brazil – e.g. building a refinery in Pernambuco that will process imported Venezuelan oil, when Brazil has achieved self-sufficiency in oil output – but reflects ideological alignment with Venezuela's president Chávez.

There are many other decisions, which should have been strictly technical, but reflect a political bias. José Sérgio Gabrielli, the president of Petrobrás, himself a PT militant, denies that there is any political interference in the company's policy decisions, and in support of this assertion mentions its excellent financial results, which are indeed significant. Nevertheless, it would appear that he himself is a faithful executor of the Government's, and PT party's directives. As part of Lula's propaganda machine aiming at his re-election, Petrobrás is earmarking from R$150-R$160 million (*circa* 69 million dollars) to advertise Brazil's sustainable self-sufficiency in petroleum production, attained with the entry into operation, in June 2006, of platform P-50, installed at the Albacora East field in the Campos basin. Petrobrás plans to close the year 2006 producing an average of 1,910 million b/d (against 1,684 million b/d in 2005).

Yet another illustration of the uneasy relationship between Petrobrás and the Brazilian state is the issue of local content in equipment and vessels for the petroleum industry As a matter of public policy, president Lula's administration has insisted on a high proportion of domestically-produced goods and services in procurement by Petrobrás, as a means to stimulate Brazilian industry – shipyards, for example – and create jobs. Both these goals are intrinsically laudable, but, given that for several items such as off-shore drilling platforms, or tanker vessels, domestic production has so far been unable to achieve economies of scale, the net effect is that prices to be paid by Petrobrás and its affiliates, e.g. Transpetro, are significally higher than those prevalent on global markets. It would be hard to disagree with the policy to promote local content, but the corollary is that Petrobrás is expected to foot the bill.

Petrobrás is notoriously unwilling to relinquish the vestiges of its former state monopoly status in every segment of the petroleum industry, which it still dominates in Brazil, with copious benefits and privileges. At the same time that all this happens, paradoxically Petrobrás is behaving overseas as an aggressive international oil company that operates – very successfully – in 22 countries, ranks as the world's 8th largest oil enterprise, achieves record profits, reaps numerous prizes for excellent relations with its investors, is traded in the leading global stock exchanges, and has earned an enviable reputation for developing advanced technologies, e.g. for deep-sea exploration.

There are numerous instances in which Petrobrás has placed its own enlightened (or not) self-interest ahead of the national interest, as any independent commercial corporation pursuing profits might do, but this reflects the company's schizophrenic dilemma. For decades the company failed to drill domestically because it was more profitable to import oil; also for decades it failed to prospect for gas because the oil business was more profitable; until recently, when a massive overhaul programme was instituted, the company's refineries (98% of Brazil's total) were unable to process the locally-found heavy crude, only imported light oil; etc. Conversely, there are examples of Petrobrás doing the government's bidding against its corporate interest. One such instance occurred in the aftermath of the national black-out of 2001 – when Brazil suffered energy shortages and had to establish a 20% electric power rationing programme – and the government required Petrobrás to invest heavily in thermo-electric power generation, which caused the company heavy financial losses.

One example of this attitude occurred earlier this year (2006), when Petrobrás, nostalgic about its former monopoly rights, did everything in its power to thwart an initiative designed to grant access by other enterprises to its pipeline network. A bill to that effect was introduced in the Brazilian Senate, late in 2005, by Sen. Rodolpho Tourinho (PFL-BA), a former Minister of Mines & Energy, as a means to partially regulate the gas sector. Prepared with the technical support of a neo-liberal think-tank in Rio de Janeiro, the Brazilian Centre for Infrastructure (CBIE), the bill reflects that ideology. Since at the time of adoption of the Petroleum Law of 1997 the production of natural gas constituted only a tiny fraction of the national energy matrix, it was then felt that specific regulation for the gas sector was unnecessary, and therefore the law applied to it residually, but when demand for the product grew exponentially in this century, such a need emerged. The government only much later was able to introduce its own much-touted bill to regulate the gas sector, and now the two bills, the Senator's and that of the government, are being considered jointly, although they reflect two widely different political philosophies. The government's bill was drafted with inputs from Petrobrás, which is understandably reticent about the loss of its monopolistic privileges.

It is easy to be critical with the benefit of hindsight, but the Bolivian episode (described below in some detail) brought to light the fact that the Brazilian state deferred to Petrobrás the responsibility to plan for the petroleum & gas sector, and, at least in respect of long-term planning, the company failed, because, among other factors, it had a short-term perspective when a much more comprehensive one would have been required. The Bolivian crisis exposed the country's utter vulnerability, in that (i) Petrobrás wagered on this single source of imported gas, a country of great political volatility and therefore unreliable as a long-term prime source of energy; (ii) having found plentiful domestic gas reserves in the Santos basin, Petrobrás failed to build in timely fashion the infrastructure required to transport it to consuming centres; and, last but not least; (iii) although it received as far back as 2002 proposals to build LNG re-gasification plants – which would have been useful if only on a contingency basis – Petrobrás declined to act on these proposals. All this is now being remedied, belatedly, and the company is committed to a multi-faceted policy (Plangás) to supply gas to satisfy the country's swiftly increasing demand, but the point is that the planning was inadequate.

C. A New Diplomatic Configuration

Perhaps in no area is Petrobrás' ambivalent relationship with the Brazilian state more evident than in that of foreign policy. The company is not a mere executor of the government's external relations, capably carried out by the foreign ministry, Itamaraty, but obviously plays an ancillary role to it. That is very much the case in Latin America, e.g. *vis-à-vis* Cuba and Venezuela. In some cases, the company formulates and implements its own foreign policy. An egregious case of initial collision between president Lula's party line i.e. the government and Petrobrás' interests occurred in Bolivia.

There is today in South America a new diplomatic configuration that poses challenges to Brazil, and specifically to Petrobrás. There is a very real question as to whether the Lula government, which – without as yet indulging in populism – is ideologically aligned with the populist regimes emerging in the region, will be able to surmount those challenges and defend Brazil's interests under threat. To be sure, the country counts on a very professional foreign service, but major foreign policy decisions are not made by Itamaraty: rather, they emanate from the president's office, and are conditioned by ideological and domestic political considerations in an election year.

– The most immediate challenge is posed by Bolivia, the source of one-half of the natural gas consumed by Brazil, which on May 1st, 2006 nationalised the assets of Petrobrás. Precisely when the Brazilian government should apply maximum diplomatic pressure on Bolivia to settle this and other issues amicably and equitably, it signed 25 agreements offering financial and technical co-operation, and followed with BNDES credits that may attain 1 billion dollars.

– Bolivia's president Morales is clearly under the thumb of president Chávez of Venezuela, and has just become a member of his "Bolivarian Alternative for the Americas" (ALBA), together with Cuba. Venezuela has joined Mercosul – which it wishes to change to suit its own preferences (including a ban on collaboration with the US) – and Cuba would thus gain back-door access to Mercosul, which it couldn't otherwise join since it cannot comply with its "democratic clause".

– Venezuela under Chávez has left the G-3 which it had formed with Mexico and Colombia, as well as the Andean Group (CAN) the latter because Colombia and Peru had signed free trade agreements with the US Brazil had made strenuous efforts to achieve agreement between CAN and Mercosul, as a prelude to forming a South American Community of Nations (CASA), in which Chile, for instance, is interested, but Chávez's Venezuela has pre-empted it with his ALBA. Latin America is disintegrating, not the reverse.

– Mercosul itself, Brazil's foremost diplomatic priority, is under threat of disruption, both from endogenous causes (e.g. the rift between Argentina and Uruguay due to two paper mills in Uruguay that Argentina claims will pollute its atmosphere) and from exogenous ones, as Chávez insists on certain conditions that would be hard to meet.

– The Chávez-proposed mega-gas pipeline (GasSur) carrying Venezuelan gas to Argentina and traversing all of Brazil, a mammoth project costing up to 25 billion dollars, which the three governments have approved but is being widely criticised by experts as being technically and economically not viable, poses some challenges of its own. The three sponsoring governments, which are spending 10 million dollars for preparatory studies, want to incorporate Bolivia, Paraguay and Uruguay, into the scheme. However, most importantly, Brazil's participation in the project is not contemplated in Petrobrás' new business plan for 2007-11.

– Chávez has stated his willingness to finance a Bolivian gas pipeline to Paraguay, providing an outlet to the Atlantic, which would completely by-pass Gasbol and Brazil, at the same time that Petrobrás wishes to expand the capacity of the Bolivia-Brazil gas pipeline in order to meet growing demand for Bolivian gas in Brazil. Petrobrás, in light of Bolivia's nationalisation, has shelved its plans for the expansion of Gasbol.

Under president Lula, Brazil has become politically closer to Venezuela than ever before, and bilateral trade is booming. In addition to a series of agreements for co-operation in a variety of sectors, Lula has pulled Chávez's Venezuela into Mercosul, which will require profound adjustments on both sides. Besides ideological affinity with the "anti-imperialist" movement – whatever that may mean, since the bulk of Venezuela's oil revenues originates in the United States – the Brazilian rationale for all that closeness is Venezuela's oil wealth. Brazil doesn't need the oil, because it will become self-sufficient this year, but can use some of the wealth. Question is, will Venezuela's good fortune last over the long term?

Following the two-month strike of 2003-04, President Chávez has plunged Venezuela's petroleum industry, and with it PDVSA, into disarray. For one thing, he fired 18,000 of its best technicians. The once-proud and technically advanced state oil company is now being steadily milked as a cash cow to finance the "Bolivarian Revolution" abroad and social development programmes at home, indeed, so much so that PDVSA is investing more on said programmes than on present and future oil & gas production (which could require 4 billion dollars p.a.). Production has declined by 20% p.a. from its level of 2,5 million b/d, unless fresh capital should be forthcoming. To be sure, PDVSA has announced a five-year strategic plan calling for investments of 56 billion dollars over the period, but these resources just don't exist. (The company contributes about 4 billion dollars p.a. to social schemes). President Chávez hopes that about one-third of this capital will come from the foreign oil companies operating in Venezuela, but they stopped investing when, in 2005, the Government billed them billions for alleged late taxes and forced them to migrate to joint ventures with PDVSA. 21,000 oil wells in Venezuela have ceased production for lack of repairs; only 14,000 are operating in the country's declining petroleum industry. Venezuela's natural gas reserves (4.27 trillion m^3) are among the largest on earth, but much of the gas produced is re-injected into oil wells in the Lake Maracaibo area in order to increase production.

A collaborative undertaking between PDVSA and Petrobrás is the *Abreu e Lima* (200,000 b/d) refinery in Pernambuco, whose keystone was placed on December 27, 2005 by presidents Lula and Chávez. The project is controversial on a number of counts, not the least of which is that the refinery will process heavy crude (100,000 b/d) imported from Venezuela (of which Brazil is already exporting 300,000 b/d from the Campos basin), and does not really need to import. Again, the political motivation behind this Chávez initiative is clear, but it is difficult to find any rational benefits for Brazil. Chávez's motivations are not only geopolitical, consolidating the "Bolivarian Revolution" etc. Domestically, he is subjecting foreign enterprises in general, and the petroleum industry in particular, to ever stricter controls, burdensome taxation, forcible joint ventures with PDVSA, and, worst of all, co-management with workers' co-operatives, a system that failed lamentably when it was tried in Communist Eastern Europe.

There seems to be a "domino theory" in action in Latin America today, with countries succumbing one after the other to the populism of president Chávez, but in the recently-held elections held in Colombia and Peru, he was rebuffed. Now, whither Ecuador? The domino theory is being realised in South America's petroleum sector, and it is not a coincidence, given the wave of nationalism that is raging in the Andean countries. The government of Ecuador decided on April 7 to increase to 50% the state's participation in the revenue of oil companies operating in the country. It is estimated that 409 million dollars, in revenue will accrue to the Ecuadorean treasury as a result; 35% of the national budget is financed from such revenues. According to the new law, the government will collect one-half of the difference between the price set at the time contracts were signed and the current price of oil sold by concession-holders, excluding only the output of marginal fields. Petrobrás has invested 430 million dollars in Ecuador and plans to invest another 300 million dollars for the development of reserves discovered in the country's Amazonian region. Petrobrás' Argentinian subsidiary, Petrobrás Energía, currently produces in Ecuador some 11,000 b/d from two fields.

On March 2, 2006, the Subcommittee on the Western Hemisphere of the US House of Representatives International Relations Committee heard testimony on the role of the Western hemisphere in fostering US energy security. One of the speakers was Dr Sidney Weintraub, head of the CSIS research project on energy co-operation in the Americas. In his testimony, Dr Weintraub noted that President Bush's State-of-the-Union address altogether ignored the Western hemisphere in the context of energy, even if it accounts for half of total US crude oil imports and 95.5% of its total gas imports (2004). He went on to mention Venezuela, which under President Chávez has become antagonistic to the US, as "the most significant country energy problem" for the US, to which it supplies 11.82% of its imports of crude oil. He also described Mexico (22.66% of US imports) as friendly to the US and willing to co-operate, but unable to fashion a policy that would lead to this result, or even to its own domestic energy needs. Canada is the largest oil exporter to the US (16% of its oil, 85% of gas), and the most reliable one, whereas there are doubts about the reliability of Bolivia and Ecuador as future sources. Peru appears to be a potential source of LNG; Trinidad & Tobago has become the leading supplier of LNG to the US, and Brazil, while a marginal oil exporter, will focus on its vast domestic market.

Dr Weintraub concludes that "the hemisphere would benefit greatly if there were energy co-operation", the main impediments to which are political rather than technical. As policy advice to the US Government, Dr Weintraub advocates that it should give higher priority to the hemisphere generally and with respect to energy in particular, and cautions that "there will be no US energy security if it is lacking elsewhere in the hemisphere." On the other hand, a recent study by US consultancy KPMG indicates that the Latin American region is an energy powerhouse, with six oil & gas exporting countries (Venezuela, Mexico, Ecuador, Colombia, Argentina and Bolivia), and Brazil becoming one later this year (2006). The study does point to some problems, however: a lack of synergy among the countries, dependence on gas pipelines for cross-border transport (when LNG plants might be cheaper and more flexible), the absence of infrastructure for gas distribution, etc. A recent study by the Brazilian Centre of Infrastructure (CBIE) in Rio de Janeiro, shows that within four years natural gas will be Brazil's second most important source of energy (after petroleum), rising from 8.9% in 2004 to 14.7% in 2010, surpassing alcohol, whose share in the national energy matrix is also rising.

Regarding the GasSur pipeline, a project in which the Lula administration, for political-ideological reasons, has implicated Petrobrás, there are great doubts as to its feasibility. A meeting of ministers and other authorities from Argentina, Brazil and Venezuela took place in Caracas on June 7, 2006, chaired by Venezuelan Energy Minister Rafael Ramírez – who also heads PDVSA – to evaluate progress on the GasSur gas pipeline project proposed by president Chávez, and thus to follow up on the guidelines established by the presidents of the three countries at their mini-summit in S. Paulo on April 26. There are seven working groups studying the project from an economic, environmental, engineering, financial and regulatory standpoint, as well as one focusing on the route to be followed by the pipeline. While the director for gas & energy of Petrobrás, Ildo Sauer, seems committed to the polemic project, probably for ideological rather than technical reasons, there are in Brazil many voices expressing their misgivings about it, from environmentalists, disturbed about the pipeline's potential damage to the Amazonian region of both countries; academics and even bankers, (who doubt the project's economic and financial feasibility); and energy experts, who worry about Brazil's hypothetical need to subsidise the flow of Venezuelan gas through its territory lest it reaches Argentina at a non-viable price. Diplomats see the project as another in the series of Chávez' initiatives to estrange South America from the US and affirm Venezuela's geo-political pre-eminence in the region, and wonder about Brazil's allegiance to such a scheme.

Finally, there are those who question the availability of sufficient gas in Venezuela to keep it flowing through the pipeline at the rate of 150 million m^3/d (i.e., five to six times the volume of gas Brazil now imports from Bolivia). Venezuela does have the largest gas reserves in South America (4.2 billion m^3), but most of it is associated with petroleum, and therefore crude production will have to increase substantially to free natural gas. The country's current output of 176 million m^3 is expected to double within six years, and PDVSA expects to invest until then over 6 billion dollars, but these plans are contingent on the maintenance of a high world price for oil as well as on the willingness of IOCs to abide by Venezuela's increasingly forceful fiscal demands, which tend to reduce the freedom and profitability of oil production in the country, now under mandatory partnership with PDVSA.

GasSur is likely to become an issue in Brazil's electoral campaign. The opposition to Lula will not fail to remind voters about the president's bowing to Bolivia's truculent nationalisation of gas, explicitly supported by Chávez. A likely hike in the cost of gas to domestic consumers will make the electorate feel the pinch. In other words, it wouldn't be safe at this stage to wager on the success of the GasSur project, notwithstanding official government statements that it is essential to Brazil's energy security.

D. A Case Study: Bolivia

The reactions of the Brazilian government and Petrobrás to Bolivia's nationalisation of its entire petroleum industry constitute a case study of the interaction between a national oil company and its government. It may be easier to comprehend the subtle nuances of that interaction by giving a chronological overview of events, preceding their analysis.

On May 1st, 2006 (Labour Day), President Lula, aboard Petrobrás giant off-shore drilling platform P-50 (180,000 b/d) proclaimed with great fanfare (with an eye on his re-election), Brazil's self-sufficiency in petroleum production – a great achievement, no doubt, but Lula announced it as if he had single-handedly made it possible, rather than the painstaking cumulative work of thousands of dedicated technicians over several decades. On the very same date, President Evo Morales of Bolivia, surrounded by Army troops, took symbolic possession of Petrobrás' gas fields and decreed the nationalisation of the entire petroleum sector in his country, every segment of it.

While nobody disputes Bolivia's sovereign right to exercise full control over its natural resources in foreign hands – not only Petrobrás was affected by the measure, so were international oil companies (IOCs) from at least seven countries – the truculent and unnecessarily aggressive manner in which this was done, in order to appeal to the nationalistic feeling of the Bolivian populace, made their governments utterly uncomfortable, including that of Brazil. What followed, however was, a comedy of errors, which over the long term may eventually turn into a national tragedy for Bolivia. Moreover, it exposes the difficult relationship between Petrobrás and the government of Brazil, with whose political leadership, Lula's, the company is nevertheless ideologically aligned.

Lula's first reaction to Evo Morales' action was to actually praise it as a legitimate expression of Bolivia's sovereignty. The Brazilian Congress and the media took him to task, and a banner press headline wondered sarcastically if Lula had been elected president of Brazil or of Bolivia. Thereupon, sensing nationwide dissatisfaction with his posture – after all, Petrobrás had invested over 1.5 billion dollars of Brazilian taxpayers' money in the Bolivian gas industry – president Lula hastily arranged a meeting on June 4, at Puerto Iguazú, Argentina, on the border with Brazil, with the presidents of Argentina (Nestor Kirchner), Bolivia (Evo Morales) – and, lo and behold! – Venezuela (Hugo Chávez) without whose inspiration and support Evo Morales would not have dared to act as he did: Petrobrás accounts for 20% of Bolivia's GDP.

The mini-summit at Puerto Iguazu, called to resolve the crisis caused by Bolivia's nationalisation of oil & gas, was a diplomatic disaster for Brazil. On May 6, Brazil's most prestigious newspaper, *O Estado de S. Paulo*, published its lead editorial under the title "Shame at Puerto Iguazu", The meeting didn't resolve anything, but the day after it took place, the Brazilian foreign ministry and Petrobrás both had second thoughts, and adopted a tougher stance *vis-à-vis* Bolivia. The Foreign Minister, Celso Amorim, said Brazil would defend the interests of Petrobrás and of Brazilian gas consumers, and would seek alternative sources of gas. The president of Petrobrás, José Sérgio Gabrielli, reiterated that the company would take the case to international arbitration and would suspend any further investments in Bolivia.

On May 5, Lula solemnly promised the Brazilian people that there would be no increase in the price of gas to consumers. In other words, whatever price increases should be exacted by Bolivia would be absorbed by Petrobrás What Brazilians wouldn't forgive is Lula's subservience to Morales-Chávez. Amb. Rego Barros, former Director-General of ANP, accused Lula's diplomacy of being a mixture of "naiveté and ideology". Amb. Ricupero, former Secretary-General of UNCTAD, said that the Brazilian government should, at the very least, activate the legal mechanisms for the defence of its rights. Amb. Barbosa, former envoy in London and Washington, said much the same thing: "Brazilian foreign policy today is characterised by the ideologisation of decision-making and the politicisation of trade negotiations". And former foreign minister Celso Lafer quipped "Itamaraty's tradition has been one of firmness without stridency; it is now one of stridency without firmness". The criticism of Lula's performance at Puerto Iguazu has escalated to a vast reappraisal of Brazilian foreign policy under his government. Spain, in order to protect the interests of Repsol, has been much more forceful than Brazil on behalf of Petrobrás. The Spanish government immediately sent a high-level delegation to La Paz, making clear its intention to invoke the bilateral investment treaty it has with Bolivia.

In the aftermath of the meeting at Puerto Iguazu, the situation can be summarised as follows:

– At the political level, Evo Morales, overnight, became a national hero in Bolivia.

– Hugo Chávez, who brazenly asserted his role as Evo Morales' mentor, will probably eventually achieve his goal to replace Petrobrás in Bolivia with PDVSA.

– Unless Lula's ideologues prevail, Petrobrás is likely to sue Bolivia for breach of contract in international arbitration courts, and if necessary in judicial proceedings. Repsol and 20 other IOC in Bolivia may do likewise.

– Politically, it would be disastrous for Lula in this election year to have Petrobrás pass on to consumers any significant increases in the price of gas, which means Petrobrás, which had no contingency plans, will have no alternative but to absorb such an increase, while it negotiates with Bolivia to bring it down to a "reasonable" level.

– The Brazilian government was obviously caught unprepared by the Bolivian move (although Evo Morales had announced it during his electoral campaign), and now Petrobrás has to scramble in order to:

a) Build two or three re-gasification plants and import LNG from wherever it can. Building the plants may take up to three years, unless floating plants can be acquired.

b) Accelerate its plans to build the pipeline infrastructure to bring gas from its deposits in the Santos basin (the Mexilhão field will now come on stream in 2007 instead of 2008, with up to 15 million m^3/d), and intensify its exploration efforts to discover new ones. (Petrobrás' E&P strategy had prioritised oil, not gas, despite the existence of resources estimated at 880 billion m^3, enough to supply Brazil for 50 years). Building the infrastructure will also require a minimum of three years.

– Petrobrás is likely to abandon its plans for further investments in Bolivia, including the 50% expansion of Gasbol (from 30 to 45 million m^3/d).

– The climate for foreign direct investment in Latin America as a whole has deteriorated markedly as a corollary of the instability evidenced by Bolivia's actions – disregarding sanctity of contracts – and this is bound to have unfavourable repercussions also on Brazil.

Brazilian foreign Minister Celso Amorim was summoned to testify on May 9 before the Senate Committee on External Relations and National Defence about the government's response to Bolivia's nationalisation of Petrobrás' assets and related questions. The Minister was quizzed by a very critical Committee, which made it clear that Senators feel that Brazil's response was not commensurate to the acts of violence already committed, or threatening to be, by Evo Morales' government.

While discussions continue to rage in Brazil about the government's leniency towards Bolivia, the Bolivian government is taking concrete steps to implement its nationalisation decree. Bolivian authorities profess themselves willing to negotiate the time frame and the amounts for paying to Petrobrás and other IOC affected, by means of gas actually produced, the costs of the nationalisation, and reiterate that the supply of gas will not be interrupted, but all IOCs will undergo an audit to determine a base for new contracts, which will have to be submitted to the Bolivian Congress (where Morales' MAS party has a majority). Morales' government insists that the investments made by Petrobrás and other IOCs in the country have already been amortised by "excessive" profits, and that Petrobrás itself had previously offered 100% ownership of its two (unprofitable) refineries to the government, which at the time (under the Carlos Mesa administration) took no decision about it.

Petrobrás has a contract for the sale of Bolivian gas to Brazil, valid until 2019. While Brazil's political leadership under Lula may compel Petrobrás to take a more positive approach towards Bolivia's nationalisation, the company regards Bolivia as a failed project, and will not invest there anymore, scrapping its plans to add 5 billion dollars to its capital outlays in the form of joint ventures. The consensus in the Brazilian company is that Evo Morales has mortgaged his country's future as South America's energy hub. What nobody in Petrobrás says openly but admits tacitly is that Chávez's grand design for GasSur is now also in abeyance, given his hostility towards Brazil, since Morales followed to the letter the Venezuelan model. The Venezuelan president announced on May 7 that a new tax would be levied on IOC operating in the country, so as to raise about 1 billion dollars in additional fiscal revenue next year.

Against the background of statements by Lula and Evo Morales – the former reassuring the Brazilian population that there will be neither interruptions in the supply of gas nor price increases, the latter saying there is a conspiracy afoot by foreign enterprises and the international media against his nationalisation of gas – negotiations have started in earnest, on May 10, between Petrobrás and YPFB. The 20 IOC operating in Bolivia have not yet agreed on a common strategy, but Petrobrás is the main victim of Evo Morales' nationalisation; the other companies principally affected include Repsol-YPF, Total, BG-Group, BP, ExxonMobil, PanAmerican, Vintage and Irving. They have all been given six months to negotiate new contracts under the nationalisation decree, and the clock is ticking.

This is well as a negotiating position, but overlooks the fact that, with his violent nationalisation, Morales had in effect torn up all contracts with IOC and thrown the scattered pieces to the wind. Confrontation is therefore inevitable, regardless of Lula's intention of having a friendly relationship with Morales. In the meantime, Brazil is revising its national energy matrix to reduce the relative weight of gas (S. Paulo industry runs on Bolivian gas), is accelerating the construction of domestic gas pipelines, and is readying plans to import LNG within 30 months, and to build the corresponding re-gasification plants. Morales may have killed the golden goose.

From Vienna, where he was attending on May 11-13, 2006, a the EU-Latin American Summit, President Morales emphatically reiterated that Petrobrás was operating both illegally and unconstitutionally in Bolivia, and therefore was not entitled to any indemnity at all. Petrobrás and Itamaraty promptly reacted with "surprise and indignation" to the statement, and reaffirmed that, in every country where the company operates, it does so strictly within the law. Morales made from Vienna other inflammatory and disparaging statements about Brazil, leaving Lula and his foreign minister "indignant and astounded". Lula was exasperated; his foreign minister reacted in a moderate tone, stressing that Brazil would defend its interests, and Petrobrás would know how to defend its own. In effect, presidents Morales and Chávez with their antics managed to overshadow if not wreck the Vienna Summit. Granted that the atmosphere was already lukewarm at best for lack of concrete mutual trade concessions, one does not convene 60 heads of state or government for nothing, but the destructive posture of Venezuela – leaving CAN, posing conditions for its entry into Mercosul, etc., and the aggressive language of Evo Morales – left most other governments perplexed. None of Brazil's foreign policy objectives at the summit (e.g. obtaining concessions for the Doha talks) could be accomplished, because Morales and Chávez stole the scene and pre-empted discussions. In effect, they wrecked the meeting. Morales denied that he had ever said that Petrobrás had been operating in Bolivia under illegal contracts and was guilty of tax evasion and contraband. He blamed the press for reporting it. (Lula pretended that he had not heard the recording of Morales' actual statements).

The Brazilian Minister of Mines & Energy, Silas Rondeau, and the president of Petrobrás, José Sérgio Gabrielli, accompanied by several company directors, arrived in La Paz on May 10 to begin negotiations with their Bolivian counterparts, Hydrocarbons Minister Andrés Soliz Rada and YPFB president Jorge Alvarado, about specific consequences of Bolivia's forceful nationalisation of oil & gas tremendous pent-up resentment against Brazil among Morales' cohorts, and this caused absolute dismay since Brazil since it sees itself as a country eminently friendly towards its neighbours and particularly Bolivia – with which there is a perfect convergence of interests revolving around gas – especially under Lula, whom Morales, until the nationalisation, had repeatedly called his "elder brother". Since Chávez's intervention and Morales' May 30 trip to Havana, no longer.

The only concrete outcome far of the talks in La Paz was the creation of working groups to discuss the principal points involved in the nationalisation. Brazil reiterated its position of "absolute respect for the sovereign decisions of the government and people of Bolivia". There was no specific mention of Petrobrás' right to indemnity, but two bilateral commissions will define "contracts" and "compensatory mechanisms". The two bilateral commissions consist of (i) the Minister of Hydrocarbons of Bolivia and the Minister of Mines & Energy of Brazil, and the presidents of YPFB and Petrobrás; and (ii) a technical commission sudivided into three working groups. The two delegations agreed that "the proposal for revision of gas prices should be treated in a rational and equitable manner, as stated in the Declaration of Puerto Iguazú and under the mechanisms established in the contract to buy and sell natural gas".

On May 16, Petrobrás president José Sérgio Gabrielli testified before the Foreign Relations Committee of the Brazilian Senate about the company's plans in Bolivia, saying that (i) all new investments in Bolivia have been suspended owing to prevalent uncertainty in the country; (ii) depending on the future course of negotiations, Petrobrás could withdraw from the refining sector in Bolivia altogether; (iii) there would only be an increase in the price of Bolivian gas if Petrobrás agreed, as it cannot be a unilateral decision; (iv) that, while negotiations proceed, Petrobrás would abide by the new Bolivian tax rules (a share of 82% in production); and (v) that Petrobrás is willing to be indemnified by Bolivia in natural gas for the expropriation (*sic*) of its assets and installations in the country, but insists on "a prior and fair" indemnity. Petrobrás received permission from the Brazilian Ministry of Mines & Energy (MME) to negotiate independently from the government its commercial deals with YPFB.

President Evo Morales on May 31 instructed Hydrocarbons Minister Andrés Soliz Rada to expedite negotiations with Brazil regarding the price of gas. Argentina and Brazil are currently the only customers for Bolivia's natural gas, but YPFB advised that it is working on a medium-term plan (4 to 5 years) to export gas (from the current level of 30 million m^3/d to 70 million m^3/d) to other South American countries – not including Brazil. When the latter decided on May 18 to cancel the planned expansion of Gasbol's capacity, from 30 to 45 million m^3/d, YPFB began to seek new buyers for its available 40 million m^3/d, among them Argentina (with which an agreement was concluded on June 29) and Paraguay.

On May 30, Minister Soliz said that his government intended to *double* the price of natural gas sold to Brazil, but Petrobrás received only on June 12 a notification to the effect that the Bolivian authorities wished to resume talks, and insists that it is abiding by the contract in force. This contract, valid through 2019 – albeit subject to quarterly adjustments – provides for the following: 3.53 dollars/MBTU for the first 16 million m^3/d, 4.21 dollars for the remaining 14 million m^3/d (under a take-or-pay clause), plus 1.70 dollars for transport. As of July 1 there will be a contractual readjustment of 11.34%, from the current 3.53 dollars to 3.93 dollars/MBTU. These readjustments are a function of price variations in a basket of three fuel oil prices with different sulphur contents. Between July 1999 and 2006, according to YPFB, the price has risen 437%. Since September last year, when Petrobrás discontinued the practice of absorbing the price differentials on imported Bolivian gas, the domestic price paid by Brazilian consumers has already increased by 26.78%. Given the cost of transport, gas prices for consumers in the southern and southeastern states of Brazil, e.g. São Paulo, will hover around 6 dollars/MBTU, a significant increase. It must be understood, however, that this has nothing to do with negotiations between YPFB and Petrobrás on the new and higher price the Bolivian government wishes to charge for its gas, independently of the much higher taxation the nationalisation decree has imposed.

Evo Morales missed no occasion, at several Mercosul summits, to appeal to Lula to apply pressure on Petrobrás in order to relent in its demands. What is being discussed is the return of Petrobrás' two refineries and compensation therefor. Petrobrás has refused to discuss the price issue, invoking the contract in force through 2019, which envisages quarterly adjustment, and these have indeed been implemented. Another topic raised, but on which likewise no progress has been made, is that of a calendar for Petrobrás to relinquish control of its nationalised Bolivian assets. The atmosphere is tense, replete with accusations against Petrobrás' alleged malfeasance. The 45-day period prior to possible resort to arbitration expired on June 23, if one counts that it started with the May 10 visit to La Paz of a Brazilian delegation headed by Energy Minister Silas Rondeau, but. dilatory tactics are evident. Petrobrás' negotiators will continue to attend these weekly negotiating sessions, however inconclusive and unproductive, in order to avoid at all costs the charge that they are breaking off the dialogue.

Apparently negotiations with other international oil companies are similarly stalled. There is a suspicion on the Brazilian side that one possible reason behind the Bolivian posture may be that president Evo Morales may be manoeuvering to have Venezuela's PDVSA pre-empt the role played so far by Petrobrás and other IOCs. President Chávez promised to invest in Bolivia 1.5 billion dollars, the same amount that Petrobrás had invested over a decade. Another hypothesis, which is quite plausible, is that Morales wants to await the outcome of Brazilian elections in October to plead again with Lula to intercede with Petrobrás on behalf of Bolivia.

E. Brazil Will Be Energy-independent by 2008

Belatedly, but nonetheless in earnest, the government of Brazil now plans to become independent from imports of Bolivian gas by 2008. As President Lula phrased it, this does not by any means signify that Brazil will cease to import gas from Bolivia, possibly in increasing volumes to meet expanding domestic demand, "as a way to help the people of Bolivia". It does mean, however, that two years hence Brazil will no longer depend, as much as it does now, on Bolivian gas, because, by a combination of policies, it will by then be self-sufficient in energy production *lato sensu*, and not only, as now, in petroleum. That is the upshot of an extraordinary meeting, on May 18, 2006, of the Brazilian National Council on Energy Policy (CNPE), a Cabinet-level advisory body to the President, and this time chaired by him, whose directive was that Brazil must henceforth be self-sufficient in *every* source of energy. That is in itself a far-reaching, strategic decision. Highlights of CNPE's meeting:

– Petrobrás will anticipate, from 2010 to 2007, domestic gas production from its reserves in the Espírito Santo offshore basin.

– The company will, accordingly, accelerate the construction of its gas pipeline network in the Southeastern and Southern regions.

– Petrobrás will install three plants for re-gasification of imported LNG, in the Northeast, Southeast and South of Brazil, with a total capacity of processing 34 million m^3/d.

– The 8th Round of E&P concessions by ANP will be anticipated, from December to August of this year. (This proved to be technically impossible, but 8R will be scheduled for October).

– ANP has since suspended the tender for expansion of the Bolivia-Brazil gas pipeline (Gasbol). The three principal bidders – Petrobrás, Repsol and Total – withdrew their proposals, while British Gas and PanAmerican Energy requested a 180-day postponement of the tender.

– Petrobrás will spend 900 million dollars over the next three years to avoid a natural gas deficit of 15 million m^3/d resulting from the suspension of its investments in Bolivia. LNG imports seem to be a key element in resolving the current crisis. While it will cost more than natural gas imported from Bolivia, it does constitute a viable alternative, and a floating plant could be operational in 18 months; land-based plants would require 2 to 3 years to be built.

Brazilian foreign minister Celso Amorim travelled to La Paz on May 21-22, 2006 in order to meet with President Evo Morales and his key Cabinet ministers. Amorim's mission was a complex and difficult one. It included an official invitation to Evo Morales soon to visit Lula in Brasília (now scheduled for September 20), hopefully leading to a more positive dialogue between the two countries. Amorim travelled to La Paz strengthened by the Brazilian government's decision to emancipate itself from dependency on gas imported from Bolivia, and by Petrobrás' decision, ratified by the government, to suspend further investments in the Andean country. Moreover, his negotiating brief emphasised Brazil's wish to be compensated for the loss of its rights and assets in Bolivia owing to the nationalisation decree. Concretely, the Minister insisted that contracts signed by Petrobrás be respected, under penalty of seeking arbitration. In addition, he insisted that Petrobrás conduct an independent audit to confront that undertaken by Bolivia. Evo Morales wants to preserve the Brazilian market for Bolivian gas, and indeed expand it. He also desires Brazilian financial and technical co-operation.

The Bolivian government had already acknowledged the Brazilian decisions of not building a second gas pipeline, of not increasing the volume of imported gas, and of installing LNG plants. These were presented to the Brazilian Congress by the president of Petrobrás on May 16. The Bolivian authorities had not, however, been apprised of the decision of CNPE, taken two days later, to anticipate to 2008 the domestic production of an additional 24.2 million m^3/d of natural gas (a volume equivalent to current imports from Bolivia) and to substitute ethanol for gas as fuel in thermo-electric plants. Thus, the situation has radically changed in relation to that prevalent on May 1st, the date of the nationalisation decree. Far from Lula's original attitude of appeasement (which earned him enormous domestic criticism). It has hardened into a tough negotiating position, which endorses and vindicates, the initial reaction of Petrobrás.

Bolivia's contribution to the net profits of Petrobrás during the first quarter of 2006 (R$6,67 billion) amounted to 13 million dollars, i.e. 0.42% of the company's revenue. Petrobrás advises that it has the capability to replace with fuel oil the entire gas supply imported from Bolivia, equivalent to 100,000 boe/day, in the unlikely event that there should be an interruption of gas supply. Current Brazilian consumption of natural gas is 200,000 boe/d. Petrobrás exported 250,000 b/d of fuel oil and other petroleum by-products during the first quarter of 2006, and could re-direct part of this volume to the domestic market. Another possibility would be to replace imported natural gas by increasing the proportion of alcohol mixed to petrol, from the current 20% to 25%, as it had been prior to the sharp increase in ethanol prices in Brazil, earlier this year. Under Petrobrás' new strategic plan, the company plans to invest 18 billion dollars through 2010 (2 billion dollars more from other companies) for gas production in the Santos basin, but may add the cost of building three re-gasification plants to process imported LNG. Having suffered a severe blow to its interests in Bolivia, Petrobrás now seeks to diversify its sources of supply of natural gas, and is investing for the purpose in Argentina, Chile, Colombia, Peru, Ecuador and Venezuela. The company hopes to gradually replace Bolivian gas with that produced elsewhere in South America, and with deep pockets (12.3 billion dollars), fully one-third of Petrobrás' new projects to be carried out this year are located outside Brazil.

During the Caracas summit on July 4, the presidents of Bolivia and Brazil had a brief private meeting. Half an hour was enough for Lula – who wished to pursue a "positive agenda" with Bolivia – to offer Evo Morales financing from Brazilian national development bank BNDES, conditioned to the supply of Brazilian-made goods and services, and the involvement of Brazilian enterprises. In the aggregate, the as yet unquantified line of credit offered to Bolivia may well reach 1 billion dollars. This decision has at least surprised well-informed Brazilians, at a time when Petrobrás is locked in battle with YPFB over the gas supply contract, and Morales' agrarian reform scheme may eventually result in the expropriation of Brazilian soya farmers from the border areas they have settled. Lula may have tried to placate the radical wing of his PT party, or he may have tried to pre-empt Chávez's financial and technical help to Bolivia, which tends to undermine Brazil's influence. The least that can be said about this offer of financing from BNDES is that it was ill-timed, and undercuts Petrobrás' tough stance in its negotiations with YPFB.

Brazilian authorities – the presidents of Petrobrás and BNDES – took great pains to try and justify, with convoluted explanations aimed at a sceptical domestic audience, the concession of credits to Bolivia at this juncture, saying e.g. that "credits and price negotiations are completely different things", that "the credits are part of the Brazilian government's policy of maintaining good relations with Bolivia", etc. BNDES has similar financing operations with six other Latin American countries, for a total amount of 3 billion dollars, and they are all guaranteed by the respective governments.

The Bolivian authorities are convinced that the negotiations between YPFB and Petrobrás depend on the outcome of Brazilian elections, scheduled for October, and that Brazil's tough stance is due to Lula's desire to avoid the opposition's criticism of his earlier leniency towards Bolivia. While Petrobrás wishes to conduct these negotiations on a purely technical level, the Bolivian side, from Evo Morales down, tries to politicise them. Since the nationalisation decree established a 180-day deadline (which expires on November 1st, i.e. after the run-off in Brazil's elections), Bolivian leaders hope for a better deal if Lula should be re-elected.

There is another aspect to this controversy. YPFB wishes to modify the criteria for quarterly price readjustments, stipulated in the contract to include aviation kerozene (which in the past year suffered a 45% increase in Brazil and is readjusted on a fortnightly basis, whereas petrol and diesel, which account for 60% of Petrobrás' revenue, have remained with stable prices since last October, despite successive records in spiralling petroleum prices).

At their negotiating session held on July 12-13, 2006, at Santa Cruz de la Sierra, Petrobrás representatives notified their YPFB counterparts that the Brazilian company would not accept price increases for Bolivian gas beyond the quarterly adjustment procedure specified in the contract in force. Bolivia had lately wanted to increase the price to "at least" 5 dollars/MBTU, i.e. a 20% increase and the same price agreed with Argentina, but lower than the 7.50 dollars originally claimed. Nevertheless, Petrobrás was irreductible, saying that under the readjustment procedure the price had increased from 1.23 dollars/MBTU in July 1999 to 4.30 dollars/MBTU as of July 1st, 2006. As a result, the Bolivian side for the first time admitted resorting to international arbitration in New York.

There are ongoing negotiations about the Brazilian company's two refineries and gas fields, and the deadline for these (180 days) expires on October. On July 18, the Bolivian government initiated an audit of the assets of nine IOCs, including Petrobrás, to verify their claim of 3.6 billion dollars worth of assets. The audit must be concluded within 90 days, and will cost 5.2 million dollars. There was another Mercosul summit, on July 20-21, at Córdoba, Argentina, when Brazil took over, for the remainder of the year, the presidency pro tempore of the block, which Bolivia was formally invited to join. President Morales again tried in vain to persuade Lula to intervene with Petrobrás to moderate its position regarding the negotiation on gas prices, but the Brazilian president was adamant that these negotiation will be conducted independently by Petrobrás.

On July 24, the Bolivian government charged both Petrobrás and Repsol-YPF with fraud in the instruments measuring output in the gas fields of San Alberto and Margherita, in the department of Tarija, operated by the two enterprises. The local companies hired by YPFB to conduct the audits also complained of lack of support from Petrobrás and Repsol-YPF, which declined to comment officially but questioned informally the impartiality of the auditors. Much is at stake, since the payment of indemnities to IOCs by the Bolivian government is conditioned by the results of the audit. Petrobrás president Gabrielli responded immediately, labelling the Bolivian charges "absurd", as control of the amper-proof measuring instruments is automatic and regularly inspected by YPFB. And the Brazilian Minister of Mines & Energy, Silas Rondeau, endorsed the protest.

F. Analysis

The crisis with Bolivia is far from over, and the case was used to highlight Petrobrás' complex interaction with its home country and the government that is its majority share-holder, but by no means the only one. The company, through no fault of its own, has a somewhat schizophrenic relationship with the Brazilian state. While acting globally as the 8th largest international oil company, with a market value of 91.2 billion dollars, and expanding aggressively overseas, the government bureaucracy in Brasília tends to regard it as an appendix to the Ministry of Mines & Energy, and indeed of the political party in power, which capitalises on the company's achievements as part of its electoral propaganda. As previously shown in this essay, on the question of pricing of domestic fuels – in regard to which Petrobrás would wish to align itself with international prices – it is systematically required to absorb the brunt of rapidly rising prices, lest inflation be fanned by passing these price increases to consumers. Again, Petrobrás is compelled by the government to deviate from its core business – production of oil & gas – to shoulder the burden of such other energy-related activities as thermo-electric power generation, and, more recently, the production, distribution and marketing of bio-fuels. All of these activities must be highly subsidised, and Petrobrás, rather than the government, is expected to defray the cost of these heavy subsidies.

Conversely, having for the first 44 years of its existence (until the Petroleum Law of 1997) enjoyed an absolute monopoly over every segment of the petroleum industry, it is understandable that Petrobrás should be pre-eminent in, e.g. oil & gas exploration and production (it has an unmatched data-base on the country's sedimentary basins), in refining (it has 98% of the country's refining capacity), in piped gas distribution (it has participation in nearly every state company established for the purpose), in petrochemicals production, and in the construction and operation of pipelines throughout the country. Thus, there are lingering after-effects of the monopoly, abolished nine years ago, and under a government such as president Lula's, which is ideologically committed to re-assertion of the paramount role of the state in the economy, Petrobrás is more than ever an instrumentality of the state.

The Bolivian episode exposed the glaring discrepancies between, on the one hand, Lula's initial appeasement policy towards Evo Morales' nationalisation, and on the other Petrobrás' intransigent defence of its corporate interests, threatened by Bolivia's de facto expropriation. In this electoral year, Lula cannot afford to have significant increases in gas prices – the inevitable consequence of that nationalisation, and its savage tax increases, even if actual price negotiations remain in abeyance – passed on to consumers, who are also voters. As a matter of public policy, Petrobrás will foreseeably have to absorb the impact of these increases, to the detriment of the company's cash flow, at least until after the election. And thus its dual role again comes to the fore.

Yet another illustration of that dualism lies in the question of foreign policy. The Brazilian government has one, and in Lula's administration it has been particularly proactive, and carried out by a highly professional foreign service. One may disagree with the policy itself, but there is no doubt that it constitutes a consistent framework for Brazil's diplomacy. On the other hand, Petrobrás, with its far-flung operations on nearly every continent, and with its own representatives around the globe, has a foreign policy of its own, geared to procuring for the company the best possible opportunities for its petroleum business. It is fair to say that it does and will pursue it independently, but without contravening the official policy defended by the Foreign Ministry, with which there is a continuing process of consultation.

Nevertheless, inevitably there are differences of perception. Arguably, the technical staff of Petrobrás would not have embarked on oil E&P in Cuba, or on President Chávez's polemic mega-project of a 10,000 km gas pipeline crossing all of South America at a cost of close to 25 billion dollars, were it not for Lula's ideological affinities with the governments in question. The company is caught between its allegiance to the government it serves and its own policy goals, which include accountability to its share-holders. To sum up, Petrobrás, like other national oil companies, must tread a delicate path between these two paradygms.

Oil Nationalism, Property Rights, and Political Regimes

A Comparative Study of Colombia and Mexico in the twentieth Century

Marcelo BUCHELI

University of Illinois, United States of America

In 1938, the Mexican government shocked the world after the expropriating the assets of the foreign oil corporations operating in Mexico. This was not the first important conflict between a national state and multinational oil corporations, nor was it the first major expropriation of oil companies. However, the magnitude of the expropriation and Mexico's proximity to the United States, home country of some of the expropriated companies, made this event particularly important. After the expropriation, the Mexicans created a national state-owned oil company (PEMEX) and forbade foreign participation in their oil industry in the years afterwards.

The events that led to the expropriation did not evolve overnight. Since 1910, Mexico had gone through a civil war, which started with the overthrown of the long dictatorship of Porfirio Díaz and was followed by a series of struggles for power between those who had originally rebelled against Díaz. A revolutionary government wrote a new constitution in 1917, which declared Mexico's subsoil property of the Mexican state, providing legal grounds for expropriation. Although the government did not use this law, it pended over foreign investors as a Sword of Damocles and was eventually used by President Lázaro Cárdenas in 1938.

Other oil producing countries were closely watching the events in Mexico. The success or failure of Mexico in changing the oil legislation could provide a model for other countries with oil multinational corporations. In this chapter I analyze the influence the Mexican events had in Colombia, the third largest oil producing country in Latin America in that period, and how the Colombian elite and the Colombian government adapted the Mexican experience to their own interests. I argue that in different historical moments the Colombian government considered the Mexican government's actions worth imitating (like declaring the subsoil property of the nation or creating a national oil company). However, they did not want to emulate the Mexicans too closely for two reasons: First, the negotiations around oil concessions in Colombia were tightly tied to the country's negotiations over Panama with the United States. Second, the Colombian elite did not want to create a national oil company through expropriation of private property, because they considered it would create a terrible precedent of lack of security of property rights. The reason why the Mexicans could do an expropriation was because the revolutionary government had the working class as its main constituency, while the Colombian government represented the national industrial or merchant elite. So, the Colombian government chose to wait until the contracts with the multinationals expired, rather than to violate the contracts and expropriate the foreign corporations. In summary, the chapter shows that although Colombia followed Mexico in several steps the Mexicans made in order to gain control over their oil resources, the fact that the Colombian government never represented the working class led it to develop a nationalist policy that did not challenge property rights.

Rafael Reyes and Porfirio Díaz: Modernization through Foreign Investment

During the first years of the twentieth century, Colombia and Mexico had similar political regimes. Colombia was recovering from the bloody "War of the Thousand Days" (1899-1902), a conflict between Liberals and Conservatives, which destroyed the country's economic infrastructure. The triumphant Conservatives, under the leadership of President Rafael Reyes, decided that the only way to jump-start the economy was through foreign investment, so after 1902, the government actively sought the arrival of foreign corporations.[1] The Conservatives remained in power until 1930, and during these years Colombia enjoyed unprecedented economic growth through coffee exports, the birth of the manufacturing industry, foreign loans, and foreign direct investment.

Mexico, on the other hand, was enjoying unprecedented times of prosperity under the leadership of dictator Porfirio Díaz. Díaz ended a long period of political instability when he took power in 1876. Ruling with an iron fist, Díaz managed to have growth rates of 8% (1876-1900)

---

[1]   Vélez, Humberto, "Rafael Reyes: Quinquenio, regimen politico y capitalismo (1904-1909)", in Tirado, Alvaro, *Nueva Historia de Colombia*, Vol. 1, Bogotá, Planeta, 1989, 193-196.

through promotion of foreign investment in oil, railroads, public utilities, banking, and agriculture. It was during the Díaz administration that most multinationals arrived to Mexico and made this country an important oil producer. Colombian President Rafael Reyes was a strong admirer of Díaz, and considered the Mexican president's agenda the best way to reach economic prosperity and political stability. Although Reyes did not manage to attract amounts of foreign investment comparable to those of Mexico, he undoubtedly created the conditions for the further modernization Colombia went through in the next three decades.

Foreign oil corporations considered Díaz and Reyes the perfect enlightened rulers for the Latin American countries. Presidents with little opposition, obsessed with modernization, and eager to attract foreign capital. In a letter to his superiors, an official of the British oil firm Pearson and Son Ltd. expressed "the sort of concession that we are trying to get does not appeal to any government and that it is very difficult to obtain in a country with a real parliamentary system; it is to my mind only easy in countries of a one man government like Mexico under President Díaz, Venezuela under Gómez, or Colombia under Reyes."[2]

Making the Subsoil State Property: Success in Mexico, Opposition in Colombia

Not all Mexicans were enjoying the economic prosperity of the Díaz era. Some members of the upper classes felt neglected by the dictator believing that only those belonging to Díaz's inner circle were getting most of the economic growth benefits. For the peasants, the economic growth had brought with it land expropriation by big landowners or multinationals leaving them as mere landless cheap labor. These tensions exploded in 1910 when some rich landowners rebelled against Díaz, sparking a national-wide rebellion from the lower classes against the regime and the economic system it had created. The first upper class rebels eventually lost control of the insurgency they had encouraged and a bloody war started between the different factions that had rebelled against Díaz in 1910 in a conflict that lasted until 1920. In that period 825,000 Mexicans died (most of them peasants) and the rural areas were devastated.

The Revolution made Mexico lose its previous advantages for foreign investors. As the revolutionaries consolidated their power, they gradually changed the oil legislation. In 1917, the revolutionary government wrote a new constitution that declared the Mexican subsoil

---

[2]   Philip, George, *Oil and Politics in Latin America: Nationalist Movements and State Companies*, Cambridge, Cambridge University Press, 1982, 32.

property of the Mexican nation opening the possibility of expropriation (Article 27). Moreover, the government got closer to the increasingly belligerent oil labor unions, raised taxation to big corporations, and even showed some sympathy towards the Bolshevik Revolution. Much to the concern of the foreign corporations the government even started considering making the article retroactive to include the concessions granted during the Díaz administration.[3]

During the period in which Mexico fell into chaos, the Colombian government was facing difficulties at attracting foreign investment due to the rise of anti-American feelings after the loss of Panama in 1903. The United States had openly supported the separatist movement of the Colombian province of Panama taking control of what would become the "Canal Zone" later on. In 1909, the Colombian government signed the Cortes-Root Treaty with which it recognized Panama as an independent state. The opposition to this treaty in Colombia was so strong that Reyes limited individual freedom in order to control criticism. This however, was not enough to stop the opposition from the press and street demonstrations against to what many considered a humiliating treaty with the US. Unable to control the opposition to the Cortes-Root Treaty, Reyes resigned in that same year of 1909.[4]

In 1913, the British firm Pearson and Son Ltd., started negotiations with the Colombian government for an oil concession. The United States government distrusted Pearson, who they saw as one of the conspirators for the outbreak of the Mexican Revolution. Pearson and Son was a very powerful company in Mexico, producing 60% of that country's output through its subsidiary El Aguila, and was looking for new sources in South America.[5] In order to reduce nationalist opposition, Pearson proposed the Colombian government to create a Colombian oil company with which Pearson would work. Although the government liked the idea, it was reluctant to go ahead because these were also times in which Colombia was negotiating the payment of reparations

---

[3] Brown, Jonathan, *Oil and Revolution in Mexico*, Berkeley, University of California Press, 1993, 239-240.

[4] López Michelsen, Alfonso, "La cuestión del Canal desde la secesión de Panamá hasta el Tratado de Montería", in Tirado, *Nueva Historia de Colombia*, 154-159.

[5] Lael, Richard, *Arrogant Diplomacy: US Policy Toward Colombia, 1903-1922*, Wilmington, Scholarly Resources, 1987, 88. For the skirmishes between Pearson and the US companies in Mexico, see Brown, Jonathan, *Oil and Revolution in Mexico*, Berkeley, University of California, 1993.

from the United States for the loss of Panama.[6] In spite of this, Pearson continued doing explorations in Colombia.[7]

The US government was following the events in Mexico more closely. Although many in Washington feared that the chaotic political situation could threaten the constant flow of oil from Mexico, the production and exports of that country only increased during the first years of the revolution. The different factions fighting the war saw oil as the only stable source of income, so they fought for the control of the oil regions, but did not want to destroy the industry. A short military adventure President Wilson ordered in 1914, proved to be a disaster. Believing that some of the revolutionary factions and the oil companies would welcome a US military intervention, Wilson sent the marines to the port of Veracruz, only generating unity among the Mexicans and rejection by the oil companies who believed that this action put them under higher risk.[8]

While intervening militarily in Mexico, Wilson was also busy trying to normalize its relations with Colombia. In 1914, the US Ambassador in Colombia signed the so-called Urrutia-Thomson Treaty in which the United States acknowledged its participation in the Panama secession and the negative effects this had in Colombia, committing to pay 25,000,000 dollars in reparations. The treaty still needed to be ratified in the US Senate and found a strong opposition from the opposition Republican Party which considered the document a *mea culpa* for getting control of the Panama Canal, which they considered "one of the great acts, of a great president, in a great era of American history."[9] However, some Democratic senators and President Woodrow Wilson considered it crucial to normalize relationships with Colombia, a country, which they considered with great potential as oil producer.[10] In addition, aware of the moves Pearson was doing in Colombia the Wilson administration

---

[6] Letter from Ribbon to Lord Murray, January 25, 1914. Pearson (S.) and Son Ltd. Papers, Reel 133, LAC. Benson Library, University of Texas at Austin.

[7] Lael, *Arrogant Diplomacy*, 94.

[8] Brown, *Oil and Revolution*, 186-203.

[9] Parks, Taylor, *Colombia and the United States, 1765-1934*, Durham, Duke University Press, 1935, 451. The London *Times* saw the opposition to Wilson's *mea culpa* as very dangerous for Wilson's political life as well as for the American control of Colombian oil. See, "More Difficulties for Mr Wilson: Colombia Treaty in Danger", *The Times* (London), April 10, 1914: 6.

[10] "Standard Oil's Interests in South American Fields: Has Extensive Holdings in Peru and Rumored Acquiring More in Colombia and Ecuador", *Wall Street Journal*, October 20, 1919: 2.

considered that the treaty was a great opportunity to open the doors of Colombian oil to American companies.[11]

Standard Oil (New Jersey) arrived to Mexico in 1917, the year of the new constitution and Article 27. The oil companies had recently created the Association of Foreign Oil Producers in Mexico, in which the newly arrived Standard had a dominant position because of its size. The main concern of the Association members was the possibility of the retroactive effects of Article 27, and the companies were pressurizing the US and British governments to directly intervene and stop the Mexicans government. For Standard Oil (New Jersey), the main problem was not the retroactivity of Article 27 but the very existence of the article. This time, however, believing that the oil companies were supporting the opposition Republican Party, Democratic President Wilson decided to simply send a formal protest. The companies accused Wilson of ineptitude and started openly supporting the Republican Party. To make things worse, the companies in the Association could not agree on whether they wanted economic sanctions (the preferred option of the big companies) or an invasion of Mexico (the preferred option of the small companies). Additionally, Texas' producers were lobbying against protecting the companies operating in Mexico fearing that a stable Mexico would become a strong competitor for Texas' oil.[12] In short, creating a producers' association did not work. The Association's lobby was unsuccessful in Washington and could not maintain unity among its members. In fact, frustrated with their differences with the big companies, the smaller pro-invasion companies eventually withdrew and created their own association.[13]

Around the times the American companies were dealing with the uncertainties created by Article 27, the Colombian government made some new moves. With the debate over the Urrutia-Thomson Treaty on the Panama reparations still going on, in 1916 Tropical Oil Company, an American corporation, purchased the territory of the De Mares concession and started drilling in 1918 and made its first discovery in 1919.[14] The De Mares concession belonged to a wealthy Colombian who never managed to exploit it and sold it to Tropical. As soon as Tropical started pumping oil, the Liberal opposition pressured the government for a more nationalistic legislation. In addition, according to the Liberal newspaper *El Tiempo* most of the Colombian territory had already been

[11] Lael, *Arrogant Diplomacy*, 93.

[12] Brown, *Oil and Revolution*, 239-252.

[13] Brown, *Oil and Revolution*, 245.

[14] Gibb, George and Evelyn Knowlton, *The History of Standard Oil Company (New Jersey): The Resurgent Years, 1911-1927*, New York, Harper, 1956, 369-370.

divided among foreign companies. The government reacted to the criticisms by writing a new legislation, which declared the country's subsoil property of the state, similar to what the Mexican revolutionaries wrote for in their constitution.[15] The oil companies considered the new legislation as a potential threat and the US government decided to postpone the ratification of the Urrutia-Thomson Treaty until the Colombian government made some changes to the oil law.[16] Fearing the loss of the Panama reparations, Colombian President Marco Fidel Suárez informed the US government and the American companies that they had nothing to fear from the new oil legislation. However, this attitude only generated more internal opposition, which eventually led to Suárez resignation.[17] In December 1919, the Colombian Supreme Court declared the law unconstitutional ending with the impasse that risked the Urrutia-Thomson Treaty.[18]

In the meantime, despite all the protests from the companies and the US government, the Mexican government kept Article 27 hanging over the oil companies, like a sword of Damocles. The companies kept operating with the constant possibility of expropriation. After 1920, the violent phase of the revolution finished, but the new revolutionary government did not act against the companies because it considered them an essential actor in the country's reconstruction. The companies kept operating in Mexico under a relative stability that lasted until 1934.

Expanding Operations in Revolutionary Mexico and Conservative Colombia in the 1920s

In 1920, Standard Oil Company (New Jersey) acquired Tropical Oil, starting operations in Colombia. The Urrutia-Thomson Treaty still needed its final ratification, so Standard sought for ways to speed up the process by sending to Colombia Colonel James Flanagan, the company's main negotiator for South America. The Colombian government had granted a thirty-year concession to Tropical Oil. Keeping his affiliation with Standard secret, Flanagan negotiated with the Colombian

---

[15] López, "La cuestión del Canal", 164.

[16] Wilkins, Mira, "Multinational Oil Companies in South America in the 1920s: Argentina, Bolivia, Brazil, Chile, Colombia, Ecuador, and Peru." *Business History Review*, Vol. 48, No. 3 (Autumn 1974): 430; Wilkins, Mira, *The Maturing of Multinational Enterprise: American Business Abroad from 1914 to 1970*, Cambridge, Harvard University Press, 1974, 27; López, "La cuestión del Canal", 164.

[17] Melo, Jorge Orlando, "De Carlos E. Restrepo a Marco Fidel Suárez. Republicanismo y gobiernos conservadores", in Tirado, *Nueva Historia de Colombia*, Vol. 3: 237-241.

[18] Colmenares, Germán, "Ospina y Abadía: La política en el decenio de los veinte", in Tirado, *Nueva Historia de Colombia*, Vol. 3: 243-251.

government the creation of a new "independent" pipeline company, the Andian National Corporation – registered in Canada. Andian would be in charge of building the pipeline and providing Tropical (or the Colombian government once the concession finished) with transportation services. In order to get the Colombian government on its side, Flanagan traveled to Washington and informally lobbied at the US government to get the approval of the Urrutia-Thomson treaty. As one of the main negotiators for Colombia in Washington, Flanagan gained a privileged position within the Colombian government, who approved the contract with Andian after the American government accepted to pay Colombia the reparations in 1922.[19] Pearson had left Colombia in 1919 after the new legislation and by pressures from the British government, so the American supremacy on the Colombian oil sector was secured after Standard's arrival.

After 1922, Colombia started a new period of economic prosperity. The Panama reparations provided free cash the government used for public works and as collateral for cheap foreign loans (a period known as the "Dance of the Millions"). The industrial sector flourished like never before and coffee exports boomed. Economic changes led to social transformations: an urban working class appeared and the industrial elite became increasingly powerful with respect to the traditional landowning class. These transformations also permitted the growth of the opposition Liberal party, which had a larger constituency due to the creation of labor unions and the enlargement of urban population.

During the 1920s, the Mexican oil sector started suffering some problems that were not related to the revolution. After 1923, the companies and the government realized that Mexico was simply running out of oil despite the efforts made by the companies to increase production. This led to a steady decline in exports during the 1920s, a period in which Venezuela and Colombia, were increasing their production.[20] In fact, in 1920, Standard Oil acquired Tropical Oil in Colombia and started operating in that country.

---

[19] The information on the role of Flanagan is taken from the unpublished manuscripts of the interviews made by Henrietta Larson for her classic books on the history of Standard Oil (New Jersey). See, Larson, Henrietta, "Reports from Interviews, Standard Oil (NJ), 1944-45", Boston, Harvard Graduate School of Business Administration, unpublished manuscript, 68-76.

[20] Haber, Stephen, Noel Maurer, and Armando Razo, "When Law Does Not Matter: The Rise and Decline of the Mexican Oil Industry", *Journal of Economic History*, Vol. 1 (March 2003): 1-30; Brown, Jonathan, "Why Foreign Companies Shifted Their Production from Mexico to Venezuela in the 1920s", *American Historical Review*, Vol. 90, No. 2 (June 1996): 243-276.

Mexican Influences on the Colombian Conservative Nationalism in the Late 1920s

The Conservative Party never changed its anti-left-wing labor union position. However, the late 1920s showed a version of oil nationalism influenced by the events in Mexico but without the labor unionism component. The Conservatives were aware of their decreasing popularity and the perception the country had of the power of the US multinationals. In 1927, the Ministry of Industries, José Antonio Montalvo, tried to increase the royalties paid by foreign multinationals from 10% to 15%. Tropical, however, rejected the idea forcing Montalvo to look for other means to increase the government's bargaining power with the company. Montalvo's strategy was to secretly approach Anglo-Persian and negotiate with them a concession in the Urabá region close to the Panama border. The government signed a contract with Anglo-Persian's secret envoy, colonel H.F. Yates in July 1927. The contract needed the Congress' final approval.[21]

Montalvo wanted to use recently expired Barco Concession to attract the British. The Barco Concession, in a territory close to the Venezuela border had been awarded to the Carib Syndicate in 1918, but the company did not comply with its obligations to exploit the oil within the time stipulated, and the concession was declared null in 1926.[22]

The secret contract between Yates and the Colombian government was filtered to the press causing an outrage in both the US companies and the opposition. Standard informed the US Department of State and lobbied in the Colombian Congress for a rejection of the contract. Although the US companies did not get the Department of State support they wanted, the British government saw this issue as a source of potential conflict with the United States in the Western Hemisphere and decided to cancel Anglo-Persian projects in Colombia.[23]

Some members of the Conservative Party also opposed the Yates contract but for different reasons. Charismatic Conservative leader, Laureano Gómez, accused the government of willing to put Colombia under the yoke of the British Empire and proposed as an alternative the nationalization of oil. Gómez, an ultra-right, Catholic fanatic, anti-Semitic, openly racist, and Mussolini admirer politician had also a strong dislike of the United States and the industrial elite of Medellín.

---

[21] De la Pedraja, René, *Petróleo, Electricidad, Carbón y Política en Colombia*, Bogotá, Ancora, 1993, 23-25; Colmenares, "Ospina y Abadía", 262.

[22] Rippy, Fred, *The Capitalists and Colombia*, New York, Vanguard, 1931, 135; Philip, *Oil and Politics*, 35.

[23] De la Pedraja, *Petróleo*, 27-28.

He believed in clear social hierarchies kept in order by the government and the Catholic Church. In spite of these beliefs, however, his proposal of oil nationalization made him popular among young Conservatives and Liberals.[24]

In spite of the opposition, the government continued with its own nationalistic agenda. In November 1927, Montalvo sent to Congress a new "Oil Emergency" law, which gave the government unlimited powers over the oil industry until a new nationalistic oil legislation was written. The "Emergency" law was approved in 1928, and afterwards Montalvo showed the press evidence that Tropical had not complied with its contract and announced that the De Mares concession would be nullified. This announcement provoked a strong reaction from the companies and the American embassy. The US Department of Commerce advised against buying Colombian bonds and the *Wall Street Journal* told its readers that Colombia was following the same steps of Mexico.[25] As a last resort, Montalvo sought the support of the Colombian elite, but was disappointed. In a poll he organized he found out that although the elite wanted an increase in royalties (as Montalvo), they did not want to conflict with the multinationals.[26]

In order to gain the support of the national elite, Montalvo proposed a new law in 1929, which dropped the idea of royalties increase, but forced the companies to sell 20% of the stock to Colombian citizens.[27] This idea got even more opposition than the previous ones. The oil companies considered it illegal, the nationalists that had supported Montalvo thought this was a step back from the previous initiatives, and many fellow Conservatives and several Liberals thought this put the US-Colombia relations in jeopardy.[28] With all these opposition, Montalvo's projects collapsed. The year after, Colombia went to new presidential elections with a divided and fatigued Conservative Party and a Liberal Party popular among the working class due to the government's actions in the banana and oil strikes. After thirty years in power, the Conservatives lost the elections and Liberal Enrique Olaya became the new president.

---

[24] Henderson, *Modernization in Colombia*, 147-148.

[25] "Colombian Senate Passes Oil Bill: Embodies Principles Aiming to Establish National Ownership of Subsoil With Retroactive Provisions", *Wall Street Journal*, November 14, 1927: 11; "Colombia Oil Laws Resemble Mexico: Provide Nationalization of Petroleum Industry and Provision for Retroactive Royalty Paymnets", *Wall Street Journal*, November 27 1917: 3; Colmenares, "Ospina y Abadía", 264.

[26] Colmenares, "Ospina y Abadía", 263-264; De la Pedraja, *Petróleo*, 28-32.

[27] Villegas, Jorge, *Petróleo Colombiano Ganancia Gringa*, Medellín, Prisma, 1971, 61.

[28] Colmenares, "Ospina y Abadía", 263-264; De la Pedraja, *Petróleo*, 32-33.

Approaching the Unions in Colombia and Mexico: Lázaro Cárdenas and Alfonso López

The decline of oil after 1923, plus the effects of the Great Depression generated new social pressures in Mexico. In 1934, the country elected left-wing presidential candidate Lázaro Cárdenas who blamed the foreign companies for the oil crisis. The foreign corporations did not hide their distrust of Cárdenas, and prepared for confrontation since the beginning. Jersey's management rejected its geologists' suggestion of proposing a joint venture with the Mexican government, as they feared it would set a precedent. Similarly, Shell's founder Henri Deterding accused the company's manager in Mexico of being "half Bolshevik" for proposing an adjustment to the new Mexican political situation. In an almost prophetic way the manager replied that "the sooner that these big international companies learn that in the world of today, if they want the oil they have to got to pay the price demanded, however unreasonable, the better it will be for them and their shareholders."[29]

The companies' strategy reflected their lack of will to work with the Mexican government, the trust they had in the US government actions, and their underestimation of the Mexican government's determination. In 1938, when the Mexican government told the companies to increase wages in proportion to their high profits, the companies threatened with leaving the country. The unions started taking over the plants while the government and the companies continued their negotiations for months. In March 18 1938, facing what he called the "rebellion" of the companies and the pressures of the labor unions, Cárdenas declared the expropriation of all the foreign oil properties.

The multinationals believed the US government would not allow Mexico to get away with the expropriation. However, the US government did not give the companies the support they expected due to a combination of foreign and domestic factors. According to the US Senate Commission investigating the US oil interests abroad, the government protection of oil companies operating in other countries started to decrease after 1930 due to the "Good Neighbor" policy, an application of the New Deal ideology at home and abroad, as well as the fact that the United States was an important oil producer.[30] The US ambassador himself even said: "it was scandalous that the companies should not

---

[29] Yergin, Daniel, *The Prize: The Epic Quest for Oil, Money and Power*, New York, Simon and Schuster, 1992, 273-274.

[30] United States Senate Special Committee, *American Petroleum Interests in Foreign Countries*, Washington, US Government Printing Office, 1946, 432.

have raised their wages to the level demanded."[31] The Senate commission acknowledged that these two factors put the American companies in a weaker position when confronting or bargaining with foreign governments.

With a new world conflict starting, President Roosevelt decided not to alienate the Mexican government and demanded a "fair compensation" for the expropriation.[32] The companies calculated a fair compensation in 250,000,000 dollars, while the Mexicans offered 7,000,000 dollars. After long negotiations in which Roosevelt personally intervened, the American and Mexican government agreed on a compensation of 29,000,000 dollars. The US government told the companies they were free to accept or reject the compensation, but that they could not expect further assistance from their government. Under these circumstances, the companies reluctantly accepted the Mexican compensation and lost their properties in that country.[33]

While the Mexicans succeeded in their expropriation project thanks to an alliance with the labor union movement and a new administration in Washington, Colombia was going through major political changes after 1930. The industrial elite of Medellín approached its former critic Conservative Laureano Gómez, who wanted to stop the rise of labor unionism. The interest of the factory owners on keeping labor cheap made Gómez their natural ally. On the other hand, the Liberals were divided in three factions. One led by Alfonso López Pumarejo, a strong advocate of labor and social reforms that was supported by the import and export merchants and the labor unions.[34] The commercial elite needed a working class with higher purchasing power and labor reforms were the best way to reach them. Another faction was Jorge Eliécer Gaitán's. Gaitán, a leader of working class origins who was very popular in poor urban neighborhoods and was a fierce critic of the way the government allied with the multinationals. Gaitán made the strongest criticism to the Abadía government after the Army's intervention in the banana strike of 1928. Finally, there was the faction led by President Olaya, who wanted a closer relationship with the US with timid social reforms.

---

[31] Philip, George, *Oil and Politics in Latin America: Nationalist Movements and State Companies*, Cambridge, Cambridge University Press, 1982, 56.

[32] Yergin, *The Prize*, 277-278.

[33] Randall, Stephen J., *United States Foreign Oil Policy, 1919-1948: For Profits and Security*, Montreal, McGill-Queen's University Press, 1985, 97-105; Yergin, *The Prize*, 275-277.

[34] Leal Buitrago, Francisco, *Estado y política en Colombia*, Bogotá, Siglo XXI Cerec, 1989, 160-165.

In 1930, Liberal Enrique Olaya took power as the new Colombian president. In order to assure the American multinationals that they were safe in Colombia, Olaya proposed the Congress a new oil law in 1930. Both the multinationals and the foreign banks expressed Olaya their interest in having a new friendlier legislation, which eliminated some clauses that survived from the Montalvo years. In addition, several New York banks informed Olaya that without new oil legislation, the country risked not having new loans in the future.[35] The law Olaya proposed to Congress eliminated the requirements to foreign oil companies had of a 25% minimum of Colombian workers, and the obligation to fully comply with the Colombian legislation without diplomatic arbitration. In addition, the law permitted the companies to finish their operations before the concession deadline, decreased royalties from 12.5-6% to 11-2%, decreased taxation on private property from 8-4% to 8-1%, and decreased taxes on pipelines operations in 50%.[36] The multinationals and the US government were not completely satisfied with the changes, however.[37] Under these circumstances, Olaya believed that the only way to get the multinationals and the foreign banks on his side was by using the Barco Concession.

The Barco Concession, as I explain above, was declared null by the Conservative government in 1926. The original grantee of the concession was the Carib Syndicate, which was later purchased by Doherty, and later sold to Gulf Oil Company.[38] Andrew Mellon, US Secretary of Treasury and founder of Gulf, suggested Olaya to re-establish the Barco Concession as a way to assure new loans in the future and to avoid more US opposition to his new oil legislation.[39] Olaya proposed the nullification of the previous nullification to the Barco Concession and found an initial strong opposition in Congress and the media.[40] However, Olaya convinced the opposition that without the Barco Concession the country's economic stability was under great risk. In June 1931, Congress approved the new oil legislation.

In 1934, the Liberals won the elections again with Alfonso López Pumarejo, also nicknamed as the "Roosevelt of the Andes." López won with the endorsement of the labor unions, and the Socialist and Communist parties. A former banker, López transformed the country through

---

[35] De la Pedraja, *Petróleo*, 40-46.
[36] Villegas, *Petróleo Colombiano*, 68.
[37] De la Pedraja, *Petróleo*, 46-47.
[38] Rippy, *Capitalists*, 143.
[39] De la Pedraja, *Petróleo*, 51-52.
[40] Estrada, Efraín, *Sucesos Colombianos, 1925-1950*, Medellín, Universidad de Antoquia, 1990, 348-359.

dramatic changes in the labor and social legislation. His main goal was to modernize Colombia following the model of the American New Deal. He approached the labor unions and got the endorsement of the Communist and Socialist parties.

López also increased taxation to big corporations. In fact, just during the first year of the tax reform Tropical Oil paid in one year as much taxes as it had paid in the preceding eight years.[41] Taxation kept increasing in the following years. From Col\$197,125 that Tropical paid in 1934, it jumped to Col\$1,108,908 in 1935, and 3,382,657 in 1936. In his 1935 report, the Minister of Industries (Jorge Perry), highlighted the way the government was making the oil companies to comply with the labor legislation and to contribute to the welfare of the producing regions.[42] The government proudly showed this as the only way with which it could increase its welfare expenses.[43]

In his first year (1934), López's sought to decrease the oil multinationals' power by proposing a law to create a state owned refinery. This project, however, faced the opposition of Standard and the US embassy. Not willing to confront the US, López changed his proposal coming with a new project in 1936 with which he created incentives for both foreign and national investors to build a new refinery in the country. In this proposal, the government permitted the operation of companies partially owned by foreign governments, something indirectly targeted to Anglo-Persian, a company López tried to attract to balance the US power in Colombia.[44] Anglo-Persian, however, did not come and Standard remained the most powerful oil company in the country.

The Creation of the National Oil State Companies: The Role of Labor Unions in Mexico and the Industrial Elite in Colombia

After the expropriation, the Mexican government started producing the oil itself through PEMEX, a state-owned monopoly. The oil multinationals had been kicked out, but Mexico remained an important producer, so the companies could not afford to simply disappear after the expropriation. Officially, after 1938, all production and distribution of oil in Mexico was done by PEMEX. However, for the newly created PEMEX, replacing companies like Shell or Jersey was not an easy task.

---

[41] Bushnell, David, *The Making of Modern Colombia*, Berkeley, University of California Press, 1993, 189.

[42] Colombia, Ministerio de Industrias, *Memoria*, Bogota, Imprenta Nacional, 1935, 62-66.

[43] Estrada, *Sucesos*, 515-516.

[44] De la Pedraja, *Petróleo*, 55-57; Villegas, *Petróleo Colombiano*, 83-84.

Since the beginning this state monopoly realized it lacked the know-how and skills necessary to develop the industry. The Mexican oil industry had been developed with foreign technology and management, and it was not possible for PEMEX to replace that overnight.[45] This problem was exacerbated by the fact that just days before the expropriation, the companies crossed the border with trucks full of equipment.[46] Finally, given that the foreign multinationals still controlled most of the international marketing of oil and exploration equipment, these companies organized a boycott against Mexican production against which PEMEX could not defend itself easily. The multinationals were closely observing the situation in Mexico waiting for the government to give up and call them back again.

As early as 1939, just one year after the expropriation, PEMEX decided that the only option to jumpstart its oil industry was by permitting some foreign participation. This was heavily constrained by the extremely nationalistic legislation written by the revolutionaries and changing it would have been a political suicide for the government. So, the way the government dealt with it was by awarding several service contracts to small American and European companies. The big pre-1938 multinationals (Standard Oil (New Jersey) and Shell) had an early big disappointment: PEMEX officials and the Mexican government punished them by making sure they would not get any of these new contracts. Permitting the return of Jersey or Shell to Mexico would have had a very high political cost for the Mexican government.

Despite being rejected by the Mexicans, Jersey continued trying to return. By the end of the Second World War the company started unofficial negotiations for new contracts with the Mexican government. This time Jersey came with a more humble attitude. They promised better behavior and higher profits for the Mexicans. Northrop Clarey, head of public relations of Jersey, said in an unpublished interview given in 1946 that he was confident Jersey would get contracts with PEMEX as long as it changed its attitude towards the Mexicans. Clarey even blamed Jersey for the resentment Mexicans felt against the company before the expropriation. "Americans scorn the natives and do not mingle with them", he said and added that the New York management was arrogant and lacked any basic knowledge about Mexico and simply did not care about learning about it.[47] Clarey's private view highly contrasted with the detailed report Jersey gave its shareholders during

---

[45] Barbosa, Fabio, "Technical and Economic Problems in the Newly Nationalized Oil Industry", in Brown, Jonathan and Alan Knight, *The Mexican Petroleum Industry in the Twentieth-Century*, Austin, University of Texas Press, 1992, 189, 194-203.

[46] *Ibid.*, 190.

[47] Larson, "Reports", 42-44.

the expropriation process on the welfare benefits it provided to its Mexican workers. The US Senate commission also made mention of the welfare expenses of Jersey in Mexico and highlighted how the Mexican oil workers were doing much better than the Mexican workers in other sectors.[48] Both Standard and the US Senate commission considered the welfare expenses made by the company as evidence of the unfair accusations made by the Mexican government. Both things are not necessarily contradictory – a company can pay welfare and be arrogant at the same time – but for the company's officials it was clear that, after the Second World War it needed to change the way it related with the local society.

Standard returned to Mexico in 1946, but not as a producer but as a marketing company. Marketing activities for the final consumer were not covered with the expropriation so Standard re-started those activities through Esso. Later, in 1956, Standard started importing chemicals from the US for the growing Mexican industrial sector.[49] Standard had to wait until the 1970s to get its first service contracts with PEMEX extracting oil in Southern Mexico for the state company.

The creation of a national oil company in Colombia was less traumatic for Standard partly because of the lack of participation of the labor force in the process, and partly because of the interests of the industrial elite. In 1938 the Mexican expropriation forced the Colombian elite to rethink what they considered the way oil should be exploited. With this event the government thought that a national oil industry was possible, so in 1940 it made its first step by creating the Ministry of Oil.[50]

Shortly after its creation, the Ministry of Oil had its first conflict with Tropical. According to the government's lawyers, the De Mares concession expired in 1946, but according to Tropical it expired until 1951. The litigations extended until 1944 when the case was taken to the Colombian Supreme Court, which eventually decided unanimously for the company settling the end of the concession in 1951.[51] This process was not easy, however. Although the company publicly showed confidence on his case and the Colombian courts, the Conservative opposition used the Supreme Court's decision to criticize the ruling party.

Despite the Supreme Court's final ruling, the Colombian elite saw 1951 as the year in which they could create a national oil company with the De Mares concession. There was, however, a debate of how this

---

[48] Standard Oil Company (New Jersey), *Annual Report*, New York, 1938, 8-11; United States Senate, *American Petroleum*, 264.

[49] "Mexico Building on a Storied Past", *The Lamp*, Vol. 86, No. 2 (2004): 4.

[50] De la Pedraja, *Petróleo*, 70.

[51] International Petroleum Company, *Annual Report*, Toronto, IPC, various years.

company should be. While some argued for a state-owned company (like PEMEX), others advocated for joint ventures between the Colombian state and local entrepreneurs, or a foreign company and local capitalists.[52]

In the 1940s, Colombian industrial capitalists organized themselves in an organization known as ANDI (National Industrial Association, in its Spanish acronym). Established in Medellín in 1944, ANDI became a powerful lobbying group with close ties with the Conservative Party. After ANDI's creation, its members paid close attention to the developments of the oil industry. Until then, the ANDI members' main concern was the constant supply of oil at affordable prices. However, after 1945, they started thinking of actively participating in the industry.[53] The Mexican events showed them that a Third World country could manage oil technology successfully.

For ANDI, the political environment changed in their favor in 1946 when the Conservatives came back to power after a disappointing López's second administration. This was clear in 1947, when Conservative President Mariano Ospina proposed Congress a new law to create a national oil company with 49% of private capital (local or foreign), which was approved by Congress in 1948 (Law 165).[54] Although ANDI wanted the new company to be completely privately owned, this still was consistent with some ANDI's goals, because they did not want a state-owned company a la PEMEX. The Medellín industrialists did not want to set a precedent of private property expropriation in Colombia.[55] The law established that the new company would acquire the De Mares concession after 1951.

In 1949, the Colombian government offered Standard to participate as part of the private investors in the new post-1951 company, but the company rejected the idea arguing that it would only participate with at least 51% of ownership.[56] After this, the government and ANDI started negotiations on how to create the company. Both the ANDI and the government wanted to have the final say in the company's decisions. The negotiations extended until 1950, when the country went to elections again. This time, the country elected Laureano Gómez, ANDI's closest ally.

[52] De la Pedraja, *Petróleo*, 76.
[53] Sáenz Rovner, Eduardo, *Colombia Anos 50: Industriales, política y diplomacia*, Bogotá, Universidad Nacional de Colombia, 2002, 55-56.
[54] De la Pedraja, *Petróleo*, 81-82.
[55] Sáenz, *Colombia*, 55.
[56] Sáenz, *Colombia*, 57.

Laureano Gómez's economic policy was highly protectionist permitting new golden years for the Medellín industry. During his administration, ANDI enjoyed incredible lobbying power in the government in detriment of the merchant class (who in 1949 created FENALCO, their own lobbying organization to advocate for free trade), and the working class (who suffered prosecution and violence from a government that never liked Liberal and Socialist influence in labor unions).[57]

Despite Gómez close relationship with ANDI, the president was open to hear proposals from both foreign and local companies for the creation of the national oil company. This forced ANDI to compete with Standard's proposal. While Standard proposed the government to provide management, technical, and refining services to the new company, the Medellín industrialists could not make a credible, viable and affordable proposal. The government gave ANDI the opportunity to come up with the capital they needed to develop their own proposal, but this did not happen. Under these circumstances, Gómez decided for Standard's proposal, which gave the government more income and saved the country more money. The government, however, agreed with Standard on decreasing the multinational's participation in the refinery's profits from 50 to 25% and on opening its distribution business to local capitalists, something the company did in 1951 when it sold 40% of its shares in Esso Colombiana to local investors.[58] In this way, Colombian industrialists could still participate in the oil business.

In August 25, 1951, Standard reverted De Mares concession to the Colombian government. Both the Colombian government and the multinational highlighted in the reversion ceremony how this constituted an example of "civilized" relationships between governments and foreign corporations. In fact, it was the first time in Latin American history that an oil concession had been transferred to the local government due to the expiration of the original contract. Moreover, contrary to what happened in Mexico, the appropriation of the concession by the new government company, ECOPETROL, did not mean that foreign companies could not apply for new concessions. In fact, Standard got new contracts and concessions in the following years.[59] In 1961, Stand-

---

[57] For a detailed study of ANDI's power in the Conservative administrations see, Sáenz Rovner, Eduardo, *La ofensiva empresarial: Industriales, políticos y violencia en los años 40 en Colombia*, Bogotá, Universidad de los Andes, 1992.

[58] "Sale of Oil Stock in Colombia is Set", *New York Times*, January 3, 1951; "Colombia Signs Oil Field Pacts", *The New York Times*, December 9, 1950; "Jersey Standard Affiliate to Run Colombia Refinery", *The Wall Street Journal*, July 18, 1951; International Petroleum Company, *Annual Report*, 1950; Sáenz, *Colombia*, 68-72.

[59] International Petroleum Company, *Annual Report*, 1951, 1952.

ard handed over the administration of the Barranca refinery, and only until 2003 ECOPETROL became public.[60]

Conclusion

In the first half of the twentieth century, Mexico and Colombia wanted to develop policies with which the countries could earn higher rents from oil production. These kind of ambitions naturally generated conflict with the foreign multinational corporations. The Mexican events had a strong influence among Colombian policymakers. However, due to the kind of political system existing in Colombia, the relationship between the government and the working class, and the relationship with the United States, both countries followed different paths in their nationalist policies.

Mexico reached its peak in nationalist policies after an armed conflict that overthrew the business-friendly Díaz regime. The pro-multinational policy from Díaz times represented the pre-revolutionary past the post-1910 Mexican leaders did not want to reproduce. In addition, the revolutionary government had to rely more and more on an alliance with the working class for its survival. This created the conditions to have a completely state-owned company with strong participation of the oil union for its management.

In the Colombian case the nationalist policies were closely affected by the electoral competition between parties. Although one party (Liberal) was closer to the working class than the other (Conservative), the Liberals never encouraged the working class masses to take fight a class war. Each party represented a different faction of the national elite, but had to attract working class votes. This system created an equilibrium in which the government could never go completely against the foreign companies. The only way to get the concessions back was by complying with its part of the contract, even when sometimes the companies did not complied with theirs. The lack of an element of class-nationalist war permitted a smooth transfer of the concession to the Colombian government and the participation of foreign companies in the oil business. So, while Mexico followed a nationalist policy that threatened private property rights (such as the 1917 Constitution and the 1938 expropriation), Colombia followed a policy by which not only did both the foreign and the national private sector not feel threatened, but also the multinationals and the national investors believed they could benefit from.

---

[60] International Petroleum Company, *Annual Report*, 1961; ECOPETROL, "Emisiones de Acciones", in ECOPETROL official website (www.ecopetrol.com.co), last accessed August 5, 2006.

Which country gained more with its nationalist policy? Does a radical measure pay off more than a respect for contracts signed under dubious ethical behavior? Further research is needed to answer these questions, but these two cases show how in less developed countries, the type of government leads to very different outcomes in terms of nationalist policy.

PART V

ALGERIA

The Relationships between the Producing Countries and the Oil Companies in the South

The Example of SONATRACH

Nadji KHAOUA & Belgacem MADI

University of Annaba, Algeria

The countries producing hydrocarbons, particularly in the South, have always assigned the various stages in the production process of their resources as well as the development thereof on the world oil market to oil companies of planetary scope, having human, technological, financial as well as political resources such as to be able to intervene at the various levels required by exploitation of hydrocarbons, resources that are so vital to the most industrialized consumers, as well as to the producing countries, that this situation gave them special strategic importance.

Beginning in the 1980s, a new tendency slowly came into being, use by the producing countries in the South of oil companies that, themselves, have come from the producing countries in the South.

In the case of SONATRACH, an Algerian oil company dating back to the 1960s and of modest size compared with the world oil firms, it intervenes in collaboration with local oil companies in more than ten producing countries, all in the South and scattered over three continents.

What are the impacts on the world hydrocarbon market of this type of relationship?

Does the cooperation between oil companies of the South and producing countries play a role on the world hydrocarbon market?

What could the local economic impacts of this fact be?

This contribution attempts to clarify these issues to a small extent. With that in mind, this work is divided into three parts: the first part will offer a succinct portrait of SONATRACH, a national oil company in

Algeria whose very existence is so closely connected with the development of the country's economy as a whole.

The second part will study the international action of the national oil company SONATRACH. The point will be to show that this action is not new and fits completely into the policy of cooperative international relations advocated by the Algerian State, with a view to extending its possibilities of exchanges and mutual economic assistance.

Finally, in the third and last part the point will be to raise questions about the present and predictable results of those South-South oil cooperation relationships, by way of the national oil companies of certain developing countries that produce hydrocarbons.

SONATRACH – a Singular National Company

SONATRACH, a national oil company, did not result from a public will that took shape little by little and led to State intervention, by way of a firm with public capital, in the oil domain, either because that domain took on a certain economic and financial importance, or for strategic reasons relating to the policy of energy independence *vis-à-vis*, for instance, international oil interests.

Nor is SONATRACH, as a national oil company that is among the most important ones in the Arab countries and the North African countries, a creation of local players or investors, in the field of exploitation of hydrocarbons in Algeria.

Its existence originated in several considerations, of equal importance, explaining and helping us understand, at present, the singular nature of that national oil company, SONATRACH – that singularity emerging, for instance, if one compares it to the majority of the national oil companies in the rest of the Arab countries and in North Africa that produce hydrocarbons.

That national oil company was created, in particular and essentially, as the tool *par excellence* in the hands of the State in Algeria, with a view to exercising its sovereignty over its available and exploitable natural resources, such as hydrocarbons.

That tool, national oil company SONATRACH, of which the Algerian State has been the sole shareholder since its creation in 1962, lets the State establish its own oil policy and plan the development of its resources in terms of hydrocarbons that can be mobilized and be exploited, depending on the financing needs of its national development policy.

One of its designers and most important managers (due to his closeness at the time to the highest political officials) writes the following about the profound reasons that led to establishment of the national oil company SONATRACH:

> The recognition by France of Algerian sovereignty over the entire territory implied, ipso facto, recognition of our sovereignty over the content of the subsoil. The Saharan Oil Code, extended for some time by the Evian Agreements, maintained the rules for exploitation of the deposits then in effect beyond the date of independence. That extension, which was the main concession made by the negotiators[1] did not mean any waiver whatsoever of the principle of ownership of the deposits – on the contrary. That Saharan Oil Code, which was the French oil law during the time of colonization, was based on royal prerogative under the terms of which the State enjoyed exclusive ownership of the content of the subsoil. Namely, the French State of the time of colonization and, since independence, to the Algerian State due to the general transfer of all attributes of the former French sovereignty in Algeria to the reestablished Algerian sovereignty, …

> … In July 1962, exploitation of the deposits was dominated by majority French companies, resulting mainly from a public establishment, the B.R.P. (Bureau de Recherche des Pétroles), to which ERAP (Entreprise de recherches et d'activités pétrolières) and then ELF (founded in 1976) succeeded, as well as minority English and American companies.

> While sovereign from the legal viewpoint, we were foreigners in the field, since the exploitation policy was determined by foreign entities. In two words as well as a hundred, we were the master … in our offices, but were foreigners at our deposits. Whence the logic that we had to accept immediately: no real sovereignty without operational control of the deposits; no control possible without the Algerians themselves being able to carry out the operations regarding each link in the entire chain, from upstream to downstream. (Ghozali S. A., *Question d'État*, Éditions Casbah, Alger, 2009)

Thus, on one hand some light is cast on the creation as of 1963 of the national oil company, SONATRACH, and on the other hand we have an explanation of that acronym "SONATRACH" (Société Nationale de Transport et de commercialisation des hydrocarbures).

By creating the national oil company SONATRACH as of the first months of national independence, the Algerian State equipped itself with the tool enabling it, on one hand, to control and manage its hydrocarbon resources in the best possible way to meet its national objectives, and on the other hand to develop an oil policy able to serve, later, the effort to follow a broader diplomatic and international cooperation policy, at international level.

---

[1] The Algerian negotiators of the Evian Agreements winding up with the country's independence in 1962.

In our view, this accounts for all of the singularity displayed by the national oil company, SONATRACH, if one compares it to the majority of the other national oil companies of the oil-producing countries in the South.

SONATRACH – a Tool for the Algerian State's Multiform International Action

With a view to being able to make a fair judgement of the international cooperation action in the field of activities connected with development of the hydrocarbons on the external markets, it is necessary to, in our view, in the first place to consider the institutional conditions proper to SONATRACH's country of origin, in order to reach that goal.

In the quotation by the former SONATRACH President and Chief Executive Officer (and, many years later, a minister and Prime Minister of the Algerian Government), Mr S. A. Ghozali (cf. below), we have indicated a few facets among the most decisive ones casting light on the institutional conditions that prevailed over the creation and development of SONATRACH.

The same author quoted above adds:

At the time of independence, everything was controlled de facto by foreign companies, headed by former French State group BRP-ERAP, whose strategy was strictly aimed at guaranteeing, whatever it might cost, the continuation of its oil empire, beyond the defunct colonial empire. It was in Algeria that that oil empire was established. The only strategy allowing a prospect of a future recovery of the national oil resources consisted in equipping the country with national means, people and economic tools able to play the role assigned de facto solely to the foreign companies, for each link in the oil chain. It was for that purpose that SONATRACH was created, ..., which means that SONATRACH was born with a roadmap, which committed itself as of the day following its foundation on tens of fronts simultaneously.

To be frank, certain such fronts or assignments were disconnected from the strict business purpose of the national oil company SONATRACH.

However, it took them over, not for its own internal needs, but rather within the framework of the country's general policy on behalf of accelerated industrialization and modernization. The typical case in this connection is the one regarding higher education, which found SONATRACH taking responsibility for organization and management of thousands of students in a very broad range of specializations and scattered over all of the world's countries, wherever there might be a university or a specialized advanced training institute worthy of that name.

SONATRACH, Algeria's sole national oil company, played a multiple role as a tool in the hands of the national institutions with a view to speeding up development and modernization, not only of the economy, but also of society in the broad sense, in Algeria.

When viewed within this global national framework, the action of the SONATRACH oil company, at international level, and in particular the relationships that it might have with the similar national oil companies of the South's other oil-producing countries, in the final analysis actually constituted only one of the elements, not the most important one, of a more global international cooperation strategy aimed at reaching national strategic objectives connected with speeding up economic development and the social modernization of a country bled white by a long colonial period.

The International Accomplishments of the National Oil Company SONATRACH

The international cooperation initiated and maintained by SONATRACH, the national oil company, was aimed at reaching the objectives set out by the sole owner, the Algerian State.

First of all, what are the most important ones?

Are they limited solely to the field of operation, development and international marketing of hydrocarbons, on a market virtually monopolized by the big private multinational firms of American origin, essentially?

Or do they also include purposes relating to international political strategy, going beyond the domain of hydrocarbons in the strict sense?

The annual report published by the national oil company SONATRACH in 2006 mentions the fact that one of the strategic goals pursued by the national oil company for many years is to win positions in its field of activity, everywhere in the world.

By pursuing that objective, SONATRACH is now present, in some connection or other, both in Africa, Asia and Latin America as well as in Europe and in the Middle East.

The stated purpose is to attempt to create value, not only by exploiting the hydrocarbons present in the national subsoil, but also by concluding international partnership agreements in the various segments of the oil and gas business.

The set of cooperation agreements and partnerships concluded throughout the world now held by SONATRACH links it with various public and private players to be found in around 50 of the world's countries (Annual report, 2006).

This international activity carried on by the oil company emphasizes some aspects more than others. In particular, the following priorities can be identified in connection with that international cooperation activity:

1 – create cooperative relationships with the oil companies of the Arab world that are members of the OAPEC (Organization of Arab Petroleum Exporting Countries);

2 – initiate oil cooperation with the oil-producing countries of Africa, including those belonging to OPEC (Organization of Petroleum Exporting Countries) in particular;

3 – obtain a foothold in Latin America thanks to institution of oil cooperation with certain countries in that zone, particularly the ones belonging to OPEC;

4 – open up a new field of cooperation in the oil domain in Asia, particularly with the two Koreas and China, as well as the other Asian countries, some of which have long-standing multiform relationships with Algeria (Vietnam, Indonesia, India, the Philippines, etc.).

These objectives for cooperation between the SONATRACH oil company and the various public and private players in the Southern countries did not prevent the development of similar phenomena of cooperation and exchanges with the countries of the North, which contain the bulk of the export markets for the Algerian hydrocarbons exported by SONATRACH.

In particular, we might mention here the most significant examples of that cooperation with players in the Northern countries:

A – taking advantage of the European energy needs, particularly for natural gas, in order to intensify the already existing relationships (France, Italy, Germany, etc.) in this field by way, *inter alia*, of the "Enrico Mattéï" (gas pipeline between Algeria and Italy via Tunisia)) and "Pedro Duran Farrel" (gas pipeline from Algeria to Spain via Morocco) gas pipelines, which supply Europe with Algerian gas.

B – intervening on the European energy market as a partner with local players (particularly in Spain and Portugal), thanks to the relative opening of the hydrocarbon distribution market within the European Union.

Those international cooperative relationships – in spite of all efforts to diversify them – are still dominated by the relationships developed with the Southern oil countries, particularly with Yemen, Tunisia, Kuwait and the United Arab Emirates, with respect to the Arab world's countries, Nigeria and Mauritania in Africa, Peru and Venezuela in Latin America, and South Korea (recently) and China in Asia.

Oil cooperation with the players in the countries of the South, which the national oil company SONATRACH has initiated and strengthened for many years now, is not limited in any way to marketing oil products.

Benefiting from institutional support at the highest level whether in Algeria or, often, in the countries of the South *vis-à-vis* SONATRACH, that cooperation has broadened as time passed so as to take in at present, with certain partners in the South, several segments of the complex oil activity.

According to the most recent available data at SONATRACH level, that national oil company has managed to develop very fruitful and promising cooperative relationships, particularly with certain players in the South, in the following segments:

1 – Cooperation in exploitation in Mali, Mauritania, Niger, Yemen and Libya,

2 – A production contract in Africa with certain countries in the Sahel and in Egypt (in the Nile Delta, offshore),

3 – An exploration and production contract in Latin America, particularly in Peru,

4 – The Trans-African gas pipeline in cooperation with Nigeria (planned).

Algeria's Relationships with the Multinational Oil Companies via the New Law Concerning Hydrocarbons

Nadji KHAOUA & Nabila GHAFOURI

University of Annaba, Algeria

The new Law concerning hydrocarbons in Algeria represents a significant break in the practices of relationships between the producing countries of the South and the multinational oil companies, which now dominate the world market for energy from fossil sources.

Those firms, the number of which is limited and the origin of which is mainly American, had managed to turn to their advantages the crisis experienced by the world hydrocarbons market since the 1950s and the abortive Iranian experiment with national control of resources by the producing country.

Since then, in spite of the creation of OPEC at the beginning of the 1960s, as well as at least three major crises spread out through the 1970s and until now (1973, 1979, 1985-86), the relationships between producer countries and multinational oil companies have always been characterised by a certain sharing – more or less negotiated – of the resources extracted, enabling each producing country to maintain at least national control of its mining domain and of the reserves that it might contain.

The new Law concerning hydrocarbons promulgated in Algeria breaks with that practice.

Aimed at speeding up Direct Foreign Investments, it allows multinational oil companies to hold at least 70% of the hydrocarbons that they might discover in the country's subsoil.

Its recent amendment and the cancellation of the measures ordered, even though the regulatory texts concerning application of the law have not yet been promulgated one year later, give rise to more questions than they settles concerning the nature of the relationships between the State and the "political power" in Algeria, with the resource par excellence, hydrocarbons.

How can one understand this apparent return to kinds of relationships similar to those characterising the first periods on the international hydrocarbons market, during which the companies operated in non-independent territories or territories lacking any local authorities?

What would the strategic implications of that Law be for the Algerian economy?

How can one understand the fact that among the producing countries in the South, Algeria is the only one to henceforth offer such a legal opportunity to the multinational oil companies?

Finally, how can one understand the logic guiding the "decision-makers" in reformulation of that law?

Finally, how is one to judge the meaning or meanings (political? strategic? etc.) of this fact: neither the first version, which was permissive with respect to the interests of the multinational oil firms in Algeria's potential hydrocarbon resources, nor the second version, which was radically different since it could be considered as renationalisation of those resources, has any legal existence as yet?

Would this be another sign, one more (see the previous signs represented by the political crises of 1962, of 1965, of 1967, of the summer of 1974, of 1979-80, of 1986, of 1988, of 1990, etc.), of the struggle at the summit of political decision-making power in Algeria, for control of the public resource?

The energy issue, within the framework of contemporary international relations, is not only a question relating to economic or commercial relationships, whether those relationships are between States, or within the framework of the globalised market, between specialised multinational firms and international speculators, on one hand, and national oil companies on the other.

It is a much more crucial and strategic question, characterised by extremely multiple and complex aspects. It involves, simultaneously, a multitude of disparate players, both political players, economic and industrial players as well as financial participants, on several levels, from local to global.

This is the general framework within which we will try here to understand and analyse the energy situation in the case of Algeria's national oil company, SONATRACH.

The particularity of this case is that it associates, on one hand, the oil policy of a producing State belonging to OPEC[1] and on the other hand

---

[1] Organisation of Petroleum Exporting Countries, headquartered in Vienna (Austria), and which, as of 2006, grouped producing countries from the majority of the world's

the medium- and long-term economic and commercial strategy of a specialised public economic business, which is among the most important businesses in the country, and also among the most important national oil companies, if one compares it with those of the other producing countries belonging to OPEC.

Finally, international trade in Algerian hydrocarbons accounts for more than 95% of that country's financial resources in international currencies and for more than 60%[2] of the tax resources in local currency.

This indicates the great importance of SONATRACH as a national oil company to the economy and to Algerian society, and the extreme importance for those elements that will immediately result from the slightest changes made in the way in which SONATRACH pursues its purpose, namely, commercial exploitation of the hydrocarbon resources available to the country (or which become available in the future), in a world economy in which the energy picture, because of its many specific characteristics, is to a great extent beyond the control of the strictly economic players on the market.

That was the general framework within which that country's governmental authorities began to lay down the markers for a new legal and regulatory reorganisation of the Algerian hydrocarbon market.

That reorganisation is aimed at attracting international investors to the hydrocarbon sector, with the ambition of maximising the country's financial income by exploitation of such energy resources under a new approach to intervention by foreign partners on behalf of that sector's development.[3]

SONATRACH and the Development of the Algerian Economy from 1980 to 2000

The relationships between the national oil company SONATRACH and the Algerian economy, due to the latter's nature and condition, by the direct and indirect financial resources generated by the activity, or rather the activities (prospecting, drilling, production, storage, transport and marketing) of the company, go beyond the normal and usual strict framework within which an ordinary government-owned business operates, in any country.

---

oil areas. They are Saudi Arabia, Venezuela, Indonesia, Kuwait, Libya, Algeria, Iran, Nigeria, Ira, Qatar and the United Arab Emirates.

[2] Abderrahmane MEBTOUL (2003), "The new legislative bill concerning hydrocarbons: SONATRACH strengthened in a competitive environment", review of the ADEM, March, p. 104.

[3] Mourad PREURE (2003), "Globalisation and the oil industry", review of the ADEM, March, Algiers, p. 23 et seq.

SONATRACH is the main source of Algiers' financial resources, and in particular of its resources in terms of convertible currencies.

When one observes the development of the discourse devoted to the hydro-carbon sector over a period of four decades of structural and institutional transformation of SONATRACH, the remarkable continuity resulting there from, at first sight, eloquently bears witness to the power of the consensus that developed concerning this "vital and strategic" resource.[4]

Hence there is a strong parallel between that company's development and the development of the country as a whole.

The role traditionally assigned to this sector and, significantly, summed up in the formula *"use oil to transform dinars into foreign currencies"* appears as a constant constructed on the basis of three essential dimensions, respec-tively, those of a source of accumulation for financial development, a source of national energy supply for the long term, and finally a source of raw ma-terials for the petrochemical industry. This function-objective assigned to the SONATRACH company even in its gestation phase found its original justification in the weakness of national savings that could be collected for the needs of the ambitious development plans then projected. It has not ex-perienced any explicit reformulation since then, even when the expansive context that had give it its high ranking had to give way, subsequently, to the profound and lasting turnaround caused by the barrel's collapse in 1986.[5]

One of the main persons responsible for the hydrocarbon sector[6] writes as follows on this point:

It is useful to remind you that the oil prospects were very pessimistic at the beginning of the 1980s: oil exploration, carried on almost solely by SONATRACH, had slowed down. The likelihood of discovery of new de-posits was considered as almost nil by the few foreign companies taking an interest in the Algerian subsoil. It was proclaimed that the recoverable oil reserves would be exhausted by 2005!

The legislative modifications introduced in 1986 and in 1991 to attract in-ternational companies and increase the exploration effort, and the introduc-tion of new technologies in connection with seismics and drilling made it possible, in particular, to discover the Berkine basin (near Hassi-Messaoud) and to reconstitute the oil reserves to bring them back to their 1971 level.[7]

---

[4]   Abdelatif REBAH (2006), *Sonatrach, a unique business*, ed. Casbah, Algiers, p. 224.
[5]   Abdelatif REBAH (2006), *op. cit.*, p. 224.
[6]   Abdelaziz KRISSAT – Former head of the ENTP (Entreprise Nationale des Travaux aux Puits) – A Sonatrach subsidiary.
[7]   Abdelaziz KRISSAT (2006), "Legal treatment of oil: a return to reason, but other changes are necessary." *Le Quotidien d'Oran*, 10 September, Algiers, p. 7.

Chems-Eddine Chitour and his colleagues[8] go farther in the analysis of the singular links between the National Company and the national economy.

In a recent publication reporting on the proceedings of the 7th energy day, they write as follows:

> A State within the State... With 95% of the country's exports, 90% of its foreign currency receipts and 25% of its GDP, the SONATRACH (Société Nationale pour la recherche, la production, le transport, la transformation et la commercialisation des hydrocarbures) is indeed more than just a business. It is one of the strategic hearts of Algeria. The history of SONATRACH is the chronicle of a business that is essential to Algeria's' life. Established in 1963, it benefited in 1971 from the nationalisation of the foreign interests in the oil sector. Since then it has constantly discovered oil and gas in the country, so much so that its production constantly increased to lift it to fifth place (in the world) for gas reserves, and to 14th place with respect to oil reserves. However, the International Energy Agency finds that Algeria is still a country that is under-exploited in terms of hydrocarbon resources (see below). Since 1991, Algeria has reopened its oil sector to the foreign countries, triggering some new discoveries of black gold.[9]

The latter remark by the authors of this passage is extremely judicious and gives rise to a legitimate question concerning the underlying motivations that pushed the State's decision-makers into proposing a new hydrocarbon law, so permissive with respect to the international interests in this strategic sector, and then into reversing course and so quickly abrogating (in less than two years) what they had decided on just previously.

Abdelatif Rebahi, on his part, observes the constancies of this development, going beyond its ups and downs due to the business cycle:

> Is one going to find, at the core of all of the explanations of reasons relative to the legislative changes in question, a constant nucleus of five arguments based on necessity and the object of consensus: the exhaustion of reserves, the decline of income, the shortage of capital and of technologies, increased international competition, and long-term energy security and inter-generational solidarity.[10]

Two rather significant periods in terms of time, since each of them lasts for approximately one decade at least, marking parallel develop-

---

[8] Pr Cems-Eddine CHITOUR is the director of the laboratory for exploitation of fossil energies at the École Nationale Polytechnique d'Alger.

[9] F. KOLAI, R. BOUFASSA, I. BENSARI, S. HADDOUM, F. MEZIANI, C.-E. CHITOUR (2005), *Algeria's energy balance since independence*, ed. OPU-ANDRU, Algiers, p. 102.

[10] Abdelatif REBAHI (2006), *op. cit.*, p. 225.

ments and having the same tendency, experienced jointly by the country's global economy, on one hand, and by the Compagnie Nationale Pétrolière SONATRACH on the other.

a- The first period begins approximately one year after the second oil shock of 1979, which brought a change of political regime in Iran, lasting until the beginning of the 1990s.

During that phase, oil prices initiated their downward tendency, in normal terms but also in real terms, on the world hydrocarbon market.

The revenue derived from exploration of the Algerian hydrocarbons gradually declined, and actually collapsed in 1985-86.

In that crisis, the system of international prices of Algerian hydrocarbons was not the only factor, because there was also the internal use made of the revenue received by the country from its energy exports.

The majority of analysts of the Algerian economy have emphasised the model of its development during that period: based on the preference given to internal consumption demand, all of the said income went toward financing imports of consumer goods.

The rate of investment in industrial production activities, which was more than 23% of all GDP (Gross Domestic Product) in 1980, then began to decline, reaching less than 12% in 1990, and without recovering at present (it was less than 7% in 2005).[11]

During that period, the expression "oil is a curse on Algeria" became widely quoted, in all discussions and other expressions of public opinion.

The fact is that everybody found his standard of living deteriorating day by day, the press reporting only increase after increase in consumer product prices, the closing of government-owned and private businesses of all sizes, and droves of workers laid off in a country in which unemployment had already been endemic.

While a few years earlier, during installation of a heavy industrialisation process that was supposed to power all the rest of the economy, the authorities responsible for the State anticipated and publicly announced – with a few proud redundancies – that by the 1980s *"Algeria would reach Spain's level of economic and social development"*.

The riots in Tizi-Ouzou in 1980 and in Constantine in 1986 and the ones that became general in a just few hours in the entire northern part of the country in October 1988 were a good indication of the strength of disenchantment and the amplitude characterising the social and economic crisis, being transformed into a political crisis of a regime and of a

---

[11] ONS (National Statistics Office), Various statistical reports, Algiers.

failing political system, in spite of the resources continually flowing to it from exports of energy raw materials.

It was this entire general framework that was instrumentalised to create apparent profound upheavals. (*In the final analysis there were apparent and finally deceptive upheavals: nothing basically changed in the way in which relationships were organised between political-decision making power and the formal State, with respect to the rent received on hydrocarbons*).

b- The second period, 1990-2006: This period began with the promulgation of a legal document underlying the stated desire for a choice of the "market economy" as the new path for upgrading the economy in Algeria: the Law concerning the Currency and Credit, also known as the "LMC" law[12]. That Law henceforth authorised private capital activity and the circulation of financial flows among operators, whatever their respective legal statuses might be.

The situation of the national oil company at that time was that it was a singular business, torn, as had long already been the case, between its basic function, looking for, putting into production and exploiting the national hydrocarbon resources, and its other equally important function as holder of part of the State's authority over the national mining domain, its hydrocarbon resources whatever the form thereof may be, their degree of economic mobilisation (producing more or fewer quantities of hydrocarbons depending on the objectives set for SONATRACH by the State at every moment,) and their exploitation on the international markets.

It is that sense that the Algerian national oil company is singular. It is not a business like the others, obeying the rules and objective constraints governing relationships between players on a market. Rather, SONATRACH is a "dismembering of the State", having the function of acting on the markets (national and international), in accordance with the directives received from the State as approach and objectives, because that company by definition is the main source of monetary resources (in local currency resulting from oil taxation, and in convertible currencies stemming from hydrocarbon exports) for the State in Algeria.

Since the State chose to liberalise economic activity, it made an implicit wager that the said choice would give rise to substantial flows of capital and of direct foreign investment, benefiting the market economy in Algeria.

---

[12] Promulgated in 1991, the Law concerning the Currency and Credit liberalised the field of organisation and of development of the economy in Algeria.

Since 1991, the date of promulgation of the law concerning the currency and credit (the LMC law), until 2004, the volume of direct foreign investment excluding hydrocarbons seldom exceeded an amount of about 200 million dollars per year!

It was partly as a reaction to that failure that an influential political tendency within the State used all of its influence to obtain extreme liberalisation of the hydrocarbon sector, to the benefit of the major players in that sector (mainly the world oil firms based in the United States).

The new law concerning hydrocarbons in Algeria, which constituted the main topic of public discussions, even if the latter has been rather mixed in this country for several years now, represents a significant break in the practices of relationships between the producing countries in the South and the multinational oil companies.

Until now, the world oil firms' intervention in the producing countries in the South has been carried out, in general, on the basis of two main systems:

The concession system

The multinational oil company generally benefits, following a period of invitation to tender and then of negotiations, from a concession the periods of which are established by contract in order to exploit the oil resources that might exist within the geographical limits of the concession.

The State concerned remains the indisputable owner of its resources, during and after the multinational oil companies' intervention.

The production sharing system

The multinational oil company intervenes in exploitation and development of the oil resources, within a precise area in the producing country in the South.

In exchange, it shares, in accordance with procedures laid down by contract and in advance, the results (in terms of actual hydrocarbon production) with the national oil company of the producing country concerned.

Discussion (Aborted in Advance) of the Hydrocarbon Law

The new law on hydrocarbons, which constituted the main subject of discussion (abortive, to be sure, since its one-way direction was well indicated as of the beginning) in Algeria wanted to break with those ordinary and well-marked practices of relations between producing countries in the South and multinational oil companies.

Nothing was left to chance to give the impression that the said law represented the most urgent wish of an entire country: all social classes were called on to contribute to noisy approval thereof, and the information organs and the media of all tendencies and types constantly tried to show that liberalisation of the hydrocarbon sector, as organised under the said new law, was the one and only solution for obtaining direct foreign investment and developing a "snowball" effect on the other neglected sectors of the Algerian economy in deep crisis.

Thus rallies and petitions for weeks, whether of labour union members, or of the media, or else of political parties and even of university people collectively or individually, constantly touted the new virtues of all-out liberalisation of the hydrocarbon sector in Algeria.

Concerning a Few Significant Elements of the "New Hydrocarbon Law"

Aimed at speeding up direct foreign investment in the hydrocarbon sector, and then in a second phase with the hope of creating a surge of direct foreign investment to the benefit of the countries entire economy, the new law would allow, if applied, the multinational oil companies to hold at least 70% of the hydrocarbons that they might discover in the country's subsoil.

Thus the draft of that law specified the following:

The search for oil and gas and exploitation thereof constitute the very heart of SONATRACH's activity. It is in this domain that the legislative bill provides for the greatest possible opening for private capital. If this text were adopted, the law would then allow any national or foreign business to acquire, on a basis of full ownership, at least 70% of the oil reserves that they have uncovered.[13]

As to articles 21 and 22 of that text, they specify the following:

Article 21 of title II of the legislative bill, dealing with the petroleum upstream sector, stipulates that "the exploration contract grants an exclusive right to the contracting party to operate within the perimeter defined by the said contract". Article 22 mentions the following: "*The hydrocarbons extracted under an exploration and/or exploitation contract belong to the contracting party...*"

As to article 45, it notes the following:

Each exploration and operation contract must contain a clause granting a participation option to SONATRACH SPA, when it is not a contracting party, that may reach thirty percent (30%), and may be no less than twenty per-

---

[13] Hocine MALTI (2002), "Reflexions concerning the legislative bill on hydrocarbons." *Le Quotidien d'Oran*, Algiers 24-25-26/11.

cent (20%). The said option shall have to be exercised at the latest thirty days after approval by ALNAFT.[14]

Thus, as a unique measure, by comparison with the laws and regulations organising relationships of the other producing countries in the South, whether or not they are members of OPEC, with the multinational oil companies, the legislative bill concerning hydrocarbons that the Algerian State wanted to apply is not explained by logical elements relating either to the development of the national economy, or to the development of the international hydrocarbon market.

Consequences of the Law

This level of opening the country's energy resources, enjoyed by the multinational oil companies under the said law, constitutes *a precedent* in the relationships between the producing country from the South and the oil multinationals.

Thus this law lastingly *alienates* the community's resources without any objective reason and without any real counterpart.

None of the South's producing countries, even the ones traditionally most permeable to the interests of the oil multinationals, such as Saudi Arabia or Kuwait, have granted, at any time during their oil history, such a level of ownership of their energy resources to the foreign oil companies.

What Are the Prospects?

Then how can one try to understand, if not explain, the real basis for such a law?

Can one understand it within the more general framework of development, during the last few decades, of the relationships between the producing countries in the South and the multinational oil firms?

Paradoxes and Policies Relating to the Energy Resource

Following years of muffled debate, limited to small circles and within the institutional forums close to civil society, the NLH[15] was promulgated in 2005.

To be valid and to be legally applicable, its publication in appropriate form in the official journal was necessary.

---

[14]   The author was a former senior executive of SONATRACH (a public management entity to be installed subsequently) of the plan for development of the commercial discovery.

[15]   NLH: New Law on Hydrocarbons.

But that never took place.

The paradoxical result was the promulgation of a Law of decisive importance, but which has no legal existence. It is as if it had never seen the light of day.

Hydrocarbons continue to be exploited under the old system of production sharing in which the CPNSH[16] is the owner of at least 51% of the resources exploited.

There is no objective reason explaining such a paradoxical situation, except the one concerning a conflict at the highest level in the State concerning exploitation of the energy resources and control of the economic rent that they generate.

At the beginning of the year 2006, and still without really associating society as a whole with the reflection, a sudden reversal took place.

Amendments were made to the NLH that emptied it of its content concerning the previous provision granting at least 70% of ownership of the new exploitable reserves to the firm that discovered the said resources.

However, to be legally valid and applicable, those amendments, issued by means of a presidential ordinance, must be approved by Parliament and the Senate, and then be published in the Official Journal.

This indispensable legal and regulatory treatment has still not taken place.

Finally and in the final analysis, the energy resources continue to be exploited in an ordinary and proven form.

The political groups headed up the State continue to neutralise each other as regards the status of those resources for modernisation of the national economy.

S.H.[17] is not a national company like the others; it is a singular business deriving its singularity from its political instrumentalisation in the Algerian politico-economic field.

---

[16] CPNSH: National Oil Company SONATRACH.

[17] SH: These letters constitute SONATRACH's official abbreviation.

PART VI

EUROPEAN DIVERSITY

Concerning the Nationalisation
of the Rumanian Oil Industry
The Mining Law of 1924
and its Rejoinders of 1929 and 1937

Gheorghe CALCAN

University of Ploiesti, Rumania

Rumania is an important European oil producer. The year 1857 brought three world "firsts" with respect to the Rumanian oil industry: the world's first officially recorded production of oil, establishment of the world's first refinery, and Bucharest becoming the world's first city to be lighted up with oil.[1]

In 1857, Rumania recorded output of 275 tons of oil, but as the First World War approached, the country's oil production reached approximately 1.9 million tons. Rumania's largest oil output during the period between the two World Wars was posted in 1936, at around 8.7 million tons. Thanks to that production, which represented about 3.53% of the world's total output, Rumania ranked fifth in the world, after the United States (61.10%), the USSR (11.13%), Venezuela (8.90%), and Iran (3.56%).[2] Thanks to its production and above all to its oil exports, Rumania held a very important position in the hierarchy of oil-producing countries during the inter-war period. Thus in 1928, Rumania ranked sixth among the world's leading exporters, with 4.10% of all world exports, after the United States, Venezuela, Mexico, Persia and

---

[1]   Gh. Buzatu, *O istorie a petrolului românesc*, Edition Enciclopedică, Bucarest, 1998, p. 24; Gh. Ivănuş, I. Ştefănescu, Şt.N.Stirimin, Şt.-Tr. Mocuţa, M. P. Coloja, *O istorie a petrolului în România*, Edition AGIR, Bucarest, 2004, p. 66-77.

[2]   See *Enciclopedia Română*, Vol. III, National Print Works, Bucharest, 1938-1939, p. 1094; The table concerning *Production and value of crude oil obtained in Rumania from 1857 through 1924*, Moniteur du pétrole roumain, (MPR), No. 6, 1925, p. 427; *Producţia mondială de ţiţei în anul 1936*, MPR, No. 19, 1937, p. 1457; the table concerning *Monthly world output of crude oil during the year 1936, by comparison with the year 1935*, MPR, No. 10. 1937, p. 852.

the USSR, while in 1937 Rumania ranked fifth in that classification. In Europe, Rumania constantly held first or second place, the latter after the USSR, in terms of world oil exports.[3]

Even if Rumania's export percentage was not represented by a figure, the country's geostrategic position substantially helped it play an important role in the hierarchy of the region's oil resources, and not only that. Thus in 1931, Rumania met more than 50% of the domestic oil needs of nine countries in Europe, North Africa and the Middle East (Bulgaria about 97%, Hungary about 98%, Spanish Morocco about 92%, Syria and Lebanon about 87%, Austria about 82%, Yugoslavia about 79%, Egypt about 71%, Palestine about 66% and Greece about 55%). In that same year, France satisfied 11.54% of its oil needs by means of imports from Rumania.[4]

All of these elements demonstrated the importance of the Rumanian oil industry, first of all for the national economy, but also for the international economic circuit. That fact attracted the attention of big international capitalists. During the period prior to the First World War, foreign capital held from 92% to 96% of all capital invested in that industry and, for the Rumanian industry, between 4% and 8%. That state of affairs led the country's political elements to think of the possibility of nationalising the Rumanian oil industry.[5]

The 1895 mining law provided for nationalising all wealth in the Rumanian subsoil, except for oil, which remained the property of the party controlling the land surface.[6]

After the end of the First World War, with the formation of a unified Rumanian State, a debate got underway concerning nationalisation of all

---

[3] Mihail Pizanty, The current problems of the Rumanian oil industry – A short statistical and economic presentation, "Cartea Românească", Bucarest, 1929, p. 39; *Enciclopedia Română*, Vol. III, p. 654.

[4] Harta petroliferă a Europei în 1931. Producţie, rafinaj, export. MPR, No. 1, 1933. See also Gheorghe Calcan, Aspects of Roumanian Petroleum industry in the inter-war period, "Annual of University of Mining and Geology", "St. Ivan Rilski Sofia", Vol. 48, part IV, Humanitarian and economic science, Sofia, 2005, p. 37-40.

[5] Gh. Buzatu, *România si trusturile petroliere internaţionale până la 1929*, Edition Junimea, Iasi, 1981, p. 143; Vintilă Brătianu, *Politica de stat a petrolului in urma constituţiei şi a legii minelor*, Bucarest, 1924, p. 6; O. Constantinescu, *Contribuţia capitalului străin în industria petrolieră românească*, Bucarest, 1937, p. 123; Ion Agrigoroaiei, *România interbelică*, Vol. 1, Edition Universitaire "Alexandru Ioan Cuza", Iaşi, 2001, p. 197; Ion Agrigoroaiei (coord.), Ovidiu Buruiană, Gheorghe Iacob, Cătălin Turliuc, *România interbelică in paradigma europeană*, Edition Universitaire "Alexandru Ioan Cuza", Iaşi, 2005, p. 188.

[6] Enciclopedia Română, Vol. III, p. 122-124; Th. Ficsinescu, Mining legislation in Rumania, Lecture given at the International Drilling Congress, Bucharest, 30 September 1925; MPR, No. 20, 1925, p. 1622-1630.

wealth in the subsoil, including oil. As those discussions took place, three stages emerged. The first one was the one preceding adoption of the new constitution in 1923, when there were discussions of the principle of nationalising the subsoil. Article 19 of the new Constitution nationalised all subsoil wealth and provided for the need of adopting a new mining law. The second stage occurred during the period between adoption of the new Constitution and up to the appearance of the preliminary draft of the mining law. The third stage covered the time between the time of appearance of the draft mining law and the time of approval of the new law.

The discussions of a change of system seemed to have been triggered on 18 January 1920 by a speech given by engineer Constantin Osiceanu, head of the company "L'Étoile Roumaine" of Campina, who called for greater involvement of national factors in extraction and processing of oil.[7] From the viewpoint of the technical report, it was necessary to have unified national legislation, above all because in Rumania, after the end of the First World War, there were 19 mining laws, regulations or statuses.[8] In January 1922, the Liberal National Party, which promoted the slogan "Thanks to ourselves", was brought to power and began to take steps on behalf of adoption of a new mining system. A committee was formed to establish a draft of the new Constitution. The project for a new Constitution had been developed in November 1922, and at the start of 1923 it was submitted for public discussion. The need for the provisions of article 19 was defended by liberal jurist C. Dissescu, who also made references to English legislation, and even to the Napoleonic Code and to the French law of 1919, which distinguished between ownership of the land and ownership of the subsoil. *Le Moniteur du Pétrole roumain*, Rumania's most important oil publication and also one of the world's best-known specialised publications (bilingual between 1900 and 1948)[9], opposed the provisions of article 19 of the Constitution.[10]

The idea of nationalising the Rumanian oil-bearing subsoil was resisted by engineer V. Iscu during two conferences, the first one being

[7] O manifestaţie importantă, MPR, No. 2, 1920, p. 62-63.

[8] Grigore Dimitrescu, D. R. Ioaniţescu, Dem I. Nicolescu, I. Predescu, N. Constantinescu Bordeni, *Legea minelor cu expunerea de motive a d-lui ministru Tancred Constantinescu*, State Print Works, Bucharest, 1924, p. 113-115.

[9] L. Mrazec, *Reflection concerning the economy on the 40th anniversary of the first Rumanian oil review*, MPR, supplement No. 13, 1940, p. 2-4; Th. Ficsinescu, *Cu prilejul unei aniversări*, MPR, No. 8, 1940, p. 437; Gh. Calcan, *Industria petrolieră din România in perioada interbelică*, Technical Editions, Bucharest, 1997, p. 1-5.

[10] Motivarea naţionalizării, MPR, No. 5, 1923, p. 331-333; V. Iscu, Naţionalizarea subsolului, MPR, 1er No., 1923, p. 33-38.

the Congress of Engineers and Technicians held in November 1922, and the second one being held at the Charles I University Foundation.[11] He tried to minimise nationalisation action in the sense that, on one hand, the lands constituting part of the State domain would not be of any value, and on the other hand that such an action would be useful to the bourgeoisie, which was initiating the law and which headed the State.

A real anti-nationalisation attitude was promoted during the discussions of the National Association of Owners of oil-bearing lands, grouped in an impressive meeting in Ploiesti, the country's most important oil-producing centre. The President of that association maintained that the nationalisation presented by the new Constitution constituted only a "disguised confiscation of property". Another participant maintained that nationalisation was only a Communist theory, and a distinguished representative of the governing party, who was present during the discussion and owned some oil-bearing lands, read some passages from the Soviet Constitution to the audience to demonstrate the violation of property rights.[12] Almost at the same time, I. G. Duca, one of the most famous P.N.L. figures, demonstrated in a lecture that opinion concerning ownership should not be absolutistic, but should be nuanced, making a distinction between ownership of the land and ownership of the subsoil[13], and suggesting that consideration be given to the possibility of expropriation on grounds of public usefulness.

The first stage of discussion, concerning adoption of the future mining law, ended with the conviction that the principle of nationalising the subsoil could no longer be avoided and that it would be incorporated into the text of the new Constitution. The adversaries of nationalisation could fear adoption of a principle underlying a new mining law. They had learned that the new law was aimed at allowing exploitation of the nationalised lands only by those companies having a Rumanian majority in their capital.

The adoption of the new Rumanian Constitution on 28 March 1924 signalled the beginning of the second stage of discussion concerning development of the new mining law. During that stage, a few foreign viewpoints were also taken into account. *The Times* published the negative views of the president of the Company "L'Étoile Roumaine British" with respect to the principle of nationalisation of the Rumanian

---

[11] V. Iscu, *Politica de stat a petrolului*. Lecture given on 16 March 1923 at the Charles I University Foundation, MPR, No. 8, 1923, p. 545-549.

[12] Acţiunea de proteste contra naţionalizării subsolului, MPR, No. 5, 1922, p. 355-358.

[13] I. G. Duca, *Doctrina liberală*, in the Doctrines of the political parties – 19 lectures organised by the Rumanian Social Institute, Bucharest, p. 108.

subsoil.[14] On the other hand, the spokesman of the governmental party, "the Future", offered the clear rejoinder that the Bucharest government's position was that "we believe that we alone are masters in our own house".[15] In turn, Henry Béranjer, general rapporteur on the budget in the French Senate, visiting Bucharest, openly informed the Rumanian Finance Minister, V. Bratianu, of his interest in protection of French capital invested in the Rumanian oil industry.[16]

The Rumanian authorities had to take foreign interests and suscepti-bilities into account, especially because they wanted to float a substan-tial borrowing abroad. Vintila Bratianu, King Ferdinand I and Crown Prince Charles visited Paris and London in 1923.[17] The Rumanian representatives pledged that foreign interests would no longer be ne-glected, but they emphasised their desire for consistent involvement of national factors.[18]

The discussions of the oil industry were subject to numerous varia-tions, meaning that there was no Rumanian capital, that the said foreign capital was going to refuse to cooperate with the Rumanian oil industry, and that the investments in the oil industry were unfavourable. The discussion agenda also presupposed other directions: recognition of the rights already won in the oil industry, the problem of the lands under concession, and the one relating to the State's oil-bearing territories.[19]

The Moniteur du Pétrole, which was sensitive to unfavourable opin-ions concerning the new mining legislation, made room in its pages for all opinions on this point. To show that the idea of State involvement in the oil industry mechanisms was undesirable, the publication also used foreign examples. Thus an article was published with the suggestive title: "The oil regime in France. Its lessons for Rumania. The National Oil Office. Its role. The way it is formed. The resources of French Government against state control of oil."[20] On the other hand, the oil review knew about the intentions of a group wanting to launch an analysis of all companies having Rumanian-majority capital in an

---

[14] *Aplicarea naţionalizării subsolului*, MPR, No. 8, 1923, p. 530-532.

[15] *Cuvântarea lui Sir Charles Greenway*, MPR, No. 8, 1923, p. 530-532.

[16] *Vizita d-lui Henry Béranger*, MPR, No. 23, 1923, p. 1732.

[17] *Punerea in valoare a bogăţiilor petrolifere ale statului. Călătoria in străinătate a d-lui ministru de Finanţe*, MPR, No. 13, 1923, p. 915-917; M.S. *Regele Ferdinand la Guidhall în Londra*, MPR, No. 10, 1924, p. 810; *Un interviu al Principelui Carol*, MPR, No. 17, 1924, p. 1421.

[18] See Emilian Bold, *De la Versailles la Lausanne* (1919-1932), Edition Junimea, Iaşi, 1976, p. 11.

[19] Gh. Calcan, *Industria petrolieră din România in perioada interbelică*, Technical Editions, Bucharest, 1997, pp. 25-30.

[20] MPR, No. 19, 1923, pp. 1347-1349.

association of the companies favourable to the idea of nationalising Rumanian oil resources. Twelve Rumanian companies responded to this initiative, headed by the company Le Crédit Minier, the purpose being as follows: "Rumanians without any connections with the big foreign groups, we must unit so as to be able, at a given time, to express our desires."[21]

March 1924 brought publication of the draft new mining law, and that marked the third stage in discussions of this issue. *Le Moniteur du Pétrole* criticised that document, holding that it had the purpose of holding back development of the oil industry, which would have favoured small companies, being implicitly against the big ones, that it would not encourage exploration of oil resources, etc. The draft mining law provided for nationalisation of the oil companies within a period of five years, meaning possession of 60% of Rumanian capital, and 2/3 of the Board of Directors and of the management had to be Rumanian.[22] However, the hope was expressed that the said draft, when submitted for discussion, would be improved.[23] As a principle, the idea of nationalisation of the oil subsoil was accepted by everybody, and what made people unhappy was the procedures and terms by which such nationalisation was planned and carried out.

The Association of Oil and Mining Industrialists held discussions about the draft law, and criticised it at several meetings. The industrialist C. Osiceanu, president of the Association of Oil Industrialists, invited each major oil company to make proposals, to be summarised in a collective document for delivery to the appropriate ministry. The head of the Company Aquila Franco-Roumaine considered that if nationalisation were not carried out slowly, there would be a real economic revolution.[24]

Those discussions also included opinions to the effect that the law bothered foreigners, who might react. The contemporary press already mentioned diplomatic intervention by France, England, the United States and The Netherlands with the Bucharest government as con-

---

[21] *Crearea unui sindicat al societăţilor româneşti de petrol*, MPR, No. 21, 1923, pp. 1634-1636.

[22] *Anteproiectul legii minelor*, MPR, No. 6, 1924, pp. 432-436.

[23] *Situaţia generală*, MPR, No. 5, 1924, p. 385.

[24] *Anteproiectul legii minelor în studiul Asociaţiei Industriaşilor de Petrol*, MPR, No. 7, 1924, p. 267; *Conferinţa Asociaţiei Industriaşilor de Petrol*, MPR, No. 11, 1924, p. 403-404; *Uniunea Generală a Industriaşilor faţă de naţionalizarea industriilor şi legea comercializării*, MPR, No. 11, 1924, pp. 904-906.

cerned the draft new law.[25] The various reactions noted, which were often contradictory, led Industries Minister T. Constantinescu to announce that he would defer parliamentary discussion of the legislative bill, but he reversed that decision a short time afterwards, proposing the project subject to parliamentary debate and approval. In that stage, one may perhaps find the combination of the discussions on the subject of the new law. Several statements were submitted to the Ministry, two of which were especially important. In principle the oil companies were divided into two camps: the ones who were against the new bill, and the ones favourable to it. The opposition included the big companies with foreign capital. Favouring the project were companies holding Rumanian capital. The statement issued by companies with foreign capital was signed by 25 oil companies, led by Astra Roumaine, Roumaine-Américaine, Aquila Franco-Roumaine, Colombia, etc., while the ones submitted by companies based on Rumanian capital was signed by 22 firms, led by Le Crédit Minier, La Rumania Pétrolière, Le Pétrole Matiţa, etc.

The statement submitted by companies based on foreign capital was broader and did not criticise the legislative branch's intention, but it clearly put forth some proposals for modifications. The Rumanian companies' statement was favourable to the legislative bill. The sharpest discussions were the ones dealing with the proportion of capital and of Rumanian staff provided for in the legislative bill: the companies based on foreign capital considered that they could not be nationalised for a period of ten years, as was provided, after all, by the legislative bill, increase their capital by 150%, and that increase should have come from Rumanians, that the companies already existing should have been accepted as is, thus recognising their efforts on behalf of development of the Rumanian oil industry, that the companies that were going to be established after adoption of the said law were constituted in accordance with the new provisions, and that the law proposed destruction of the major oil companies.

The statement submitted by companies based on Rumanian capital considered that the legislative branch was justified in its intention to encourage the national economic factors. It came out for maintenance of the ratio of 60% Rumanian capital and 40% foreign capital for the companies wanting to carry on economic activity in the oil domain. It wanted to maintain the numerical superiority of Rumanians in the management organs, even suggesting an increase of that proportion to 75% (compared with 2/3, as provided for in the bill). We must point out

---

[25] Gh. Buzatu, *România si trusturile petroliere...*, p. 168; "Politica noastră economică. Răspunsul finanţei internaţionale", *Argus*, 3 July 1924; *Demersurile diplomatice în chestia legii minelor*, MPR, No. 12, 1924, p. 994.

that this proportion was initially suggested in a statement submitted by engineers and technicians working in the mining industry. The statement of the companies based on Rumanian capital detailed, at the same time, the merits of the Rumanian themselves with respect to the birth and development of the oil industry, as a rejoinder to the pessimistic estimates made by companies based on foreign capital as concerned the technical and financial possibilities of the Rumanians in developing that industry.[26]

In June 1924, Parliament approved the mining Law, and the Law was promulgated on July 4. Tancred Constantinescu, the minister of Industry, had urged adoption of the law. He said that oil, such an important source of wealth, necessarily had to belong to the Rumanians, and should no longer be claimed by the major international trusts, "Royal Dutch" and "Standard Oil". The Rumanian minister indicated that laws protecting national wealth had already been adopted in England, France and the United States. He rejected charges that the law was aimed at foreign capital. What lesson should be drawn from all this? In his opinion, it was the following: one must accept foreign capital. "Letting it into the country helps us, and one must treat it well and accept it. But at the same time one must guide everything Rumanian, capital, energy, labour, into industry [...]. That is the basis of this law, its economics. Hence we are not forcing anybody, but on the contrary one must act fairly and firmly [...]. We are not going to reject foreign capital, but are also going to introduce our own capital into those businesses".[27]

The legislative bill concerning mines laid down the following principles for exploitation of the subsoil wealth: at least 60% Rumanian capital and a maximum of 40% foreign capital, and the chairman and 2/3 of the Board of Directors of any oil company should be Rumanian. The text of the law softened a few requirements, thanks to major protests by foreign capital. Thus the law reduced the share of Rumanian capital to 55%, and increased, from 5 to 10 years, the period for nationalisation for companies having foreign capital that wanted to receive oil-bearing lands belonging to the State for exploitation.

In Parliament, the discussions entailed a choice between, on one hand, ideas to the effect that the law was conditional on the principle "everything thanks to the Rumanians and for the Rumanians", and on the other hand the opinion that the said law was "anti-democratic". In the Chamber, the members approved the law by 134 votes for it, the

---

[26] Gh. Calcan, *Industria petrolieră din România...*, p. 37-44.

[27] *Ibid.*

parliamentary opposition having abstained. In the Senate, the law was adopted by a vote of 83 to 4.[28]

The adoption of the mining law in the year 1924 marks an important stage in Rumanian economic legislation. That law stimulated the involvement of the national element in economic development of Rumanian society. The basic principle of this position – state control of the subsoil wealth – was accepted by all parties interested in that aspect. The concrete application of that principle was viewed differently. Companies with foreign capital wanted a delay, a dilution, and if possible elimination of that requirement. The mining law of 1924 became a veritable "mining choir", the text of which was much more precise and complex than the one of the 1895 law. The law became part of the legislative complex adopted after the unified Rumanian national state became a reality, in 1918. It may be considered as the most eloquent expression of the motto of the Liberal National Party: "thanks to ourselves". Thanks to the importance attached to and the new view of oil exploitation, the mining law of 1924 could be considered as a real oil law. It was the result of the collaboration of a few elite Rumanian experts: geologists, jurists, mining engineers, chemists and economists, but also of a few very valuable liberal politicians.[29]

However, voting on and adoption of the mining law of 1924 were far from being the end of discussions of the oil industry. *Le Moniteur du Pétrole* emphasised the fact that after adoption of the law, discussions would intensify, also including the aspects of implementation of the legal provisions.[30]

"Le Moniteur du Pétrole" published the full text of the law and stated that it had been significantly modified by Parliament, and that fact had been also appreciated by opponents of the law.[31] Tancred Constantinescu, the minister of industry, believed that the law took remarks made concerning the project into account, with the exception of the point concerning maintenance of a majority of Rumanian capital. A few representative companies with foreign capital indicated that they were prepared to collaborate with the Rumanian State, accepting the conditions laid down in the law. Those companies included "Concordia" and "L'Etoile Roumaine". Others, including two of the biggest ones,

---

[28] Gh. Buzatu, *România şi trusturile petroliere...*, p. 164; *Legea minelor în Parlament*, No. 13, 1924, p. 1075.

[29] Ion Agrigoroaiei, *op. cit.*, pp. 195-196; Gh. Ivanuş, I. Ştefănescu, Şt.N.Stirimin, Şt.-Tr. Mocuţa, M. P. Coloja, *op. cit.*, pp. 217-219; Gh. Buzatu, *România şi trusturile petroliere...*, p. 171.

[30] *După votarea legii minelor*, MPR, No. 13, 1924, pp. 1007-1009.

[31] *Ministrul industriei despre legea minelor*, MPR, No. 14, 1924, pp. 1099-1101.

"Roumaine-Américaine" and "Astra Roumaine", made their decision not to collaborate with the Rumanian State public. Those companies based their decision on the fact that they would have found it impossible to invest 60% of their shares in Rumanian capital. With respect to those aspects, we should point out the fact that the Rumanian Minister even supplied the newspaper *Le Temps* with part of this information.[32]

Vintila Bratianu, the Minister of Finance, maintained his position, which was already known: he was not against foreign capital, but for collaboration with it. However, the Rumanian minister was firm: national capital should not play a passive role.[33]

Abroad, the law did not get a sympathetic reception. There were very few positive reactions. *Le Moniteur du Pétrole* published an article with a significant title: *An English demonstration on behalf of the mining law*. E. Manville, Chairman of the Board of Directors of the Company "Phoenix Oil" and "Transport Co.", addressed himself to the shareholders by means of a circular, combating their fears created by the English press, thus assuring them that the new mining law as well as the Rumanian State did not intend to affect "seriously the interest held by invested foreign capital". The opinion that the oil industry's foreign investments enjoyed "the required safety, even under the conditions of the new law", was expressed by Leon Wenger as well, representing Franco-Belgian interests.[34]

The opponents of the mining law continued to criticise it. They maintained that the law was voted without serious parliamentary discussion. Gogu G. Anagnoste, a doctor of law, published an assessment in which he synthesised the negative opinions concerning concerning the legislative bill on mining, also concerning himself with the problem of the rights earned. That problem continued to be analysed by the *Le Moniteur du Pétrole*. A note issued by the English legation in Bucharest drew the Rumanian government's attention to the fact that it had promised the English government "that the established rights will be respected". In turn, the Association des Industriels de Pétrole organised several meetings and submitted several statements criticising the restrictive provisions of the new mining law.[35]

---

[32] Gh. Buzatu, *România şi trusturile petroliere...*, p. 185; *Ministrul industriei despre legea minelor*, MPR, No. 14, 1924, pp. 1099-1101; Gh. Buzatu, *O istorie a petrolului...*, p. 209; *Domnul Tancred Constantinescu şi legea minelor*, MPR, No. 23, 1924, p. 1907.

[33] *Ministrul de Finanţe si capitalul străin*, MPR, No. 15, 1924, p. 1270.

[34] Gh. Buzatu, *România şi trusturile petroliere...*, pp. 202-204; *O manifestaţie engleză în favoarea legii minelor*, MPR, No. 14, 1924, p. 1196.

[35] Gogu G. Anagnoste, *Legislaţia minieră şi petrolieră română*, tipografie "Aurora", Ploieşti, 1924; *Chestiunea autorizării de noi sonde şi distanţele dintre ele*, MPR,

The foreign press was generally hostile to Rumania's new mining law. Some important publications, such as *The Times*, *PetroleumTimes*, *The Economist*, *Manchester Guardian Comercial*, *Daily News*, *Chicago Daily Tribune* and *The Sunday Times*, etc., criticised the mining system and the Rumanian State. Finance Minister Vintila Bratianu held that the roots of that opposition were to be found at home, whence their continuous nature. Abroad, this opposition was headed by the "O.P.Q." association, constituted by five national groups: American, English, Dutch, Belgian and French. That association was formed for the purpose of acquiring the oil-bearing lands of the Rumanian State, offering a foreign loan to Rumania in exchange. The association had submitted its proposals in 1921 and 1923. After the adoption of the new mining law of 1924, the association announced that it was withdrawing its offer. The English newspapers "The Times" and "Financial Times", taking advantage of a visit to London by the Rumanian Finance Minister, brought this problem up. Vintila Bratianu seemed intransigent on this problem. Asserting that behind the "O.P.Q." action, there were actually the big international trusts "Standard Oil" and "Royal Dutch", the Rumanian minister repeated that the Rumanian State had decided not to drop those principles, which could even affect the State's political independence. "Le Moniteur du Pétrole" defended the "O.P.Q." association.[36]

The first big oil company that decided to restructure its organisation and activity in accordance with the provisions of the new law was "Colombia". On 15 October 1924, the decision was made to increase its share capital from 138,000,000 leu to 300,000,000 leu. Six Rumanians joined the Company's Board of Directors, and the board Chairman was now Dr I. Cantacuzino. The nationalisation of "Colombia" was followed by other oil companies.[37]

Also in the autumn of 1924, the Rumanian State decided to institute a concession of 500 hectares (ha) of its oil-bearing lands. That could be considered as a historic decision, above all because starting in 1900, the State had not established any further concessions of its lands. Much was at stake, because the lands contained rich deposits that were granted in

---

No. 21, 1924, p. 1727; *Asociaţia Industriaşilor de Petrol şi chestiunile la ordinea zilei*, MPR, No. 19, 1924, pp. 1554-1557.

[36]   Gh. Buzatu, *România şi trusturile petroliere...*, pp. 203-207; Gh. Buzatu, *O istorie a petrolului*, pp. 211-216; *Declaraţiile d-lui ministru Tancred Constantinescu în chestia noii legi a minelor*, MPR, No. 17, 1924, p. 1417-1419; *Sindicatul "O.P.Q." şi terenurile petrolifere ale statului*, MPR, No. 16, 1924, pp. 1341-1343; *Petrolul român, finanţele statului şi capitalul străin*, 1341-1343; *Petrolul român, finanţele statului şi capitalul străin*, MPR, No. 18, 1924, pp. 1441-1452.

[37]   Gh. Buzatu, *România şi trusturile petroliere...*, pp. 200-201; Gh. Buzatu, *O istorie a petrolului*, p. 209.

accordance with the new provisions of the new law, and hence to companies accepting the principles of nationalisation. The area granted under concession was divided into 42 perimeters, for which 78 applications were filed. The companies not wanting to nationalise themselves were not affected by this problem, since during the year they had purchased oil bearing lands that could exploit as they wished, thanks to the acquired rights. That situation could continue for another fifty years, the period for the lands in question to join the category of "vested rights". After that time, the lands came under State control, but without having any mineral resources.[38]

In 1925 the major discussions in the oil world were held on the subject of a grant of the State's oil-bearing lands. The companies that were nationalised or promised, under firm agreements, that they were going to do so, accepting the conditions of the law, and the Rumanian companies were favoured in granting such perimeters. L'Étoile Roumaine received 9 perimeters that were rich in oil reserves, having an area of 124 ha. The company offered the Rumanian State 75,000 shares and committed itself to having at least 55% Rumanian capital, within a period of ten years. "Colombia" company was given two perimeters, each of 10 ha, that company having complied with the provisions of the mining law. The companies "Vega" and "Concordia" were also nationalised. The companies "Le Credit Minier", "I.R.D.P.", "Pétrole Govora" and "Le Pétrole Roumain", etc., received oil-bearing lands.

The "O.P.Q." association in turn made efforts to obtain oil-bearing lands under concession, but Vintila Bratianu was intransigeant, not wanting to take account of the fact that the problem of an external loan was conditional on the State's oil-bearing lands: "Don't you realise the nature of the principle now followed by England, by the United States, and even by France, which lack oil, and of the way those countries are trying to buy it? And as to us, these days we are free, and when that policy is asserted anywhere, we will throw it out!" – those words were spoken by the Rumanian minister in the National Parliament.[39]

The discussions of the mining law continued in 1926 as well, with opinions both for and against. Agreeing with application of the law, mining engineer L. A. Ianculescu held that the grant of oil perimeters to the Rumanian companies "Le Crédit Minier" and "I.R.D.P." and also to the other companies accepting nationalisation represented "the beginnings of a national oil policy". In turn, G. Damaschin, the director-

---

[38] *Declararea terenurilor petrolifere ale statului ca miniere si concesionate*, MPR, No. 23, p. 924, p. 1851; *Repartiţia terenurilor statului*, MPR, No. 23, 1924, pp. 1905-1907; *Industria română de petrol în anul 1924*, MPR, No. 2, 1925, pp. 97-99.

[39] Gh. Calcan, *Industria petrolieră din România...*, pp. 54-56.

general of mining, believed that recognition of the vested rights repre-sented a great shortcoming in the Rumanian mining system, since 70,000 ha were affected by those rights, which would have meant that "the mining reform would bring the State almost nothing". There were criticisms of the law by the association of owners and concessionaires of oil-bearing lands, which, by way of several statements sent to the super-visory minister, precisely requested simple recognition of the vested rights.[40]

During the autumn of the year 1926, the review *Le Moniteur du Pétrole* republished an article that had appeared in *Le Courrier des Pétroles*, offering harsh criticism of the negative attitude adopted by certain parties close to the Minister of Foreign Affairs of France, who had forbidden collaboration with the Rumanian oil companies. The French publication considered that attitude as wrong, injuring French interests. The article considered that the proper attitude was a rejoinder to the nationalisation adopted by the Rumanian State. The French publication indicated that the Rumanian decision was not unusual, being found in the legislation of several States, but in addition one could point out that "to be precise, the legislation that inspired Rumanian legislation was the French mining law". The article wondered "whether there was a country that had thought of closing its borders to French mining inter-ests on the grounds that our legislation requires a majority of the mem-bers of the Board of Directors to be of French nationality."[41]

The arrival in 1926 of the government led by Alexandru Averescu to lead the country led "Le Moniteur du Pétrole" to express a hope that it "will have to adjust to reality, by changing the provisions of the new law that have proven to be inapplicable". The publication maintained the same attitude during the liberal governments of 1927-28, making an ever stronger connection between the problem of the planned loan and "the normalisation" of relationships with foreign capital, the latter meaning, in a cryptic but obvious way, a softening of the provisions concerning nationalisation of the oil companies.[42]

The arrival in power in the autumn of 1928 of the National Farmers' Party led by Iuliu Maniu triggered a change in the Rumanian mining

---

[40] L. A. Ianculescu, *Industria petrolieră din România. Aspecte şi consideraţiuni*, MPR, No. 22, 1926, pp. 2120-2126; G. Damaschin, *Reorganizarea direcţiei generale a minelor din Ministerul Industriei şi Comerţului*, MPR, No. 6, 1926, pp. 499-501; *Doleanţele proprietarilor şi concesionarilor de terenuri petroliere*, MPR, No. 24, 1926, p. 2309-2311.

[41] *Petrolul românesc şi politica petrolieră franceză*, MPR, No. 19, 1926, pp. 1892-1893.

[42] *Noul guvern şi industria de petrol*, MPR, No. 8, 1926, p. 718-719; *Noul guvern*, MPR, No. 22, 1928, pp. 2049-2050.

system. The Farmer's Party came out for the penetration without any constraints of foreign capital in the Rumanian economy by virtue of its slogan "open doors". At the time of taking power, Iuliu Maniu asserted that the new government planned to make the national wealth available to foreign capital. At the start of the year 1929, "Le Moniteur du Pétrole" published the basic principles of the future mining system: total equality of foreign and Rumanian capital in exploitation of the subsoil wealth and the removal of provisions restricting the staffs of the mining companies.[43]

The work on installation of a new mining law took place rapidly, a fact that surprised "Le Moniteur du Pétrole", which was favourable to a change in the mining law. The Presiding Judge of the Supreme Court of Appeals, Em. Miclescu, was appointed to head the committee that had to draft the new law. Virgil Madgearu, the new Minister of Industry and Trade, had clearly expressed his opposition to "aggressive nationalism", which characterised the law of 1924 and which, in his opinion, had been a mistake. The Rumanian minister held that the 1924 law did not have the purpose it indicated, that it was inspired by "false nationalism", and that grants of the State's oil-bearing perimeters should be made in the future in the light of the technical and financial possibilities of the companies, and not in accordance with the kind of capital of those companies.[44]

During the process of developing the draft new mining law, several trade associations expressed their opinions at several meetings by way of statements sent to the competent minister. The association of oil industrialists of Rumania requested stronger support for companies exploring oil-bearing lands, simplification of formalities with respect to official factors, and a fairer breakdown of taxation aspects. The companies having a majority of Rumanian capital submitted their own statement maintaining that the law in effect (contained) provisions that were "indispensable to our existence and to our development". Without naming them, it was obvious that the Rumanian companies were contemplating the provisions referring to maintenance of the capital percentage and of Rumanian staff. Those companies showed that the 1924 law had helped them develop and to acquire a certain importance in the oil industry. They gave the example of concrete figures, including the

---

[43] *Cronica financiară*, MPR, No. 23, 1928, p. 2101-2102; *Capitalul străin şi legea minelor*, MPR, No. 1, 1929, pp. 61-62.

[44] *Reforma legii minelor. Alcătuirea comisiei şi a subcomisiilor pentru întocmirea proiectului de lege. Direcţiile date de dl. Virgil Madgearu, ministrul industriei şi comerţului*, MPR, No. 2, 1929, p. 105-107; The new mining law. The Ministry of Industry and Trade briefed the press on the principles of his reform in *La Roumanie Pétrolifère*, 22 March 1929.

fact that in 1927 the company "Le Crédit Minier" held first place in the country's oil production.[45]

The companies that had refineries drafted a separate statement. They requested maintenance of the provisions of the law of 1924, pursuant to which "all oil production must be processed by the country's oil refineries". Those companies appreciated the fact that if exports were to become unrestricted, the development of those companies would have been endangered. On the other hand, the oil companies that did not have any refineries submitted a statement demanding the contrary. They asserted that the prices obtained in Rumania represented 50% or 75% of the ones gotten abroad, for which reason they requested freedom of exploitation of oil. That statement maintained that the provisions of the law of 1924 were justified in any case by the fact that the country's oil production was then three times less than at present. The statements submitted by the Association of Engineers and Technicians of the Mining Industry requested selection of the party for exploration in the light of its technical and financial capacity, a viewpoint promoted by the official governmental circles, but with respect to staff the statement requested "maintenance of the proportion of 75% Rumanians, without any exceptions". The "Association of the Owners and Concessionaires of Oil-Bearing Lands" produced a statement showing that the provisions of the 1924 law represented a confiscation of property rights and had negative results, requesting the grant of 50% of the fees due to the State to the owner of the oil-bearing lands.[46]

In the economic press, the problem of adoption of a new mining law received nuanced analyses. Thus at the same time as the newspaper *Argus* was enthusiastic about the principles of the new law putting an end to the xenophobic system, and minister Virgil Madgearu was characterised as a clairvoyant, *La Roumanie pétrolifère* was more cautious. The latter judged that the new law would not put Rumanian companies in an inferior position, and the national capital and Rumanian experts would not be discredited.[47]

In mid-March 1929, Virgil Madgearu proposed a bill concerning the new mining law to Parliament. When explaining his reasons, he criticised the law of 1924, which created the illusion that it was protecting the national economy, but actually only managed to irritate foreign

---

[45] *Şedinţele Asociaţiei Industriaşilor de Petrol din România în legătură cu modificarea legii minelor*, MPR, No. 4, 1929, p. 313-314; *Industriaşii petrolului şi modificarea legii minelor*, MPR, No. 5, 1929, p. 396-399.

[46] Gh. Calcan, *Industria petrolieră din Romania...*, p. 64-66.

[47] Viator, "Legea minelor şi petrolul", *Argus*, 27 February 1929; "Legea minelor, capitalul străin, statul şi întreprinderile de petrol", *La Roumanie Pétrolifère*, 10 February 1929.

capital. He indicated that the new law complied with the principle of nationalisation of the subsoil, contained in the constitution, but the law instituted a complete change in the mining system. The Liberals withdrew from Parliament, refusing to take part in the discussion and in voting on the new law, so the parliamentary discussion was not very lively. On 28 March 1929, the new mining law was published in the Moniteur Officiel.

The mining law of the year 1929 established complete equality between Rumanian capital and foreign capital interested in exploiting the wealth contained in the Rumanian subsoil, complete freedom of companies to appoint their managements, the right of the State and of companies doing exploration without refineries to export the oil, pursuant to a few conditions, and recognition of the requests for concessions filed before adoption of the 1924 law, for a period of fifty years. In conclusion, the 1929 law reversed the basic principles introduced by the law of 1924: a guarantee of superiority for Rumanian capital and staff in oil companies.

"Le Moniteur du Pétrole" considered the new law as the concrete result of the "open door" policy followed by the National Farmers' Party, which was in power at that time. The liberals criticised the new law, considering it an enormous error. G. Damaschin felt that the said law was adopted by the governing party because of its servile attitude toward foreigners, and Vintila Bratianu said that the law caused prejudice to national interests because it granted, to the foreign trusts, control over the "country's principal energy" factors. Abroad, "The Oil Bulletin" of Los Angeles considered that the Rumanian law amended foreign capital's participation in the Rumanian oil industry.[48]

The Rumanian experts considered that the law of the year 1929 was adopted at an unfavourable time from the economic and political viewpoint, because the Rumanian State had borrowed 1,000,000 pounds sterling in the interest of domestic monetary stabilisation and accepted the conditions imposed by the foreign oil trusts, which were interested in the Rumanian oil industry. Historian Gh. Buzatu said that the persons guilty for the emergence of this situation were Iuliu Maniu, president of the National Farmers' Party and head of government, and Virgiliu Madgearu, the Minister of Industry and Trade, who offered additional

---

[48] Parliamentary discussions. The meeting of the Deputies, on 22 March, in *Le Moniteur Officiel*, No. 57, 1 June 1929, p. 2126; *Ibid.*, The Senate, the March 20 session, in *Le Moniteur Officiel*, No. 38, 1 June 1929, p. 1919; Gh. Buzatu, *România şi trusturile petroliere...*, p. 222-226; *Proiectul noii legi a minelor*, MPR, No. 6, 1929, p. 461-523; *Noua lege a minelor la Senat*, MPR, No. 6, 1929, p. 539-549; *O revistă americană despre industria de petrol din România*, MPR, No. 8, 15 April 1929, p. 487.

commitments, committed themselves to changing the mining system, and made public declarations along those lines. Both of them went beyond the permissible limits, the negotiations concerning the external borrowing made in 1928 by Vintila Bratianu with results that suited the Rumanian State and did not presuppose a reversal of the principles that constituted the basis for the law of 1924.[49]

The general view was that the 1929 law had produced negative effects on development of the Rumanian oil industry.[50] It is true that with respect to judgement of the context in which the oil industry developed after 1929, one must also take account of the effects of the 1929-33 economic crisis.

The return of the liberals to power at the end of 1933 put the problem of Rumania's mining system back on the table for discussion. Thus the year 1935 brought the official triggering of the mechanism for adoption of a new mining law, the Ministry of Industry and Trade designating a committee led by the great geologist Ludovic Mrazec. "Le Moniteur du Pétrole", watching such changes closely, expressed the hope that the oil industry would be consulted about implementation of the new law. Subsequently, coordination of that committee was undertaken by Gh. N. Leon, undersecretary of state at the Ministry of Industry. He published an article in which he pointed out the domains that could be the object of changes. Leon found that after seventy years, the system for exploiting oil was anti-economic and there was disregard of the operating distances between oil wells, a fact that tended to make exploitation irrational. He also criticised the fact that the types of exploitation at the time disregarded the question of creation of reserves for the future. Then the undersecretary of state asserted that 85% of Rumania's oil output was in the hands of foreigners, a situation caused by the law

---

[49] Gh. Ivanuş, I. Ştefanescu, Şt.N.Stirimin, Şt.-Tr. Mocuţa, M. P. Coloja, *op. cit.*, p. 219-220; Gh. Buzatu, *România şi trusturile petroliere...*, p. 211-228; Gh. Buzatu, *O istorie a petrolului...*, p. 226-227.

[50] The most recent monograph dedicated to the Rumanian oil industry, bearing on the law of 1929, indicates that the said law "seriously affected the Rumanian producing industry and caused substantial prejudice to the Rumanian economy.

Under the circumstances mentioned above, it is obvious that the big and powerful oil companies with foreign capital definitively benefited, the companies with Rumanian capital, generally of modest size and financial potential, being unable to compete with them. The negative consequences of the mining law of 1929 for the 'Rumanian' oil industry quickly appeared, earlier than had been anticipated. The mining law of 1929 was a law resulting from an economic and political context that was unfavourable to Rumania, in particular, but due to its provisions and its toughness, in spite of the uncontrolled increase of production, it caused great prejudice to the Rumanian economy" (Gh. Ivanuş, I. Ştefanescu, Şt.N.Stirimin, Şt.-Tr. Mocuţa, M. P. Coloja, *op. cit.*, Éditions AGIR, Bucharest, 2004, p. 220.)

of 1929, which granted the operating perimeter as a function of the companies' technical and financial capacity, that in 1928 the Rumanian companies held more than 30% of the country's total output, and at the time in question in 1929, they controlled less than 15%. In criticising the mining system based on the law of the year 1929, Gh. N. Leon was working for state control of oil, considered as "a source of energy underlying the development of industry and of national defence".[51] Those principles had already been adopted in other countries, such as England, where the "Anglo-Persian Oil" company was established, and in France, where "La Compagnie Française de Pétrole" was instituted. Those opinions expressed by Gh. N. Leon were contradicted by "Le Moniteur du Pétrole".

In 1935, several statements were sent to the minister. They essentially expressed the opinions of two major oil industry interest groups. The companies with foreign capital requested maintenance of the provisions of the law of 1929, while the companies with Rumanian capital did not agree with granting operating perimeters as a function of technical and financial capacity, and requested adoption of new criteria for awarding such perimeters.[52]

The discussions concerning the new mining system also continued during the year 1936, and they concentrated on the problems concerning recognition of the rights earned and of the criteria concerning the grant of operating perimeters belonging to the State. In February, the legislative bill concerning the new law was proposed to Parliament's Specialisation Committee. The association of oil industrialists intervened, asking the Ministry to defer the discussion of the law in Parliament so that the text of the draft could be more effectively analysed by the industry's representatives.

During the debates concerning the rights gained in 1936, an interesting problem turned up, concerning recognition of certain rights that contributed to the fall of the law on secularisation of the monasteries' fortunes in 1863, and of Teodor Mehedinteanu's lands granted under concession in 1864. The governmental factors intervened immediately, changing article 262 of the mining law, which claimed to take account only of the papers that went into effect starting on 4 July 1924. The modification gave rise to organising a large meeting in Ploiesti, in which the owners and concessionaires of the departments of Prahova, of

---

[51] *Mişcarea petrolului*, MPR, No. 5, 1935, p. 358; *Modificarea legii minelor*, MPR, No. 6, 1935, p. 437-438; Gh. N. Leon, *Considerations concerning the national oil policy*, MPR, No. 10, 1935, p. 685-687.

[52] În *legătură cu noile norme pentru acordarea perimetrelor de exploatare*, MPR, No. 21, 1135, p. 1505-1508.

Dambovita and of Buzau, the richest ones in terms of oil resources, took part. The dominant note of the discussions was criticism of the government initiative. A very important fact to be pointed out is that the objectors also included parliamentarians of the governing party. The protestors sent a request to king Charles II. The government made the decision to reanalyse that question. Valer Pop, the new Minister of Industry, criticised the idea of increasing the sphere of the vested rights, meaning that the State had to remain the sole owner of the subsoil wealth.[53]

The new mining law was put up for parliamentary debate in January 1937. The presentation of the reasons emphasised the goal of guaranteeing new oil reserves and more rational operation by way of a system for distribution of the operating perimeters. And it still wanted to protect companies with Rumanian capital. The newspaper *Argus* held that the new law was aimed at nationalisation of the oil industry and *La Roumanie pétrolifère* expressed the opinion that the law had to take account of two aspects: Rumanian interests, but also foreign interests.

The two groups of companies drafted statements. The Rumanian countries considered the fact of enjoying priority as justified, since the context of the law of 1929, because of competition, did not grant them any perimeters for exploitation either of the State sector or of the private sector. They requested a grant of at least 50% of the operating perimeters as a benevolent gesture, and not by way of public auction.

The companies with foreign capital believed that the legislative bill contained some imperfections, disagreeing with the preferential system for granting operating perimeters, and they found that the law was unfair to foreign capital.[54]

The discussions in Parliament were held rapidly. Madgearu, the author of the law of 1929, told the Chamber of Deputies that it was acting in haste. In the Senate, the discussions were almost non-existent. Voler Pop, the minister of industries, stated that the law represented a devel-

---

[53] G. Damaschin, "În jurul modificării legii minelor. Recunoaşterea şi validarea drepturilor câştigate asupra petrolului", *La Roumanie pétrolifère*, 5 Februay 1937; Gh. D. Dimitrescu, *Drepturile câştigate. Situaţia creată prin decretul nr.2536 din 12 noiembrie 1936*, MPR, No. 3, 1937, p. 151-152; *Mişcarea proprietarilor şi concesionarilor de terenuri petrolifere*, MPR, No. 24, 1136, p. 1825-1826; *Retragerea decretului privitor la art.262 din legea minelor*, MPR, No. 24, 1936, p. 1827; J. Pitar, "Drepturile câştigate în materie minieră", *Argus*, 11 February 1937; "Cum se modifică legea minelor", *Argus*, 3 February 1937.

[54] *Modificarea legii minelor*, MPR, No. 2, 1937, p. 121-122; *Industria de petrol şi modificarea legii minelor*, MPR, No. 4, 1937, p. 237-239; A. Corteanu, "Politica petrolului", *Argus*, 7 February 1937; Raul Culianu, "Politica petrolului românesc", *La Roumanie Pétrolifère*, 22 December 1936; *Revendicările acţionarilor societăţilor cu capital naţional*, MPR, No. 3, 1937, p. 190; *Societăţile cu capital românesc*, MPR, No. 4, 1937, p. 275.

opment of which he could be proud, "today and tomorrow". Grigore Gafencu, Rumania's future foreign minister, who was marked by a farm orientation, said all the same that the law meant a compromise with groups of liberal interests. "Le Moniteur du Pétrole" published the text of the new law in French and in English.

Mihail Constantinescu, the director of the most important Rumanian oil company, "Le Crédit Minier", told the World Oil Congress that was held in Paris in 1937, that the law was characterised by moderate nationalism. The new law was praised at a conference at the Summer University of Valenii de Munte, organised by the historian Nicolae Iorga, where participants felt that the tendency to promote national capital was a general focus in Rumania and everywhere.

Contrasting with those opinions was the opinion of the Board of Directors of the company "L'Etoile Roumaine", which believed that the provisions of the law of 1937 were onerous.[55] The French review called "La Revue Pétrolifère" in turn held that the new law contained some chauvinistic ideas targeting the relationship of "an operating monopoly in favour of the Rumanian companies".[56]

It is obvious that the purpose and the central content of the provisions of the new mining law of the year 1937 attempted to encourage companies with Rumanian capital by introducing new procedures for granting operating perimeters. The way in which such a distribution was to be made was specified in the application rules of the mining law. The activity of implementing those rules began in 1937. The oil companies feeling the application of those rules, contained meetings and the ritual of production of statements for the responsible ministry. Again in 1937, there were the first modifications of the law, which had barely been adopted. As of 1938, people talked openly about the need for adopting a new mining law[57] or, more concretely, about a special oil law. The debates in expert circles considered that prospect. Discussions, opinions, meetings, statements, special committees, etc. The internal context and above all the international situation prevented finalisation of these intentions. It was only in 1942 that an oil law could be adopted.

The 1937 law fit into the framework of the domain of the *command economy* and of encouragement of the *national factor* in the economy.[58]

---

[55] Gh. Calcan, *Industria petrolieră din România...*, p. 78-80.

[56] *The effects of Rumania's new "mining Law"*, MPR, No. 11, 1937, p. 877-978; Nic. E. Ionescu, *Legea minelor din 24 martie 1937 nu are caracter şovin*, MPR, No. 2, 1938, p. 109-112.

[57] *Enciclopedia Română...*, Vol. III, p. 127.

[58] Gh. Buzatu, *O istorie a petrolului...*, p. 264. The historian Gh. Buzatu considered that the essence of the new law was to be found in the provisions that "from four operating perimeters due to any corporation, one is going to reserve a perimeter for the

It was one of the laws of the liberals wanting to return to the principle of the law of 1924.[59] The law did not make the problem of the nature of the capital a discussion topic. The problems concerning staff were settled by a social protection law in 1934 that guaranteed numerical superiority of Rumanian staff.

Thanks to the analysis made, it could be seen that the most important law of the period between the two world wars was the one of the year 1924. That law introduced a new mining system based on the principle of nationalisation of the subsoil, and then on the one of encouraging national factors. That is why the said mining law gave rise to the greatest number of debates.

The results of the law were obvious. In only 5 years, the Rumanian oil companies increased the percent of all national oil output by 100%. The companies that had foreign capital protested and put on a negative press campaign, in Rumania and abroad.

Actually, the laws of 1929 and of 1937 made modifications of the structure of the law of 1924. Thus one could say that they are rejoinders to the law of 1924. In the debates concerning adoption of a new mining system, every time there were two groups characterised by completely opposing interest: the group of companies with Rumanian capital, and the one of companies with foreign capital.

From the political viewpoint, each group of companies obtained help from a new party: the National Liberal Party had the slogan "thanks to ourselves", supporting encouragement of the national factors, and there was the National Farmers' Party with the slogan "open doors", which wanted to let foreign capital flow into the Rumanian economy without any constraints. Thus one can assert that each of the government's political parties had its own mining system. The historical perspective has validated the mining system that was aimed at supporting national factors by way of the law of 1924. The law of 1937 was aimed at obtaining at least a partial return to the principles contained in that law.

Rumanian companies", and on the other hand 50-60% of the reserves of oil-bearing lands of the State had to be allocated, for exploitation "in a benevolent way" to companies "the majority of whose capital must be held by Rumanian parties and whose Boards of Directors consist entirely of Rumanians [...]" (*Ibid.*, p. 263).

[59] Gh. Ivanuş, I. Ştefanescu, Şt.N.Stirimin, Şt.-Tr. Mocuţa, M. P. Coloja, *op. cit.*, p. 220.

The Norwegian State and the Oil Companies

Einar LIE

University of Oslo, Norway

The history of the Norwegian oil industry, though brief, is relatively eventful. The first field, Ekofisk, was discovered in 1969 and came on stream some years later. During the 1970s, 1980s and 1990s a number of new fields were discovered and developed. Production of oil and gas from the Norwegian sector climbed steadily from the mid-1970s until about 2000, when growth flattened out. Norway is the world's eighteenth largest producer and third biggest oil and gas exporter. The petroleum sector accounted for roughly a quarter of the country's GDP, a third of state revenues and more than half of total Norwegian exports.

The discoveries of oil and gas have presented successive Norwegian governments with two separate problems. One of these is how to handle the enormous revenues from the sector; how to ensure that oil revenues are not consumed so quickly that other industries, more exposed to competitive forces, are threatened with extinction. The other problem, which logically and chronologically takes precedence, is how to organize the recovery of petroleum resources. What role should major non-Norwegian oil companies play, and to what extent should Norwegian expertise be developed to meet the challenges posed by the offshore petroleum industry? And what should be the mix of private and state-owned ownership with regard to overall Norwegian involvement in the oil business? The rest of this article discusses the latter aspect of the challenge against the backdrop of the systematic development of a petroleum industry in Norway.

From an historical point of view the encounter between Norwegian political and industrial traditions and oil industry's distinctive identity, with the challenges it brought, is tremendously interesting. A main feature of the Norwegian political economy has been the desire to maintain national control over important areas of the economy, especially where the utilization of the country's natural resources is concerned.

This feature is also found to a greater or lesser extent in most countries, but there are grounds for asserting that it is particularly characteristic of Norway. One of the dominating themes in the Norwegian debate regarding EU membership, which the electorate has rejected in two referendums, has been the country's desire to maintain control over its natural resources. In addition to this, there is the fact that large companies have been looked upon with some scepticism throughout recent Norwegian history. Since the 1800s the aim has been to exercise as much democratic influence as possible on society's development. This has meant that powerful and influential units in the economic sphere have been resisted and subjected to extensive regulation.

It was not easy to harmonize offshore oil and gas operations with Norwegian industrial policy traditions. Offshore oil operations cannot be run by small, locally based companies. Their complexity and capital requirements made it necessary that foreign companies played a central role. If Norwegian units were developed, these would of course create and manage considerable wealth. The Norwegian oil industry was developed at a time when state-run oil companies were in vogue and it was obvious that the issue of state participation in the petroleum industry would be raised. State-run business operations were, at least in principle, a way of creating large units that were subject to democratic control to a greater extent than private enterprises. The question of public versus private enterprise was, however, one that defined a major area of conflict in Norwegian economic policy. While the Labour party had traditionally looked favourably upon state-run industry, the more conservative and liberally inclined opposition was more sceptical and restrictive in its attitude to state ownership.

These tensions between Norwegian traditions and the distinctive character of the oil industry led to extensive debate and to much conflict with regard to how the industry should be organized. In this article I shall attempt initially to describe in more detail Norway's traditional attitudes to major industrial enterprises. I shall then take a closer look at the challenges posed by the oil industry, along with the solutions found and adjustments that were made.

The Establishment Phase

Foreign companies played a central role in the early days and it was not until 1971-72 that dedicated efforts commenced to increase Norwegian participation in the oil industry.

This was primarily the result of the Norwegian authorities' uncertainty concerning the extent to which oil was present on the Norwegian continental shelf during the 1960s. Exploration for petroleum deposits was considered to be a game of chance. The authorities saw little reason for Norwegian companies to launch themselves into costly competency development programmes in petroleum exploration. While it seems clear that the civil servants, who in practice shaped oil policy at the time, envisaged the possibility and even the probability of finding oil on the Norwegian continental shelf, nobody predicted that the oil industry would grow to the extent that it subsequently did. The clearest evidence of this is the fact that the entire continental shelf south of the 62nd degree of latitude – which covers the whole of the North Sea, where expectations of a discovery were greatest – was put out to tender in the first licensing round in 1965. In principle, all the major fields could have been allocated before the institutional system – ensuring that revenues, supplies and competency development also benefited Norway – was established[1].

The thinking at the time of the first licensing round was that the state's revenues from discoveries would come exclusively in the form of taxes and duties. Prior to the second round, however, the idea of state participation by means of "carried interest" was launched in order to increase the government take from a possible future oil enterprise. The arrangements that were made meant that the state and the oil companies negotiated the size of a "carried interest" agreement for each one of the blocks likely to be allocated to the companies. The system was time-consuming and the cause of some friction between the government and the oil companies. Indeed, Gulf and Shell refused to accept the idea of state participation at all[2]. As a result, the ground was prepared for a system which would assure the Norwegian state of a greater share of revenues in a more efficient way.

The discovery of the gigantic Ekofisk field in late 1969 changed the oil policy debate in Norway for good. At the time one Norwegian company, the industrial company Norsk Hydro, was quite heavily engaged in the oil industry. Hydro was an industrial conglomerate, particularly involved in fertilizers and the production of the light metals aluminium and magnesium. The company had been set up in 1905 to capitalize on a new fertilizer production method, developed in Norway. From its inception, the majority of the company's shareholders were French and associated with the major bank Paribas. After the First World War the Norwegian state became majority shareholder with more than 45 percent of the shares. But French ownership influence remained considerable and there were still two Paribas representatives on Hydro's

---

[1]   Hanisch, Tore Jørgen and Gunnar Nerheim, *Fra vantro til overmot*, Oslo: Lese-selskapet, 1992, p. 59.

[2]   *Ibid.*, p. 153f.

board of directors in the 1960s. It was these French connections that brought Hydro into the oil business, as the French board members actively established contacts with French oil companies. Along with Hydro these companies set up the Petronord group, which was awarded a relatively large allocation in the first licensing round. Of greater importance, however, was an extremely fortunate exchange of assets with the Phillips group in 1967 that provided the group with assets in the field subsequently known as Ekofisk. Besides Hydro, a number of smaller and often recently started companies were allocated small licences in the field.

In 1970 industry politicians in the Labour party voiced their desire of seeing a purely state-run oil company established. However, the sitting coalition government of centre-right parties made a different move. At the direct initiative of the prime minister, the government purchased shares in Norsk Hydro thus increasing the state's ownership share to 51 percent. This move has to be seen as an attempt to avoid the establishment of a purely state-run company, at least as far as some of the coalition parties were concerned, the Conservative party in particular. One year later, however, a majority Labour government was formed. This government began to express most forcibly its conviction that the government had to ensure the strictest possible national governance and control of the industry. One of the instruments put forward was the establishment of a state-run company that would attend to the state's commercial interests on the shelf. It soon became apparent that there would a majority in the Storting in favour of establishing such a company. Questions remained, however, regarding the role and authorities of such a company, and how closely and directly it should be governed by the political authorities.

The Political Debate Regarding the Role of Public Companies

Throughout much of the post-war period there was considerable disagreement in Norwegian politics regarding the extent of state ownership in the economy and the scope of commercial freedom that established public enterprises should enjoy. Both of these closely related and conflicting issues were brought to bear on the debate regarding a Norwegian state-run oil company.

The various Labour party governments that held power in Norway between 1945 and 1965 did not adopt a policy of nationalization of private industry. Governments did attempt, however, to gain greater control over the industrial sector through certain forms of legislation and regulatory measures that we need not look at in detail here. In several areas it was decide to set up wholly state-owned companies, as was customary where abundant natural resources were to be utilized. Government ownership was also seen as the solutions wherever investments had to be made that were presumed to exceed the funding capabilities of existing private enterprises. Public companies were established in areas particular political or strategic importance, such as defence and in certain key metal industry sectors.

As far as the Labour party was concerned, these public companies were part of a bigger picture in which the aim was to gain greater political control over the economy. In the light of this, it is apparently paradoxical that it was the Labour party that argued for as little direct governance and political control of public companies. The centre-right parties advocated stricter political control of these companies on a number of occasions. This viewpoint is primarily explained by the more laissez-faire economic convictions of the liberal and conservative parties. They did not want the state to run large-scale industrial operations as these should be the preserve of the private sector. The opposition wanted the Storting to ensure transparency, and have at its disposal a range of controlling options, in areas where state participation in the economy was increasing. The Labour party had created the public companies and wished to protect them. One of the forms of protection was to argue that public enterprises had to be given considerable freedom of action commercially speaking, and not be burdened with reporting routines and decision-making processes that weakened their ability to compete with other companies in their fields[3].

The debate regarding public ownership can also be seen in an historical perspective as a major element in the relationship between politics and industry in Norwegian history. The historian Francis Sejersted has pointed out how powerful industrial interests were viewed with scepticism in Norway from about the middle of the nineteenth century. The position and legitimacy of popularly elected representatives have been strong elements in the development of capitalism in Norway and there has been an accompanying tendency to favour tighter political control of commercial and industrial interests than in other countries. One does not have to venture further than Sweden to find major ownership concentrations in industry and finance, which have played important roles in the modernization and industrialization of the country, and which are also found in Germany. In Norway, however, the growth of the largest banks has systematically been curbed, at least up until the 1990s. Not only have the Norwegian authorities been sceptical to foreign banks; large Norwegian banks have met with resistance as they tend to lead to the

---

[3]   Grøndahl, Øyvind, "Frihet og styring. Arbeiderpartiets og Høyres styringsfilosofier og styringspraksis overfor statsbedriftene 1945-1986", LOS-report 9202, Bergen: LOS, 1992.

centralization of economic power. Locally or regionally based banks have been more compatible with the political norms of the country. The second industrial revolution early in the twentieth century involving Norway's hydroelectric power resources created several big companies. Much unease and criticism arose as a result, especially because the rights of ownership to many waterfalls fell into foreign hands, and the ensuing debate culminated in a series of relatively restrictive concessionary laws[4].

The Labour party looked more positively on the big enterprise as an economic unit, though firmly believing that political control over the enterprise should be extended. The use of public companies and purchase of a majority shareholding in Norsk Hydro can therefore be seen as two related strategies intended to promote large companies – presumed to be more efficient – without the state losing influence to industry and commerce.

The positions in this long established debate about public companies were clearly evident in the discussion of the new state-run oil company's role and authorities. In 1971 a recently elected Labour government put forward a proposal regarding the organization of the state's commercial and administrative activities in connection with the oil industry. The proposal included the setting up of a purely state-run oil company that would manage the state's commercial engagement in the oil sector. The centre-right parties were sceptical of this proposal. Høyre was, and has subsequently proved itself to be opposed to the entire concept[5]. However, after a pragmatic appraisal of the situation, the party decided to support the establishment of such a company while attempting where possible to restrict its scope for independent action. The underlying discussion centred around the question of whether matters of major importance should be submitted to the company's general meeting, the ministry of trade and industry, whether they should be presented to the Storting, or whether they should be dealt with by the company's board of directors. The discussion also revolved around how, and by whom, the company's budget and accounts should be handled. In principle, the practical consequences of such a decision could have been reduced by placing civil servants from the ministries on the board of directors. For historical reasons, however, such a solution was deemed inappropriate.[6]

---

[4] Sejersted, Francis, *Demokratisk kapitalisme*, Oslo: Universitetsforlaget, 1993.

[5] Hanisch and Nerheim, *op. cit.*, p. 282.

[6] In 1963 there was an accident in a coal-mine on Spitsbergen in which many lives were lost. The mine was wholly owned by the state and a number of civil servants sat on the mining company's board. Conditions in the mine later came under harsh criticism and the incident culminated in a government crisis and extensive discussion regarding the relationship between politicians and civil servants. The government

The final articles of association of the state-run oil company, which was given the name Statoil, were drawn up in the course of a process that lasted throughout the first two years of the company's existence. One of the solutions found was that items of major significance should be submitted to the Storting. But Statoil's board chairman and company president gained acceptance for their proposal that the company should not be made to present its annual budgets to the ministry, only loosely defined plans for the year to come. Neither were specific routines drawn up to ensure that Statoil always acted in accordance with the opinions that held sway in the ministry of trade and industry.

The public debate about Statoil, from before its formation until at least ten years later, did not mainly revolve around how the politicians should govern the company. Perhaps the most important underlying theme was how to construct a powerful tool for national self-assertion in a conflict of interest with the multinational giants. It was precisely this argument that weighed most heavily when the state-run company was being set up. The 1972 debate about whether Norway should join the Common Market mobilized some forceful national arguments, especially where the economy was concerned. National control should be retained, both in relation to supranational bodies and the might of international capital[7]. The referendum, which resulted in a clear majority for rejecting Common Market membership, had severe repercussions on Norwegian domestic politics in the ensuing years. In particular, the main course of industrial policy was altered in a more radical direction. The establishment of Statoil should perhaps be seen in this light. The company would hardly have been set up unanimously, and granted such authority, if it had been set up in the 1960s, and certainly not if it had been established in the 1980s.

Statoil's Growth and Relationship with Saga and Hydro

But it was with the allocation of ownership shares and the granting of specific financial privileges in association with them that Statoil's role became truly controversial. Statoil was given a flying start when, in 1972, it was allocated the blocks where the Statfjord field would later be

---

crisis and debate were largely triggered by the principle that a civil servant always act on behalf of his minister. The board was therefore not looked upon as a purely independent body, but as one directly subordinate to the authority and instructions of the minister of state. In the light of this event, very great caution has been exercised in Norway since 1963 in placing civil servants on the boards of commercial enterprises and administrative companies.

[7] Benum, Edgeir, *Overflod og fremtidsfrykt*, Oslo: Aschehoug, 1998, p. 14ff.

found. Today, Statfjord is the North Sea field that has produced the most oil; in terms of its total reserves, only the Ekofisk field is larger. Even before the first exploratory well was drilled, the area was considered extremely promising because oil had been found in what were, apparently, neighbouring structures in the British sector (the Brent field).[8] The Norwegian state allocated 50% to Statoil, 15% to Mobil, 10% each to Esso, Shell and Conoco, and 5% to Saga[9]. Hydro was not granted an ownership allocation because the company chose not to apply. Saga's real share was soon reduced to around two per cent due to a collaboration agreement the company had entered into. But this small share was decisive for Saga's ability, despite a number of problems, to stay in business for two decades, until it was acquired by Hydro in 1999.

The creation of a national oil company was no peculiarly Norwegian phenomenon. On the contrary, this way of looking after the interests of the state and society at large with respect to ownership of a country's natural resources became increasingly common internationally in the 1970s[10]. It seemed obvious that this company, on behalf of the state, would be allocated major ownership shares in promising fields. And so it was to prove. In the licensing round following the allocation of the Statfjord area, Statoil also received 50% of the blocks it had applied for. But the debate was to be most intense in relation to a couple of additional privileges which the state oil company was granted. Statoil was exempted from having to pay a share of the cost of exploring these fields. These costs were shared among the other co-owners. Such costs were often high, and they came – at best – long before any development and production activities could be established. A so-called sliding scale scheme was also introduced. This meant that Statoil, according to the terms of the licences allocated in 1974-76, could increase its ownership of a field from 50% to 66-75% in the event that any viable deposits were found. In the licences granted up until the new government took office in 1981, the sliding scale went all the way up to 80%[11]. Taken together, these terms meant that Statoil avoided paying the costs of exploring bad blocks, but came in with large ownership shares when good finds were made.

---

[8]   It was later discovered that the Brent structure did not provide the largest deposits of oil in the blocks concerned. Statfjord was an autonomous geological structure, independent of the Brent field.

[9]   Hanisch and Nerhei, *op. cit.*, p. 303f.

[10]   Klapp, Merrie Gilbert, *The sovereign entrepreneur. Oil policies in advanced and less developed capitalist countries*, London: Cornell University Press, 1987.

[11]   Helle, Egil, "Saga i norsk oljehistorie", in Bjørn Glenne (ed.), *Sagaen om Saga*, Sandvika: Saga Petroleum, 1997, p. 80.

The substantial share of ownership in good fields, the use of the sliding scale and provisions requiring other companies to bear Statoil's exploration and research costs gave the state-owned company an excellent financial starting point. In addition, decisions regarding the various production licences were made on the basis of ownership share. This made Statoil an unsurpassed power on the continental shelf. The centre-right parties – and, once again, the Conservative Party in particular – were critical of Statoil's role. The party would to a great extent ally itself with Norsk Hydro in the effort to slow Statoil's growth in ownership shares and influence. After the centre-right government had increased its shareholding in the company to 51% in 1971, the company's management believed that it would be Hydro which would be given a crucial role in the build-up of a Norwegian oil industry. Now Statoil was not only given the most important privileges, but also a powerful influence on the continental shelf. For years there was a strong antagonism between Statoil and Hydro, which became the industrial parallel to a political conflict about how strong and independent Statoil's role should be.

At the company level the entirely privately owned company Saga also played an important role. Following the establishment of Statoil, the Storting decided that three fully integrated Norwegian oil companies should be built up. An important aspect of these three companies' shared history is the rapid emergence of an extensive downstream activity. Hydro was quick to enter the refining and processing business. Statoil followed suit shortly after the company was formed. Furthermore, to exploit the wet gas from Ekofisk, a major petrochemical complex was built up in the Grenland area, towards the mouth of the Oslo Fjord. Here the Norwegian state created a framework where the three companies shared operatorship and ownership. The solution presumed that the Norwegian companies were able to cooperate on a commercial level. But developments within the refining and, in particular, the petrochemical sectors, which we shall not go into here, resulted in bitter differences, which contributed to an escalation of the antagonisms between them offshore.

The build-up of three Norwegian companies led in the 1970s to these being given strong preference with respect to the allocation of ownership shares in promising fields. This culminated in 1977-78 when two particularly promising blocks came up for allocation. The most promising of these was Block 34/10. This was referred to as the "Golden Block", and it contained what was subsequently to become known as the Gullfaks field. The block was allocated by means of an extraordinary licensing round in 1978, which generated much political debate. Signals had been given that a purely Norwegian solution would be chosen. But since relations between the companies were still not clarified, the government tabled a proposal to the Storting that Statoil should be given 100% of the block. This led to enormous disappointment, particularly on the part of Hydro. Past and future were now interpreted on the basis of the allocations of recent years. The producing fields that Hydro had a stake in had all been allocated before Statoil had been created. An intense lobbying campaign ensued. In March 1978 the matter was debated in the Storting. The government had now modified its opinion slightly and recommended that Hydro and Saga should each receive five per cent of the Golden Block. The centre-right parties not happy with this proposal. The parliamentary opposition presented an alternative proposal: 15% to Hydro and 10% to Saga. Shortly afterwards a compromise was reached, in which Hydro was given nine per cent and Saga six per cent. The rest went to Statoil. This proposal was adopted by a large majority. Shortly afterwards the so-called "Silver Block", the location of the Oseberg field, was allocated. Here Hydro was given slightly larger ownership shares. The government indicated at the same time that Statoil and Hydro would each have the operatorship of one of these extremely promising fields when exploration work had been completed. This allocation ended in a compromise, and pointed to a situation in which strong disagreement would be replaced by a high degree of consensus with respect to Norway's oil policy.

During these years a large part of the political debate in Norway about the state's relations with the oil industry was linked to its relationship with the Norwegian companies. But how were therelations between the government and the international companies during this period? In the early 1970s a set of "ten commandments" was drawn up for Norway's oil policy, with, as previously mentioned, national control playing a key role. Reserving a place on the continental shelf for the three Norwegian companies, and Statoil in particular, was an important part of a more complex picture. The organization of the international companies' activities was an important part of this "Norwegianization", and it had more immediate consequences.

In general, from the mid 1970s both the British and Norwegian sectors of the North Sea were characterized by a growing level of state-sponsored protectionism of each country's national supply industries. This was probably due to the international recession which caused problems for both Norwegian and British shipyards. In Britain protectionism took the form of informal measures, of calls for the operator companies to choose British yards as far as possible. The Norwegian system was more openly protectionist, particularly from the late 1970s on. One measure which received a lot of attention came in 1976, when Statoil, through its majority vote in the Statfjord licence, forced the operator, Mobil, to have four modules for the Statfjord A platform built at Norwegian yards, even though they were asking a significantly higher price than competing foreign bids. This decision had been cleared beforehand with the Ministry of Industry. From 1978, regulations about how the companies should contribute to Norwegianization through the selection of suppliers and technology transfer were included in the licence conditions[12]. This led not only to a sharp increase in the Norwegian offshore supply industry's level of activity, but also provided a boost to technological environments outside this sector.

The Clipping of Statoil's Wings

The end of the 1970s saw Norwegian politics take a right turn, with a sharp upswing in support for the Conservative Party in particular. After the 1981 general elections the Conservative Party took office on its own. The prime minister was Kåre Willoch, who was openly critical of Statoil's position of power. To top it all, he chose to appoint social scientist Terje Osmundsen as his political advisor. This was the man who that same year published the book, "Cuckoo in the Nest. Should Statoil run Norway?" The book was a scathing attack on Statoil's position of power. Using examples, it claimed to show that Statoil was systematically working to acquire political power. Local politicians were extremely preoccupied about where major supply contracts or parts of Statoil's growing land-based activities were placed. According to Osmundsen, Statoil could exercise significant influence over these politicians, as well as the MPs representing outlying constituencies.

The majority of the centre-right parties eventually united behind a proposal to reform the way the Norwegian state's business interests on the continental shelf were managed. Forecasts from the Petroleum and Energy Ministry showed that under the existing system Statoil's revenue stream would, by the mid-1990s, constitute around 70% of the economic activity taking place on the Norwegian continental shelf. This in turn would correspond to the economic value created by Norway's entire land-based industry. The most important element in what was later to be described as the "clipping of Staoils wings" was therefore intended to limit those revenues and the influence that came with them. One possibility which was floated at the time was to set up a new operative state-owned company to limit the influence which, up until then, had been concentrated in Statoil's hands. However, the solution chosen was to divide the state's participation in the oil industry in two: one part belonging to Statoil, and the other directly owned by the state. This was intended at the same time to restrict Statoil's long-term growth and

---

[12] Nerheim, Gunnar, *En gassnasjon blir til*, Oslo: Leseselskapet, 1996, p. 91ff.

prevent the automatic voting majority the company had within the individual licences. At the same time more detailed reporting routines were introduced between Statoil and the ministry (Proposition No. 73 to the Storting, 1983-84). These measures were adopted unanimously by the Storting. One of the concessions which the government made to the Labour Party was that Statoil would be allowed retain its full share of the rich Statfjord field.

At that time a more interventionist policy with respect to Statoil was just as important. In several of the confrontations between Statoil and Hydro, the Minister of Petroleum and Energy[13] would overturn Statoil's decisions. The first such occasion came in 1983 in connection with the choice of development concept for the Oseberg field. The Statfjord and Gullfaks fields had been developed using large, fully integrated concrete platforms. These were expensive, but were reckoned to be a well-established technology that would not cause difficulties in the construction phase. As a co-owner of the Gullfaks field Hydro had favoured a split platform solution, with separate accommodation and production platforms. The solution would be slightly more expensive, but the construction time would be significantly shorter. Hydro was voted down, but returned to the proposal ahead of the Oseberg development. The company had the backing of its French friends, ELF and Total, while Statoil and Mobil voted against. After considering the proposals, however, the Ministry of Petroleum and Energy instructed Statoil to vote in favour of Hydro's plan.

Shortly afterwards the issue of where the oil from the Oseberg field should be brought ashore came up for discussion. As operator Hydro wanted the oil to be piped ashore in Norway. At that time this was considered impossibil due to the depths off the Norwegian coast. Not long before, the owners of the Gullfaks field had decided that the oil from this field should be pumped up to a loading buoy and brought ashore by tank ship. The decision to build a pipeline from the Oseberg field prompted a heated debate abut localization. Statoil wanted to bring the oil in to its refinery at Mongstad, a longer and more expensive solution than the one Hydro preferred. The licence owners approved the solution that Statoil wanted, but the decision was overturned at the political level after pressure from Hydro.

A more spectacular situation arose shortly afterwards, when Hydro wanted to use gas from the Troll gas field some 50 km away as pressure support for the Oseberg field. The company's concept was to build a subsea installation on Troll that would transport unprocessed gas to Oseberg through a pipeline. There it would be injected into the reservoir

---

[13] This was created after being spun off from the Ministry of Industry in 1977.

to increase the amount of oil recoverable. This project was to prove extremely successful. But it was technologically innovative, and Statoil and Shell in particular were critical of a project with so many untried elements. The two companies voted against the proposal in 1985, but Statoil was once again instructed by the ministry to vote in favour of Hydro's scheme.

However, the most important event which reduced Statoil's enormous formal and informal influence from the 1970s was the development of one large, single project: the expansion of the Mongstad refinery. This was jointly owned by Statoil and Hydro, and Statoil was to be operator for the expansion. Along the way Hydro pulled out due to persistent disagreements with Statoil and dissatisfaction with Statoil's cost estimates. In 1987 it became clear that the project was considerably over budget. The expansion had originally been estimated to cost around NOK 4 billion, but ended up at somewhere between NOK 11 billion and NOK 12 billion. The budget overrun led to a collapse in public and political confidence in Statoil. The issue also led to the resignation of both Statoil's board of directors and CEO. The situation from the 1970s, when Statoil had been given wide-ranging authority in the management of Norwegian interests in the oil sector, was definitively over. That authority had been significantly "reined in" several years before, but the Mongstad case and, to some extent, the company's more conservative approach in the projects mentioned above, also led to a long period of reduced confidence in Statoil's industrial competence.

The most important consequence of the reduction in Statoil's formal and real influence was that state agencies, under direct political control, took the lead in determining oil policy. Seen in the light of Norwegian industrial policy traditions, this was a return to a more normal situation. The centralization of so much influence in one company – albeit a state-owned company – was not in line with Norwegian industrial policy traditions. If we look at the oil sector in particular, the 1980s also brought a levelling out and normalization of relations between the companies operating on the Norwegian continental shelf. Since the early 1970s there had always been geological structures which were considered so promising that insiders felt the state was almost "giving away" money through licence allocations. For this reason Norwegian companies were given strong preference, for example, during the Gullfaks allocation. But the Troll field and Block 34/8, called the "Diamond Block", were the last allocations in which all the companies felt certain of finding very large deposits.[14] Although by the late 1980s there was

---

[14] 34/8 was, however, to prove a disappointment. The field, later called Visund, was viable, but with much smaller deposits than expected.

still optimism with respect to further finds on the Norwegian continental shelf, particularly along the coast of central and northern Norway, it was expected that the rate of discovery would be lower and that it would require considerable exploration and costs to establish viable fields. So the gains to be achieved by influencing the political decision-makers were considerably reduced.

Greater Internationalization

Block 34/8, which contained the last "certain" major fields, was allocated in December 1985, some months before the collapse of oil prices in the winter of 1986. Both the slightly lower expectations with respect to future fields and the low price of oil led to the state giving the international oil companies better conditions. Several foreign companies had indicated that they would limit their involvement on the Norwegian continental shelf. At the same time both the Norwegian and the international companies presented plans for a sharp cut in exploration and research activity in the years ahead. It was decided in 1986 that international companies would no longer have to "carry" Statoil and the state's share of the exploration costs. Furthermore, in the 11th licensing round in 1987 and the 12th in 1988 foreign companies were granted much larger shares than in previous allocations[15]. In both rounds these companies were granted shares of over 40%, compared with around 35% on average in the previous two rounds. They were also given the majority of the operatorships in the 12th licensing round. However, in subsequent rounds in the early 1990s, the allocations fell back and were in part smaller than had been the practice in the period 1981-86 (Norwegian Petroleum Directorate's annual reports).

As the 1990s progressed the Norwegian oil policy landscape would gradually change. Around the middle of the decade, through the 14th and particularly the 15th licensing round, there was a tightening up of allocations to Norwegian interests. This was due to low and falling oil prices. The Norwegian authorities still wanted to keep foreign companies and their competence in place on the Norwegian continental shelf. This had a particular impact on the 15th licensing round, when as much as 46.7% of the ownership shares went to foreign companies. This trend was at the expense of allocations to Statoil and the State's Direct Financial Interest (SDØE), not of allocations to Saga and in particular Hydro, which did very well out of these rounds.[16]

[15] Ryggvik, Helge, *Norsk oljevirksomhet mellom det nasjonale og internasjonale*, Oslo: Unipub, 2000, p. 110.

[16] "The 15th Licensing Round, a Summary" memo from U&P, 29.1.1996; Hydro's archive.

At the same time the Norwegian companies were becoming extremely keen to establish an international foothold, in order to safeguard their existence after the major development projects on the Norwegian continental shelf had been exhausted. All three Norwegian companies had previously been engaged in activities outside the Norwegian continental shelf, but it was particularly from the mid-1990s that international operations became important. It helped the Norwegians to be seen as "more like" the international companies. In certain situations, however, it led to the Norwegian companies intensifying their lobbying of the Norwegian authorities in the run-up to the allocation of important operatorships. Both Statoil and Hydro have turned their attention to northwest Russia, particularly the up-coming major offshore developments. In this connection it has been important to have the opportunity to continually develop their position as offshore operators.

This became particularly evident in the manoeuvrings surrounding the major gas field Ormen Lange, off the central Norwegian coast. This is a deep-lying field discovered by Hydro after a seismic survey in the early 1990s and confirmed by exploratory drilling in 1997. Hydro also owned the largest share of the field. However, when the operatorship of the field's development and subsequent production phases was due to be allocated, Shell seemed to be a strong competitor. Shell also had a significant ownership share and could demonstrate a more extensive track record with similar field developments. At the same time Shell was Hydro's presumably strongest competitor for Block 34 off the Angolan coast. When it was rumoured that ministry civil servants had recommended that Shell should become operator, Hydro initiated an intense campaign to lobby government ministers. The argument was that it would be impossible to convince the Angolan authorities of the company's capabilities as a developer if the Norwegian authorities did not publicly signal their confidence in Hydro. As a result it was decided to grant shared operatorship, with Hydro responsible for the development of the Ormen Lange field and Shell taking over as operator for the production phase.

Structural Changes in the Norwegian Oil Industry around the Year 2000

An important element present when the Norwegian oil system was set up in the 1970s was the tripartite division into one large, public company that merged politics and business, one semi-public company and one private company. The "reining in" of Statoil changed one of these premises in that Statoil should be able to operate as a business enterprise. Then, around the year 2000, came important new amendments to the decisions made back in 1971-72.

The first of these came when Hydro acquired the Saga Petroleum. The acquisition was not a friendly one; relations between Hydro and Saga had never been particularly good. The political maxim that there should be three fully integrated oil companies in Norway had never gained acceptance in Hydro. These three companies would be too small – size would be a critical issue, even with two companies. Hydro's management had for many years maintained a high level of alertness with respect to Saga. Back in the early 1980s, when Saga got into financial difficulties because of its involvement in petrochemicals, Hydro undertook some very detailed calculations of the value of Saga. A purely stock-exchange based acquisition was not considered feasible, because of the clear political signals indicating that the tripartite structure should be maintained. Political opinion was furthermore tested by the acquisition of DnC's shareholding in Saga in 1989. The political reactions to the acquisition were, however, exclusively negative[17].

Still, the company was very well prepared to seize an opportunity should it arise. The two companies were to a great extent involved in the same North Sea fields, so Hydro was exceptionally well positioned to assess the value of Saga on a continuous basis. When Saga – despite its preferential position as the third Norwegian oil company – got into financial difficulty in 1998 and 1999, Hydro's opportunity arrived. Saga's profitability was weaker than Statoil's and particularly Hydro's, and the company's financial position was relatively weak in the late 1990s[18]. The acquisition of the Santa Fe oil company in 1996 proved to be less than fortunate. When the price of oil in 1998 fell from around 15 to 10 dollars per barrel, Saga was in serious difficulty. The company's management made the unfortunate decision to enter into long-term futures contracts as a hedge against further price falls at a time when the price of oil was at a historically low level. This meant that Saga was not able to profit from an eventual price rise. In the spring of 1999 Hydro submitted a bid for Saga without having discussed the matter with Saga's board of directors and management. Following a brief round of bidding in which ELF also participated, Hydro acquired Saga. In accordance with a previously signed agreement with Statoil, the latter obtained roughly a quarter of Saga's field licenses, while Hydro acquired the remaining three-quarters plus Saga's organization.

At the time Statoil's board and management were working on an extensive proposal to reform their corporate model. Statoil wished to move in the direction of a Hydro model, in which the state held a major,

[17] Lie, Einar, *Oljerikdommer og internasjonalisering*, Oslo: Pax, 2005, p. 412.

[18] Nore, Petter, "Norsk Hydro's takeover of Saga Petroleum in 1999", Oslo: Maktutredningen, 2003.

controlling stake, but the company had considerable commercial free-dom. One of the reasons for this was the desire to list Statoil on the stock exchange in order to fund stronger international expansion in the future. Another stated goal was to expose the company to externally determined requirements to profitability and return on investment. It was acknowledged that Statoil's cost position could be substantially improved. This could be achieved by enhancing operations and tackling the challenges presented by project execution. A second Statoil CEO had been dismissed, along with the company's board, in the previous year following cost overruns in connection with a field development. These overruns were big, though not uniquely so, in the North Sea at that time. The perception in Statoil at the time, perhaps a fairly accurate one, is that the dismissal of the board of directors and management was closely linked with Statoil's form of ownership. The minister of state responsible was under some pressure to react against the cost overruns and this was the most readily available form of reaction.

An extensive debate, which also covered the State's Direct Financial Interest (SDØE), took place in Norway round about the year 2000. One proposal submitted at an early stage, was to list Statoil on the stock exchange and sell between a quarter and a fifth of the shares on the open market. Part of the SDØE should also be sold, while a purely state-run management company should be set up based on the main portion of the SDØE. By means of the purchase and sale of licenses in certain fields, this company would enable the field operators to hold greater shares than they held to start with. It was considered problematic that the operators did not previously have strong enough incentives for cost and resource efficient operation as each of them held relatively small stakes. By re-allocating licence shares, operators would achieve a greater share of the savings made during field operation.

The partial privatization of Statoil triggered the most heated oil sec-tor political debate since the system was established in 1971-72, with the same basic industrial policy assumptions coming to the fore in both discussions. The centre-right parties, especially the Conservatives, wanted to see a relatively substantial sale of state shares in Statoil. They also wanted to see a greater divestment of SDØE shares to the oil com-panies. This proved to be a particularly difficult matter for the Labour party, where powerful forces were opposed to both the sale of shares in Statoil and in the SDØE. The parties reached a compromise, however, whereby the government was authorized to sell up to 25 percent of its shares in Statoil, and offer 21.5 percent of the SDØE to Statoil and Hydro. The remaining SDØE shares were to be transferred to a recently established company, PETORO, which was also ear-marked to obtain licences in attractive fields in the future. These solutions were in many ways an adjustment to the requirements and norms that were clearly being looked for by the industry itself and by international capital markets. The basic ways and means of governing Norwegian oil policy were, however, little changed by the decisions affecting Saga and the SDØE.

Conclusion: The Norwegian State and the Oil Companies

In his book *The Struggle for North Sea Oil and Gas* Svein S. Andersen has compared Danish, British and Norwegian oil policy[19]. Denmark and Norway represent two diametrically opposed approaches in the ways the three states have dealt with the sector's main players. Denmark chose early on to leave operative involvement to the major A.P. Möller enterprise; the state itself played a very passive role. Norway is at the other end of the scale, with its extensive state ownership and powerful ambitions to govern activity in the sector by means of its twin roles as owner and regulator at a detailed level. The UK's approach is somewhere in between. The British state was active, though not as dominating and interventionist as the Norwegian state. And while British policy moved in a more liberal market direction in the 1980s, Norwegian policy is still characterized by a considerable degree of state interventionism. There was a purpose and direction for such interventionism in the 1970s, and to a certain degree in the 1980s, given the desire to maintain the industry in Norwegian hands and under national control. Andersen points out elsewhere that though such an over-arching goal no longer exists, this has not led to the state relaxing its grip on the oil industry.

The perception of the state's relationship with the oil companies as control driven and interventionist does accord with the opinions of major industry participants. It acknowledges the fact that the Norwegian authorities had a number of ambitious goals for the oil industry in the early 1970s, as they also had had for traditional industry in previous decades. This ambition led to the need for effective instruments. In a more mature oil province, especially one governed by EEA regulations, that sets clear limits to the extent that national companies can be favoured, one would normally have expected reduced state ownership, and not the establishment of a new company for the active management of the state's ownership interests.

As mentioned above, Francis Sejersted's analysis of the political and economic structure of Norway from the nineteenth century to the present day reveals how Norway became a country of small companies adhering

---

[19] Andersen, Svein S., *The Struggle for North Sea Oil and Gas*, Oslo: Scandinavian University Press, 1993.

to strong democratic and egalitarian norms. The state has played an important role in Norwegian banking and industrial history. On some occasions it has acted as an owner, where private Norwegian interests were not sufficient to fund major investments. In particular it has acted as regulator, modifying and to a certain extent curbing the growth of heavy, dominating centres of influence in industry that have stood outside political control. In Norwegian politics there is often an unspoken, but deeply anchored basic principle that business should be the "junior partner of government", to turn Alfred D. Chandler's American-inspired maxim on its head. In Sejersted's history, this principle lasted up until the oil age, when big business finally moved into the plucky little Viking settlement in the North.

But even though major international companies arrived in Norway and other big Norwegian companies were established, there is every reason to assert that the same political norms continued to govern the state's behaviour. The state was, relatively speaking, reluctant to let the oil companies have too much influence on the shelf. An A.P. Möller solution would have been unthinkable in Norway, although such a solution was proposed to the Norwegian authorities. In 1962, in the same year that the A.P. Möller agreement was signed in Denmark, Phillips Petroleum asked for exclusive exploration rights on the Norwegian continental shelf. Their request was, however, not taken quite seriously by the governing officials of the country.

The 1972 solution involved the setting up of a major state company and the development of two other fully integrated Norwegian companies, which would cooperate and compete with a number of other international companies. This would ensure the spread of national influence in the sector, improving the opportunities for political control. The fact, however, that Statoil was given such powerful authority did not accord well with accepted political norms. But the politicians believed that they would able to steer Statoil. The solution also needs to be seen against the background of the strong national feelings aroused in the wake of the 1972 Common Market debate. The "reining in" did, however, bring with it a normalization, whereby the state retracted some of the authority previously granted to Statoil.

Not only was an A.P. Möller solution an impossibility, but a large merger, like the French Total-Fina-ELF solution, was fore a long time unthinkable in Norway. There is no doubt that rivalry between the Norwegian companies, especially Statoil and Hydro, has provided the state with much more information and much greater autonomy than if one had just had one Norwegian company on the shelf. And Hydro's acquisition of Saga in 1999 generated much reaction. The politicians were certainly relieved to see Saga acquired by a Norwegian company, as there was no doubt that Saga could not have continued alone. The political milieu nevertheless had problems in accepting that the old maxim regarding three fully integrated Norwegian companies had been rejected – especially because rejection had been initiated by the industry itself, and not by the politicians. Former Prime Minister Kåre Willoch has described this process in critical tones as "an overruling of Norwegian oil policy, whereby the managements of Hydro and Statoil set aside the decisions of the Storting". According to Willoch, the *grand old man* of Norwegian Conservative politics, the process illustrated "the power of company managers and the lack of power of elected representatives"[20]. The political milieu also reacted very negatively in 2003 when it became known that the managements of Statoil and Hydro had held informal discussions regarding a possible merger of the two companies. Industrially speaking, such a merger would be would have been advantageous because the two companies where strongly committed on the international front in open competition with much bigger companies.

A new attempt to merge the two companies in 2007 appears to have a greater chanche of success. This time, a formal proposition of a merger was made by the companies' boards shortly after the Russian energy company Gazprom had announced that they would not involve any foreign companies in the development of the giant Schtockman gas field in the Barent Sea. Both Statoil and Hydro had expected to get a role in the development of Schtockman. During the qualification phase, they hade made a number of detailed suggestions for technological solutions in this complicated deep water project. In the aftermath of the competition, severeral observers questioned the wiseness of letting the two national companies compete with each other and expose their relatively similar core competence for a foreign company.

Literature

Johannessen, Finn E., Pål T. Sandvik and Asle O. Rønning 2005, *Nasjonal kontroll og industriell fornyelse*, Oslo: Pax.

---

[20] Willoch, Kåre, "Oljemakt på hjemmebane. Myter om oljepolitikken", in Maiken Ims, *Oljemakt*, Oslo: Maktutredningen, 2003.

Index

Contributors

Juliana Bastos Lohman, Federal University Fluminense Rio de Janeiro, Brazil, julilohmann@gmail.comet

Alain Beltran, CNRS, France, beltran@univ-paris1.fr

Marcelo Bucheli, University of Illinois, United States of America, mbucheli@uiuc.edu

Gheorghe Calcan, University of Ploiesti, Rumania, calcan@xnet.ro

Martin Chick, University of Edimburgh, United Kingdom, martinchick@btinternet.com

Nicolas Chigot, Paris-Sorbonne University, France, nicolas.chigot@tiscali.fr

Armando João dalla Costa, Federal University of Paranà, Brazil, ajdcosta@uol.com.br

Armelle Demagny-Van Eyseren, Paris-Sorbonne University, France, armelle.demagny@libertysurf.fr

Benoît Doessant, University of Paris IV, France, and in charge of the historical archives of Total, benoit.doessant@total.com

Nabila Ghafouri, University of Annaba, Algeria, nabila_ghafouri@yahoo.fr

Constance Hubin, Paris-Ouest University, France, constance.hubin@gmail.com

Nadji Khaoua, University of Annaba, Algeria, khaoua_nadji@yahoo.com

Georges Landau, University Tancredo Neves, Sao Paulo, Brazil, prismax@terra.com.br

Morgan Le Dez, Le Havre University, France, le-dez.morgan@wanadoo.fr

Einar Lie, University of Oslo, Norway, einar.lie@iakh.uio.no

Belgacem Madi, University of Annaba, Algeria, khaoua_nadji@yahoo.com

Roberto Nayberg, Panthéon-Sorbonne University, France, nayberg@wanadoo.fr

Jose Benedito Ortiz Neto, State University, London

Daniele Pozzi, University of Milan, Italy, dpozzi@mail.liuc.it

Samir Saul, University of Montreal, Canada, samir.saul@umontreal.ca

Ilaria Tremolada, University of Milan, Italy, ilaria.tremolada@unimi.it

"International Issues"

Studies in international relations, particularly historical, stem from the changing face of diplomacy over time, where the deeper forces at play, such as those once defined by Pierre Renouvin, are taken into account. Individual states, and those who define and implement their policies, are placed at the heart of global life. According to this concept, countries pursue a course of action by taking advantage of the most diverse range of tools they can rely on, such as economic or cultural resources, which act alone or interact with others.

The study of international relations grew into different fields of analysis during the twentieth century, but it is now subject to a new scrutiny in this era of globalisation. This concept, which coincides with the development of neo-liberal analysis since the 1980s, reveals a new awareness about the increased number of actors – NGOs and multinational companies, for example – but also the large autonomy they enjoy when it comes to action.

This series aims to portray these new perspectives and their impact on current research. Without casting aside studies in international relations that focus on states, it tries to better understand the diverse range of factors that play out on the world stage and how they relate to each other – from the high stakes in sport to the use of colonial memory. This series targets academics and analysts who wish to apply twentieth century history to contemporary thought.

Series editors

M. Éric BUSSIÈRE, *Professeur à l'Université de Paris IV-Sorbonne*

M. Michel DUMOULIN, *Professeur à l'Université catholique de Louvain (UCL), responsable du Groupe d'études d'histoire de l'Europe contemporaine*

Mme Geneviève DUCHENNE, *Docteur en histoire de l'UCL, chercheur qualifiée de l'UCL*

M. Sylvain SCHIRMANN, *Professeur d'histoire contemporaine, directeur de l'Institut d'études politiques de Strasbourg*

Mme Émilie WILLAERT, *Docteur en histoire contemporaine*

Published Books

N° 1 – Catherine LANNEAU, *L'inconnue française. La France et les Belges francophones (1944-1945)*, 2008, ISBN 978-90-5201-397-8

N° 2 – Frédéric DESSBERG, *Le triangle impossible. Les relations franco-soviétiques et le facteur polonais dans les questions de sécurité en Europe (1924-1935)*, 2009, ISBN 978-90-5201-466-1

N° 3 – Agnès TACHIN, *Amie et rivale. La Grande-Bretagne dans l'imaginaire français à l'époque gaullienne*, 2009, ISBN 978-90-5201-495-1

N° 4 – Isabelle DAVION, *Mon voisin, cet ennemi. La politique de sécurité française face aux relations polono-tchécoslovaques entre 1919 et 1939*, 2009, ISBN 978-90-5201-496-8

N° 5 – Claire LAUX, François-Joseph RUGGIU & Pierre SINGARAVÉLOU (dir./eds.), *Au sommet de l'Empire. Les élites européennes dans les colonies (XVIe-XXe siècle) / At the Top of the Empire. European Elites in the Colonies (16th-20th Century)*, 2009, ISBN 978-90-5201-536-1

N° 6 – Frédéric CLAVERT, *Hjalmar Schacht, financier et diplomate (1930-1950)*, 2009, ISBN 978-90-5201-542-2

N° 7 – Robert JABLON, Laure QUENNOUËLLE-CORRE et André STRAUS, *Politique et finance à travers l'Europe du XXe siècle. Entretiens avec Robert Jablon*, 2009, ISBN 978-90-5201-543-9

N° 8 – Alain BELTRAN (ed.), *A Comparative History of National Oil Company*, 2010, ISBN 978-90-5201-575-0

N° 9 – Sarah MOHAMED-GAILLARD, *L'Archipel de la puissance ? La politique de la France dans le Pacifique Sud de 1946 à 1998*, 2010, ISBN 978-90-5201-589-7

N° 10 – Marie-Anne Matard-BONUCCI, Anne DULPHY, Robert FRANK et Pascal ORY (dir.), *Les relations culturelles internationales au vingtième siècle. De la diplomatie culturelle à l'acculturation*, 2010, ISBN 978-90-5201-661-0

N° 11 – Yves-Marie PÉRÉON, *L'image de la France dans la presse américaine, 1936-1947*, 2011, ISBN 978-90-5201-664-1

N° 12 – Léonard LABORIE, *L'Europe mise en réseaux. La France et la coopération internationale dans les postes et les télécommunications (années 1850-années 1950)*, 2010, ISBN 978-90-5201-679-5

N° 13 – Catherine HOREL (dir.), *1908, la crise de Bosnie cent ans après*, 2011, ISBN 978-90-5201-700-6

N° 14 – Alain BELTRAN (ed.), *Oil Producing Countries and Oil Companies. From the Nineteenth Century to the Twenty-First Century*, 2011, ISBN 978-90-5201-711-2

N° 15 – Frédéric DESSBERG et Éric SCHNAKENBOURG (dir), *Les horizons de la politique extérieure française. Régions périphériques et espaces seconds dans la stratégie diplomatique et militaire de la France (XVIe-XXe siécles)*, 2011, ISBN 978-90-5201-717-4

N° 16 – Alya AGLAN, Olivier FEIERTAG et Dzovinar KÉVONIAN (dir.), *Humaniser le travail. Régimes économiques, régimes politiques et Organisations internationale du travail (1929-1969)*, 2011, ISBN 978-90-5201-740-2

N° 17 – Pierre JOURNOUD & Cécile MENÉTREY-MONCHAU (dir./eds.), *Vietnam, 1968-1976. La sortie de guerre / Vietnam, 1968-1976. Exiting a War*, 2011, ISBN 978-90-5201-744-0

N° 18 – Louis CLERC, *La Finlande et l'Europe du Nord dans la diplomatie française. Relations bilatérales et intérêt national dans les considérations finlandaises et nordiques des diplomates et militaires français, 1917-1940*, 2011, ISBN 978-90-5201-750-1

N° 19 – Yann DECORZANT, *La Société des Nations et la naissance d'une conception de la régulation économique internationale*, 2011, ISBN 978-90-5201-751-8